POPULAR APPEAL IN ENGLISH DRAMA
TO 1850

OF

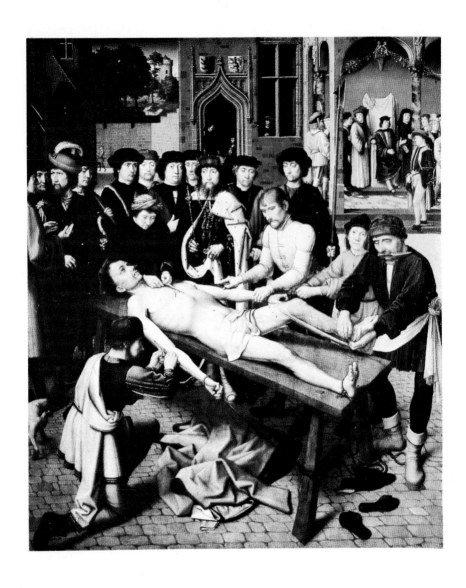

'The Flaying of Sisamnes' by Gerard David

POPULAR APPEAL IN ENGLISH DRAMA TO 1850

Peter Davison

BARNES & NOBLE BOOKS
TOTOWA, NEW JERSEY

First published in the USA 1982 by
BARNES & NOBLE BOOKS
81, Adams Drive, Totowa,
New Jersey, 07512

ISBN 0-389-20231-2
LCN 79-55528

Printed in Hong Kong

For Sheila

Contents

Preface

The origins of this study go back to my doctoral thesis 'Humour as a Tragic Force in Modern Drama in English' (University of Sydney, 1962) in which, among other things, I discussed the popular tradition of drama in the previous hundred years or so, and its influence on contemporary legitimate drama. This led to my being invited to give a Kathleen Robinson lecture at the University of Sydney in 1963, 'Contemporary Drama and Popular Dramatic Forms', in which the routines of Dan Leno, Arthur Roberts, and Flanagan and Allen were compared with aspects of the drama of Beckett and Pinter. A little later, in a book on music-hall songs, I touched on a number of occasions in which the worlds of legitimate and illegitimate drama interacted, and, in particular, the effect this had on the production in Britain of drama involving alienation.[1]

At about the same time, I was also teaching Jacobean and Caroline drama and this led to a re-examination of the accusations that this drama is decadent and escapist. It seemed to me that in Massinger's *The Roman Actor*, for example,[2] there was clear comment on the role of the king — and King James VI and I in particular — and that this was dramatised through theatre imagery. In addition, Massinger pointed to parallels between the stage and contemporary life as epitomised in James I's speech to Parliament of 21 March 1610: 'Kings Actions (euen in the secretest places) are as the actions of those that are set vpon the Stages, or on the tops of houses.'[3] I also argued that Massinger's use of allusions to Shakespeare's work did not stem from a lack of inventive power, but because reference back to the idea of the player in *Hamlet*, *Macbeth* and *Richard II* enabled him to make more tellingly the points he wished to get across. Massinger, to adapt his own words, was 'deciphering on the stage, *to the life*, what honours wait on good and glorious actions, and the shame that treads upon the heels of vice' (*The Roman Actor*, I.i.22–5).

I tried also to argue that even work of a kind so readily dismissed as showing a 'withdrawal from the pursuit of reality'[4] might have a serious concern with then current political events. Indeed, tragicomedy might have owed part of its popularity in the time of Beaumont and Fletcher to the fact that it attempted, through drama, to reconcile conflicts of

ix

absolutes that, in the event, only civil war would resolve. The relationship of *Philaster* to contemporary affairs, it was suggested, was not only to
be found in the many parallels between that play and James I's speeches
and writings, but in the link between the publication of Q2 in 1622 and
the bitter Parliament of January 1621–January 1622. The ending of Q2,
with the degradation and brutal baiting of Prince Pharamond, is very
different from the much more restrained conclusion to Q1 of 1620. It was
also suggested that the curious victory over royalty of the buffoon-like
Country Fellow made use of *dramatic* tradition in an important *political*
way: 'A poor man that is true is better than an earl, if he be false.'[5]

In this study I have taken this interest in the relationship of the real and
play worlds back to the late Middle Ages, in particular to *Fulgens and
Lucres*. I discuss Shakespeare's relationship with the clowns and show
how their material (including the bad pun) was used in the Elizabethan
period. The use of the induction is discussed, in masques (by Jonson and
Shirley) as well as in plays, and in the final chapter the origins of the
rehearsal play are traced, and the way Fielding and later dramatists used
this form is analysed. The major break in the English dramatic tradition is
seen as occurring, not with the closing of the theatres in 1642, but some
two hundred years later, with the end of a drama that consciously drew
attention to the nature of theatre. I have tried not to repeat what has
already been well done by S. L. Bethell, Olive Mary Busby, Leonard
Dean, Doris Fenton, Robert J. Nelson, Anne Righter, Thelma
Greenfield, Alan Somerset and Robert Weimann, referring to their work
when it will make my points for me.[6] I agree with much of what Anne
Righter has so lucidly put in her *Shakespeare and the Idea of the Play*, but
cannot agree with her conclusion:

> Europe was moving away from the Renaissance, with its complex
> balances and clarity of form, into the Baroque. In England, this
> movement spelled the end of a great theatrical tradition. Long before
> the closing of the theatres in 1642, the Elizabethan relationship of
> actors and audience, a near-perfect accomplishment, a brilliant but
> perilous equilibrium, was gone beyond recall.   (p. 207)

As my analysis of *The Roman Actor* (published in the same year as Anne
Righter's book) will suggest, I see the use made of 'the great theatrical
tradition' by Massinger as still lively and significant. That Massinger was
not the playwright Shakespeare was is not to prove that he could not
achieve that 'perilous equilibrium', even though his drama is less
remarkable. Much of this study attempts to argue that 'the idea of the

theatre' was kept alive in the theatre, often, but not always, in the irregular drama, in an important way. The succeeding volume, *Contemporary Drama and the Popular Dramatic Tradition in England*, argues that this delicate balance has recently been restored to us, often brilliantly but affected by Continental experience.

As many of the plays referred to are not well known, dates, normally of first performance, are given. Paradoxically, but for the same reason, the more obscure a work, the more likely is it to be quoted.

In addition to the countless debts I have to those who have studied this subject before me (and specific indebtedness is acknowledged in the traditional manner), I have four important acknowledgements to make. The first is to my good friends in the Department of English at St David's University College, Lampeter (among whom I would particularly include the secretary, Elsie Davies), who took upon them my work so that I could have a term free of teaching and administration. The second is to the Rockefeller Foundation, which invited me to spend a month as a scholar-in-residence at its magnificent Study and Conference Center at Bellagio, Como, and in particular to Dr and Mrs Olson who made me so welcome there. Indeed, I owe the Foundation and the Olsons additional thanks for enabling me to spend an extra week at Bellagio in order to complete this book and its companion volume. I am also grateful to the Pantyfedwen Fund for contributing nearly a third of the cost of my travel to and from Italy. Fourthly, I owe a very great debt to my wife, Sheila, who has not only helped me in countless ways to study and to write, but who typed out the whole of the first draft from my execrable handwriting when she might instead have been sunning herself by Lake Como, and who also typed the fair copy. It is owing to such generous help that I was able to accomplish more in a very short time than in years of disturbed and piecemeal effort. I am indeed grateful for the opportunity, peace and encouragement that these people and institutions so freely gave me.

Villa Serbelloni,   P.D.
Bellagio

December 1978

1 Introduction

There is no wholly acceptable term to describe the two kinds of theatrical experience with which I am concerned. Between the Licensing Act of 1737 and the Theatre Regulation Act of 1843, which ended the monopoly of the Patent Theatres (Drury Lane, Covent Garden and, to a limited extent, the Haymarket, in London), it was technically correct to speak of the Legitimate and Illegitimate Stage — as Planché characterises them in *The Drama's Levée* (1838). The terms would have been understood long after that date and, in the theatre, the expression 'to go legit.', as Marie Lloyd did for a very brief period, is still to be heard. What is more, it would still be understood today in American theatre. Apart from the inaccuracy of using these terms before 1737, it was often very difficult in practice to distinguish the kinds of drama so categorised between 1737 and 1843, except at their extremes. Much that was put on at the Surrey would have been at home at Drury Lane, just as, two centuries earlier, *The Winter's Tale* (1610) could be performed at the Globe and the Blackfriars — public (i.e. open-to-the-skies) and private (i.e. enclosed) theatres, respectively. However, that the different traditions were clearly understood as such is plain from Planché's extravaganzas (see pp. 158–64).

Despite the uncertainty of scholars, there seems no doubt that the distinction was also understood by Shakespeare, though his terminology is different. When Polonius describes to Hamlet the players who are visiting Elsinore he says, 'Seneca cannot be too heavy, nor Plautus too light. For the law of writ and the liberty, these are the only men' (II.ii.376–8)

Scholars interpret 'writ' and 'liberty' variously, to say the least. H. H. Furness in the Variorum *Hamlet* (1877) gives among other authorities:

Capell: 'pieces written in rule, and pieces out of rule'.
Malone: '"Writ" is used for *writing* by Shakespeare's contemporaries' — and he gives two examples.
Caldecott: 'For the observance of the rules of the drama, while they take such liberties as are allowable . . .'
Walker: 'Read *wit*. "Writ" for *composition* is not English.'

1

> *Clarendon*: 'Probably the author did not intend that we should find a distinct meaning in Polonius's words.'
>
> *Corson*: 'heavy and light'.

John Dover Wilson, in the *New Cambridge Shakespeare* (1936), took 'the law of writ' and 'liberty' to be terms defining the jurisdiction of the Sheriffs in and about the city of London, and Cyrus Hoy in the Norton *Hamlet* (1963) interprets the phrase as 'plays according to strict classical rules, and those that ignored the unities of time and place'.

If this confusion seems unwarrantable, it should be borne in mind that whoever produced this part of the text for the Bad Quarto (1603) — that is, in Shakespeare's day — was also puzzled:

> *Seneca* cannot be too heavy, nor *Plato* too light.
> For the law hath writ those are the only men.   (E3ᵛ)

The interpretations nearest to the mark, I believe, are those of Collier and Dowden. Collier, quoted in the Variorum, distinguishes between written productions and extemporal plays, 'where liberty was allowed to the performers to invent the dialogue, in imitation of the Italian *commedie al improviso*'. Edward Dowden, in the Arden edition of 1899, suggested that the phrase probably referred to written plays and extemporal parts and he referred to Middleton's *The Spanish Gypsy* in which gypsy-actors were said to be able to perform in 'a way which the Italians and Frenchmen use'.

Whether *commedia dell'arte* is intended or not (and it is certainly possible, Kempe having only recently, in 1601, made his famous journey to Italy where, according to *The Travels of Three English Brothers* (printed 1607) he was invited to join in an 'extemporall merriment' with an Italian Harlequin), there seems to me little doubt that the distinction is between acting from texts fully written-out and *ad lib* performance. Hamlet's advice to the clowns to 'speak no more than is set down for them' is significant (and see pp. 40–2) and it is reasonable to suggest that 'the writ and the liberty' epitomise two kinds of dramatic experience which might be called, in different contexts, legitimate and illegitimate; overheard and direct address; *théâre de boulevard* and music hall; scripted drama and what Falstaff calls 'a play extempore' (*1 Henry IV*, II.iv.313). In traditional, West End or Broadway, fourth-wall-removed drama, the audience 'overhears' what is being performed; the actors act as if the audience were not there, yet they not only hope they have a house, but, in fact, direct their voices and gestures to that outwardly unacknowledged audience./ Furthermore, they *need* that audience to complete their performance; they may well feel as strongly as did one nineteenth-century tragedian who appealed across the footlights to the audience, 'How can I act if you don't applaud?' Nevertheless the fundamental distinction between 'overhearing' and direct address will be clear, even though the contrast in modes may not always be so simple. Thus, in a double act, one performer may directly address the audience whilst the duologue as a whole is 'overheard' — the appeal being made directly, through the proscenium arch, or even 'through the camera' to a film or television audience, as in the routines of Bob Hope and Bing Crosby, the Marx Brothers, and Morecambe and Wise.

It will be suggested that this tradition of direct address, still familiar to us through music hall and its descendants, goes back long before music halls came into being. Shakespeare and Marlowe used such acts as did many of their contemporaries and predecessors. In the Tudor period, however, it is as awkward to speak of overheard and direct appeal drama as it is to distinguish these forms by the terms legitimate and illegitimate, if only because, in the soliloquy, we often cannot be sure to what extent a performer is being 'overheard' and to what extent he is directly addressing the audience. Hamlet's soliloquies may be explained as the outpourings of a man, near to distraction, puzzling aloud over what he must do; Launce on the subject of his dog beneath the Duke's table, where Crab had not been but a pissing-while before the whole room smelt of him, is very clearly addressing us. But Richard III's soliloquies? Or Launcelet Gobbo wondering if he should leave his master? Both *can* be directly addressed to the audience but need not be. Richard III, in the BBC television series, *An Age of Kings* in 1961, could, with tremendous effect, exactly in the tradition of the Vice, make his appeal direct to the audience, seeking to seduce it as it were, look directly into the television camera and say

> The son of Clarence have I pent up close;
> His daughter meanly have I match'd in marriage;
> The sons of Edward sleep in Abraham's bosom,
> And Anne my wife hath bid this world good night.
> Now, for I know the Breton Richmond aims
> At young Elizabeth, my brother's daughter,
> And, by that knot, looks proudly on the crown,
> To her go I, a jolly thriving wooer.
>
> (IV.iii.36–43)

Paul Daneman, who played Richard III, lingered over that last line: 'A *jol*-ly — *thriv*-ing — *woo*-er', and then, in a big close-up, he winked outrageously into the camera, directly involving us.

Often, however, terms such as overheard drama, or direct address, are too positive for comfort. There is something to be said for distinguishing these forms by calling one 'popular' and the other — what? 'Serious', 'straight', 'sophisticated', *commedia erudita*? The popular origins of English drama are of considerable importance, and they were reinforced in the nineteenth century by the music halls, but little drama has been exclusively popular and the word 'popular' can be unclear when related to literature: folk-originated; by the people; for the masses?[1]

Another way of distinguishing these dramatic forms is by considering the ways in which the performers present themselves. Again, at the extremes the differences are obvious. The actor wholly engrossed in his part, trained in 'the Method', or even the nineteenth-century actor who assumes his role like a well-fitting overcoat as he walks on from the wings, can readily be distinguished from Chaplin — who is always Chaplin — or Morecambe and Wise, who, though dressed as Napoleon and Josephine, yet maintain simultaneously their own persona. But, again, there is a grey area. In this one might place Charles Laughton as Captain Bligh, giving a very fair interpretation of Charles Laughton, or an actor performing, as Paul Kornfeld suggests, in a way appropriate to Expressionist Drama,[2] or Brecht's account of Chinese acting.[3]

Thus, as there is no terminology appropriate to all circumstances, from time to time I shall use, as seems appropriate, 'music hall', 'direct address', 'popular', *théâtre de boulevard*, 'fourth-wall-removed drama', and so on, in the reasonably sanguine hope that the context, coupled with the explanations given, will make the meaning plain. An example or two might further clarify these distinctive kinds of performance, and the different relationships of performers to audiences.

One of the anxieties which some actors in 'straight' drama must face is that, in the midst of an impassioned declaration of love, or, indeed, at any 'exposed' point in a play, their false teeth will fly out. Bram Stoker tells of just such an occasion. Vandenhoff, for his farewell performance in 1858 in *The Merchant of Venice*, played Shylock to Irving's Bassanio. At his first entry on this emotional occasion (Act I, Sc. iii), he got no further than 'Three thousand . . .' at the start of his very first speech when there was 'a sort of odd click'. Vandenhoff's teeth had fallen out. Irving surreptitiously picked them up, keeping his body between Vandenhoff and the audience and Vandenhoff, having hidden his face in his hands (as if overcome with emotion, presumably), slipped his teeth back, turned to the audience and said, quite strongly and clearly, 'Three thousand ducats — well!'[4]

Now, by a happy, indeed hilarious, accident I saw the very same sort of incident in Sydney in about 1961 when a not-so-young leading man lost his teeth while declaring his love to a not-so-young ingénue. Our suspension of disbelief had in any case been already strained, but as the wretched actor stooped to pick up his teeth and slip them into his mouth with surreptitious obviousness, we could only thereafter be all disbelief. Actuality had broken in with a vengeance. 'Continuity' was fatally breached.

Now, the curious thing is that, even for the same audience, had this happened to a music-hall performer, appealing directly across the footlights to us, (a) we should not have known whether or not it was an accident; (b) we should have laughed thinking it part of the act; (c) even if 'continuity had been broken', so different is the illegitimate art, we should immediately afterwards have been able to switch back to that superficial involvement in the routine being performed, without the performer fatally slipping out of the persona he was adopting; and (d) if it was an accident, the music-hall artist might well 'write it into his act' thereafter. It is such relationships that I wish to explore.

Anne Righter has suggested in *Shakespeare and the Idea of the Play* that the medieval dramatists who wrote the cycles could 'regard their audience not only as Mankind in general, but also as a specific crowd of people gathered together for some perfectly natural and realistic reason' (p. 21); the popular morality, however, 'held a glass towards its medieval audience and showed them a grim, unflattering image' (p. 24). When the play moved into the banqueting hall, universality was lost, she argues, and we have, instead of a sense of 'everywhere and nowhere', continual specific references to time and place (pp. 31–2). She suggests that after 1550 direct address to the audience 'not only decreases, but tends to be relegated in its surviving forms to a routine slightly outside the action of the play. Only the aside . . . can now be delivered directly to the audience in the presence of other actors' (p. 56 — but compare Doris Fenton and Alan Somerset, pp. 36–7 below). Thus, she argues, there is a growing emphasis on 'the illusory, dreamlike quality of the play' which extra-dramatic address, though it never died out altogether, would fracture and 'by waking the sleepers, destroy the fabric of the dream prematurely' (pp. 58–60). Between 1550 and the early work of Kyd and Marlowe 'the play was beginning to establish itself as illusion' (p. 63). The soliloquy is then interpreted by Anne Righter as a mediating device 'by which the audience might be referred to indirectly without disturbing the illusion of the play' (p. 86), and it was this play metaphor, 'Essentially a technique for maintaining contact with the spectators' which is so pervasive in Shakespeare (p. 89), but which, long before the closing of the theatres in 1642, had been 'robbed of its value'.

Anne Righter's closely argued account cannot be given full justice in so few lines, but its authority requires that I give in her terms how the 'idea of the play' developed up to Shakespeare. It is a very persuasive argument and, in the main, I am in agreement, but it does seem to me that there were more serious intrusions into the play-world than she allows, and that these could not but make an audience aware that it was in a theatre. One cannot be absolutely certain that the name Jaques conjured up the suggestion of a privy; or that his 'Nay then, God be wi' you, an you talk in blank verse' (*As You Like It*, IV.i.34–4) reminded the audience that it was watching a play; or that at least some of the audience would not find Jaques's 'All the world's a stage,/ And all the men and women merely players' (II.vii.139–40), a deadening cliché (like those ironically uttered by the new-inspired Gaunt in *Richard II* [II.i.33–9]), fatally undercut by the Globe's reputed motto 'Totus mundus agit histrionem'. One cannot be sure, but it seems very likely. The motto, it is true, is reported no earlier than by Malone, but it is certainly in accord with the way Jaques is undercut — 'placed' — elsewhere in the play. Even before he has appeared, Jaques's claim to be taken seriously is undermined by the First Lord's description of his weeping into the stream as he moralises on behalf of the deer (II.i.46 ff.). Just prior to his 'All the world's a stage' set piece, he is described in loathsome, excretory terms by Duke Senior (II.vii.64–9), and there is again reference to the world outside the play when he is called by Touchstone 'good Master What-ye-call't' (III.iii.79). I cannot wholly accept (as later discussion will show) that the play-world remains intact and the audience left to enjoy a dream world. Jaques may well be 'a professional pessimist concerned to point out the bitter comedy of man's progression from swaddling clothes to shroud' (Righter, p. 165), but he is so 'placed' in the play that he is not to be taken at his own estimation — as the entry of Orlando and Adam as soon as he has finished his set piece stresses. The 'old Adam' may be Jaques's concern, but he knows nothing of the love and loyalty that are immediately demonstrated before us.

Interpretation of *As You Like It*, and many other plays, depends in part upon the fracturing of the dream and whilst I cannot but agree that *the idea of the play* is strong Shakespeare and his contemporaries, that image was more persistently related to the real (especially the political) world than *Shakespeare and the Idea of the Play* allows.

A number of things need here to be taken into account even at this preliminary stage. The first is that capacity of Elizabethan audiences and modern audiences of illegitimate drama (music hall, film comedy from Harold Lloyd to the 'Road' films, and television comedy routines such as those performed by Frankie Howerd as Lurcio in *Up Pompeii*) for 'multiconscious apprehension'. This was excellently described in 1944 by S. L. Bethell: 'a popular audience, uncontaminated by abstract and tendentious dramatic theory, will attend to several diverse aspects of a situation, simultaneously yet without confusion.'[5] The idea that if the suspension of disbelief is broken the audience is irretrievably lost — and this underlies the argument that the sleepers must not be awakened from the dream world of the play (a beautiful but not very happy image) — is false. An English audience can have its attention broken and then, with the right performers in the right play, become even more involved after such a break. I would liken the audience's response to two kinds of experience spanning five centuries.

About the year that *Fulgens and Lucres* (1497) was performed, there was painted one of the most horrifying pictures I know: Gerard David's execution by flaying of the corrupt judge, Sisamnes. The agony of the condemned man and the workmanlike impassiveness of the executioners, are dramatically apparent in their faces. As we look, revolted and appalled, our attention is caught by the apprentice executioner's face. He gazes out of the picture, his head inclined a little to our right, away from the live body he is helping to skin, mute pain in every feature of his young face. It is, I think, the triumph of the picture. To find this beautiful would defy even Lessing — how can Sisamnes's revolting agonies be 'beautiful'? — but David's answer is even more remarkable than that of the sculptor of the Laocoön. By 'breaking the continuity', instead of gazing obscenely upon barbarity, we respond to the direct, mute appeal in the young executioner's eyes. We respond multiconsciously. We are enabled simultaneously to witness the horror and feel the pity. But the pity does not mitigate the horror. Indeed, David, painting at a time when *décor simultané* was practised in staging as well as in pictures, not only shows Sisamnes being flayed but, in the background, his whole skin stretched across his judge's chair in order to remind his successor of the price of corrupting justice.[6]

It is a commonplace to think of the composition of an audience at Shakespeare's Globe as ideal, all-inclusive: groundlings, apprentices, ordinary men and women, lawyers, aristocrats. If it is difficult to be sure how accurate is this romantic picture, it is even harder to reconstruct the response of such an audience, though several scholars, notably

S. L. Bethell, have made valiant attempts. I am inclined to think that the nearest we can nowadays get to participating in what it was like to be at the Globe for *As You Like It* in 1599, or *Hamlet* in 1601, is attendance at a Royal Albert Hall Promenade Concert. I do not mean simply the extravaganza of the last night (though there are lessons to be read there), but any full house in which the piano has to be moved, its 'A' struck, or some incidental event occurs which produces a childlike response from the huge company of promenaders, a response so endearing because it is set within a context of total rapture. It is remarkable how that audience can break out in near-rowdyism and yet, within a moment, be hushed, still, and entranced, crushed though its promenaders are, standing like Elizabethan groundlings.

At the end of the first decade of the seventeenth century, theatres like the Globe faced competition from the private theatres. The epithet 'private' is misleading. Such theatres were only private in being closed-in from the elements. They were thus much smaller, artificially lit, and, in consequence, more expensive. An apprentice who could barely afford the Globe could certainly not pay for entrance to the Blackfriars. Inevitably, 'a different class of person' was to be found at the private theatres. Nevertheless the same companies and the same plays might be seen at both kinds of theatre. After all, from 1609 to 1642 the King's Men — the company to which Shakespeare belonged — performed at both the Globe and the Blackfriars.[7]

Few theatres survived closure from 1642 to 1660 and none of the open-to-the-skies theatres was used for performance after the Restoration. It is tempting to see a dramatic tradition which had appealed universally in England from the time of the mystery cycles to Shakespeare as fatally fractured when Parliament closed the theatres at the outbreak of the Civil War. Because it was the private theatres which survived, it is assumed too readily sometimes that the Restoration audience at such theatres was akin to their coterie audiences of 1642. It is difficult to be certain, but it seems at least likely that the Restoration and eighteenth-century theatre audience had far more in common with the Globe audience than with coterie, quasi-aristocratic audiences. In the early nineteenth century one has only to think of the Old Price Riots of 1809, when performances at Covent Garden were disturbed by riots for sixty-seven nights, or read Hazlitt on the Minor Theatres or Dickens on 'The Amusements of the People' (*Household Words*, 30 March and 13 April 1850), to realise that audiences were as lively then as any depicted by Beaumont in *A Knight of the Burning Pestle*.

It also seems likely that it was not until after the ending of the Patent

Theatre Monopoly in 1843 — not the Licensing Act of 1737, nor the closure of the theatres in 1642, nor even the re-opening of the Blackfriars in 1609 — that the theatre as a distinctively middle-class institution, in ambience if not wholly in composition, began to emerge. If, decrying the middle-class audience as is fashionable, we wish to look back with nostalgia we might pick 1809 as readily as 1609, or even 1617, when apprentices wrecked the Cockpit Theatre, destroyed the play manuscripts and costumes, and hastened the dissolution of the company using that theatre (Queen Anne's Men) two years later.

The capacity of an Elizabethan audience for multiconscious apprehension was not lost with the Globe. It was to be found in theatres legitimate and illegitimate at least until the year when those terms were formally abolished. There is no doubt that the proportion of 'overheard', fourth-wall-removed drama increased after the Restoration, but even in theatres which might be expected to concentrate upon such drama, there were also to be seen, for nearly two-hundred years after the theatres re-opened, plays which *deliberately* drew attention to the theatre and the drama. In this study attention is directed almost exclusively to the latter form, it being assumed that readers will be very familiar with the history of that drama which has endeavoured to sustain completeness of illusion.

It is remarkable how frequently theatricals have expressed in performance and later in film, the very medium of their art. Often (especially in the eighteenth and nineteenth centuries) this has been in 'irregular' forms — in rehearsal plays, burlesques and extravaganzas — but, to take a single example from the medium of realistic film at the high point of that genre, Preston Sturges was not only saying something ironic in *Sullivan's Travels* (1947) about Hollywood's then current passion for the socially-conscious film, but, in Joel McCrea's and his fellow convicts' response to a Walt Disney film shown to them — a film within a film — he was saying something pertinent about the nature of film and its social function. The 'Idea of the Film' was here used seriously and many examples could be given of the comic use of 'The Idea of the Film'.[8]

What one does find from the mid-nineteenth century is that not only does the *théâtre de boulevard* attract an audience of a more homogeneous character, but that the kind of drama and the mode of presentation in such theatres led to total and continuous suspension of disbelief that precluded multiconscious apprehension. At the same time, however, music halls were developed and they maintained that capacity in their audiences. From the music hall that inheritance was passed to film and television.

In his Neale Lecture in English History given at University College,

London on 3 December 1976, Professor Keith Thomas, speaking of 'The Place of Laughter in Tudor and Stuart England',[9] discussed the repression of certain kinds of inversionary laughter — that is, laughter arising out of inversion in social role, as in the custom at Oxford in which the Terrae Filius vilified and burlesqued his superiors. This, he said, was the first great change in what was thought fit for laughter in the Tudor and Stuart periods. The second change was the attempt 'to demarcate certain areas in which laughter was no longer allowed to penetrate' (p. 79). He also pointed to the way that 'The cult of decorum led to a profound divergence between the streams of polite humour and folk humour' so that

> Farce and buffoonery were rejected by the neo-classical theorists as intolerably 'low'; suitable only for that 'rabble of little people', who, in Shadwell's words, were 'more pleas'd with Jack Puddings being soundly kick'd; or having a custard handsomely thrown in his face, than with all the wit in plays'. Bawdy was also denounced as another false form of wit, while even puns and quibbles were spurned as 'mean and boorish', the relics of 'an infantile, unpolish'd age'. The upper classes thus deliberately distanced themselves from the humour of their inferiors.

A little later he says 'The new cult of decorum thus meant that it was only the vulgar who could go laughing without restraint.'[10] Not surprisingly, perhaps, the last king or queen of England to employ a court fool was Charles I.

However, against this shift, which certainly took place, needs to be set the work of Davenant, Duffett, Gay, Fielding, Foote and Planché, sometimes specifically mocking heroic, neo-classic pretentions, always using the 'Image of the Play', and capitalising on their audiences' capacity to respond 'to several diverse aspects of a situation, simultaneously without confusion'. Of course, in the rehearsal and burlesque formulae is often what Anne Righter incorrectly attributes to Massinger's *The Roman Actor* (1626) — 'delight in playing with illusion for its own sake' (no bad thing surely). Nevertheless, so seriously was the illusion played with that Walpole's Licensing Act was brought in in 1737 to prevent the performance of such plays and as a result Fielding gave up writing drama. And Planché, in his extravaganzas, sought by just such means to give a new dignity and a certain delicacy to the stage of his time.

Thus, although there were changes even prior to the closing of the theatres in the idea of the play and the role of laughter, I would date the really significant shift in the theatre some two hundred years and more after the theatres were closed in 1642. Paradoxically, the end of the monopoly of the Patent Theatres hardened the distinction between legitimate and illegitimate dramatic forms — straight, overheard drama and music hall. This was in part a result of social change, but also because of three innovations in the theatre. One was the coming of realism into the drama, starting in England with Robertson's plays of the mid-1860s; second was the change in lighting in the 'straight' theatres — a brilliantly-lit stage from 1817 with an increasingly dimmed auditorium until, by the time Irving took over the Lyceum in 1878, the audience sat in complete darkness; and third, a decrease in rowdyism in the theatres, variously dated between the 1840s and 1860s, the legitimate theatre becoming a middle-class institution, in style if not wholly in make-up.

Separation of the 'Writ and the Liberty' only became complete about the middle of the nineteenth century and it lasted less than a century until, say, Wilder's *Our Town* (1938) and *The Skin of our Teeth* (1942); Beckett's *Endgame* (1957), Osborne's *The Entertainer* (1957) and Arden's *Live Like Pigs* (1958); yet we tend to view drama as far back as that of the Restoration, and even sometimes Elizabethan drama, as if it were on all fours with less than a hundred years of legitimate, middle-class, realistic, darkened-auditorium, drama, a drama which, as Stanislavski argued in *An Actor Prepares*, 'actors may not maintain contact directly with the audience . . . with [our partner on-stage] our contact is direct and conscious, with the [audience] it is indirect and unconscious'.[11] But this is to anticipate the concerns of this volume and *Contemporary Drama and the Popular Dramatic Tradition in England*.

2 The Medieval Tradition

The cultural traditions of the Middle Ages have been described in broad terms as comprising two streams. In the 1930s, Robert Redfield, a social anthropologist, described 'the great tradition' as that of the educated few, and 'the little tradition' as that of the unlettered majority. These traditions, though independent, 'have long affected each other and continue to do so'. Peter Burke, who quotes Redfield,[1] modifies this model in an important way. He suggests that these two cultural traditions 'did not correspond symmetrically to the two main social groups, the elite and the common people. The elite participated in the little tradition, but the common people did not participate in the great tradition.' The great tradition was closed, being available only to those who had attended grammar school and university whereas the little tradition was 'open to all, like the church, the tavern and the market-place, where so many of the performances occurred'. The upper classes, Burke later states, withdrew from participation in the little tradition in the seventeenth and eighteenth centuries and although it was argued (by Swift, for example), and is still sometimes asserted, that the culture of the lower classes is a debased form of an earlier higher-class culture (as opposed to the view of 'the discoverers of popular culture, such as Herder and the Grimms — that creativity came from below, from the people'), 'it can be stated with confidence that there was a two-way traffic between them'. Between these two cultures, mediating between them and facilitating interaction, was a 'chap-book culture', which he likens to an early form of what Dwight Macdonald has termed 'midcult'.[2]

There are fairly obvious parallels between this model and English drama of the Middle Ages. One might say that the cycles were a part of the little tradition in which the elite participated — attending the Feast of Corpus Christi performances and, probably, writing the texts. Who wrote the cycles is not known, but in the work of the Wakefield Master (c.1435–50) one can certainly see the use of popular, or little tradition, elements. This is apparent in the *First Shepherds' Play* where the Third Shepherd responds to the Second Shepherd:

12

> Yey, torde.
> I am lever ete;
> What is drynk withoute mete?
> Gett mete, gett,
> And sett us a borde.
>
> (ll. 192–6)

And 'turd' appears again in the *Second Shepherds' Play* when the Scotch robber, Mak, is told by the First Shepherd to stop pretending he has a Southern accent:

> Bot, Mak, is that sothe?
> Now take outt that sothren tothe,
> And sett in a torde.
>
> (ll. 214-16)

Peter Happé says in his introduction to these plays

> One of the most striking things about the Wakefield Master is his learning. He carries it gracefully, but clearly he is well taught and sets out to establish important religious truths in traditional terms. Even though his characters are earthy and speak coarsely, he transmits through them the learning of the medieval Church. Besides this, he is sensitive to folk-tales, to the partly non-Christian religion of the people, and to classical learning. There is also evidence, in his choice of incident, that he knew something of French farce, and something of other treatments of the Nativity, particularly in the Chester plays.[3]

Rather than being wholly in the little tradition, therefore, it could be argued that the cycle drama came close to fulfilling the role of mediator, at least from the point of view of the dramatist. As a cultural activity it was 'popular', 'open', and in these two characteristics it had much in common with one of its supposed sources: the sermon. In his monograph, 'The English Moral Plays',[4] Elbert N. S. Thompson suggested that 'the sermon in dialogue on allegorical themes' was the forerunner of the morality play. He pointed to the way in which, at first, tales were used to drive home a point (a method with, it could be argued, divine authority) but that, and he quotes T. F. Crane, 'speakers developed the story at the expense of the sermon, and did not scruple to use ribald tales and scurrilous jests. Without exaggeration Dante could protest

Now men go forth with jests and drolleries
To preach, and if but well the people laugh,
The hood puffs out, and nothing more is asked'[5]

Apart from the obvious similarity with cyclical and morality drama, the fusing of learning and low wit, and the implied abuse of method, it will be noted that in the sermon the speaker is addressing the audience directly, as will the actor in the later illegitimate dramatic tradition. The next stage has the effect of bringing together direct address and the overheard in embryo. As Thompson puts it

> Not, however, in these anecdotal excrescences, but rather in sermons on the most serious and exalted themes, did dialogue find its fullest opportunity. After learning to rehearse the simple dialogue contained in the Scriptural lesson of the day, preachers took soon to the next obvious step, and simulated as real a more extended dialogue that might plausibly have been carried on by Bible characters. To add to the reality of the words, some brief description of the scene could be added, or more effectively developed, and the preacher would then be virtually reciting, as men were supposed during the Middle Ages to have read in public the comedies of Plautus and Terence, a religious play.

It is easy to capture the effect of such a sermon technique from a dramatic monologue influenced by it: Launcelot Gobbo's routine in *The Merchant of Venice* (1596, II.ii.1–33), in which he considers whether or not he should leave Shylock. The appeal to conscience and the acceptance of the Fiend's 'more friendly counsel', are particularly interesting. The text has here been so lineated as to bring out the dialogue form. Note Gobbo's reference to his father in the form of an 'aside-within-a-monologue'.

> Certainly my conscience will serve me to run from this Jew, my master. The Fiend is at mine elbow, and tempts me, saying to me:
> *Gobbo, Launcelot Gobbo, good Launcelot —*
> or:
> *Good Gobbo —*
> or:
> *Good Launcelot Gobbo, use your legs, take the start, run away!*
> My conscience says:
> *No! Take heed, honest Launcelot. Take heed, honest Gobbo —*
> or, as aforesaid:
> *Honest Launcelot Gobbo, do not run; scorn running with thy heels.*

Well, the most courageous Fiend bids me pack:
Via!
says the Fiend —
Away!
says the Fiend —
For the heavens, rouse up a brave mind
says the Fiend —
and run!
Well, my conscience, hanging about the neck of my heart, says very wisely to me:
My honest friend Launcelot, being an honest man's son —
or rather, an honest woman's son — for, indeed, my father did something smack, something grow to, he had a kind of taste. Well, my conscience says:
Launcelot, budge not!
Budge!
says the Fiend.
Budge not!
says my conscience.
Conscience — say I — you counsel well.
Fiend — say I — you counsel well.
To be ruled by my conscience, I should stay with the Jew, my master, who, God bless the mark!, is a kind of devil; and to run away from the Jew, I should be ruled by the Fiend, who, saving your reverence, is the Devil himself. Certainly the Jew is the very devil incarnal and, in my conscience, my conscience is but a kind of hard conscience, to offer to counsel me to stay with the Jew. The Fiend gives the more friendly counsel:
I will run, Fiend. My heels are at your commandment.
I will run!

Thompson gives a number of examples including one sermon attributed to St Bernard which contains 'a definite suggestion of the scene, brisk dialogue, and an effective close' (p. 307). Compare also Coomes in *The Two Angry Women of Abingdon*, p. 88 below.

Nothing convinces me more of the 'drama in the sermon' than the similarity of response required by both forms — response to a combination of direct address and overhearing, and what George Hunter calls 'multiplicity'. Pointing out that 'the sermon was the most widely practised and most generally esteemed form of discourse till long after Lyly's day', he goes on:

> The structure of the sermon, like that of the cathedral, is in terms of idea not of recognizable unity. The separate sections of the sermon may make a direct appeal, to prayer, to amusement, to horror, to awe, but the relation of one section to another may have nothing to do with such affects, depending on the intellectual scheme which was adopted at the beginning.[6]

Such 'multiplicity' is a feature of sixteenth-century drama and the narrative methods are common to sermon and drama. Obviously, with several characters to play the roles, the possibilities open to the dramatist are more varied than those available to the preacher. It is easy to see how 'continuity can be broken' yet attention retained: indeed, attention made the deeper through being broken, exactly as it can be to this day in the successor to the music hall, when the television comic directly addresses his audience through the eye of the camera. It will be noted, too, that the way in which Gobbo dramatises his characters, his conscience and the Fiend, speaking their lines in direct speech, is combined with his describing the situation and speaking to them, exactly in the manner of a nineteenth- and twentieth-century comic.

In a peculiarly intricate way, play-acting and real life were intertwined (perhaps one should say confused, or at least not distinguished) in medieval drama when it was performed by local people.

It was not merely that local people — local personalities — played specific roles (what, for example, was the relationship between the man who played Herod and his known character?), but that whole plays were the property and pride of particular groups. Although many cycle plays had nothing in common with the occupations of those who presented them, when there was a direct link — as between those who carried water from the River Dee and those who presented The Deluge in the Chester Cycle, or between the Pinners of York and the Crucifixion play of that city's cycle — the world of daily routine cannot have gone entirely unnoticed. 'Have done, dryve in that nayle' must have had an added edge to it when the speaker was a known nailmaker in York. This congruity might have struck the watcher less to the extent that the faith being enhanced by such drama was as much a natural part of life then as it was supernatural. Nevertheless, it indicates how sophisticated was the onlookers' capacity for multiconscious apprehension. Simultaneously, they could see Christ, as it were, being nailed to the Cross; make the link with the life of their own time; and, even more amazing, respond to the buffoonery attendant upon the execution of Christ.

Some interesting comparisons can be made with the Welsh-language mystery play, *The Three Kings of Cologne* (*c*.1490–*c*.1520). This, it has been argued by Gwennan Jones, is an independently written play. (Jones does not exclude the possibility that the author was working under the influence of English mystery plays, in particular those of Chester and the Coventry Shearmen and Tailors' play; continental sources are also possible.[7]) The play bears the inscription: 'Llyma yr ymddiddau a vy ryng y tre Brenin o gwlen' ('This is the conversation that took place between the three kings of Cologne'), which might suggest a dialogue rather than an acted drama.

The play differs significantly from those in the English tradition. Herod does not rage, for example, and the innocents are slaughtered off-stage. Most interesting is a scene in which Mary, when escaping with the Child Jesus from Herod's wrath, has to pass the gatekeeper at the city wall. This may be correct for the time of Christ, though historical accuracy is not likely to have been in the forefront of the dramatist's mind. It reflects actual life in a fortified Welsh border town of the time. The play is being made appropriate to the daily experience of those who are to see it. Translated into English, the dialogue reads:

Porter: I am watching here
         where I was told to watch well.
         How like thou art to a nurse;
         what hast thou there?
Mary: I am escaping with my Child
         after hearing that some are seeking me.
         I have the Child of grace;
         I shall not try to deny him.
Porter: Go, and may God go with thee.
         I shall not say otherwise to thee;
         thou art having a long conversation.
         If he were here thou wouldst not stay so.[8]

In isolation, on paper, this says little enough, but, in the vernacular — Welsh — in a town guarded by a gatekeeper who represented an alien authority, it would have had an immediate reality, rooting the past in the present in a way which historical perspective would make incongruous.

With the coming of the morality play and the interlude, this kind of relationship of play-world and real-world is no longer as intimately interwoven as it had been in the cycles. Such plays were not necessarily performed at a specific festival at which the players could expect to gain a hearing. An occasion to be heard had to be sought or made. A play will often, therefore, begin with a plea for attention and it is not surprising that this tradition goes back to the very beginnings of the extant secular drama in English. The actor's part known as the *Dux Moraud*, which probably dates from about 1300, half a century or more before the mystery cycles were first performed, starts with an address to the audience, bidding it be silent and pay attention:

> Emperourys and kyngys be kende,
>   Erlys and barunnys bolde,
> Bachelerys and knytys to mende,
>   Sueyerys and ȝemen to holde,
> Knauys and pagys to sende,
>   So parfyt þat aryn to be solde,
> I prey ȝow, lordyngys so hende,
>   No yangelyngys ȝe mak in þis folde
>   Today;
>   Als ȝe are lovely in fas,
>   Set ȝow alle semly in plas,
>   And I xal withoutyn falas
>   Schewe resounus here to ȝoure pay.[9]

The speaker then goes on to introduce himself much as does Aristorius in *The Play of the Sacrament* some 150 years later:

> Syr Arystory is my name,
>   A merchante myghty of a royall araye;
> fful wyde in this worlde spryngyth my fame,
>   Fere kend & knowen, the sothe for to saye.
>   In all maner of londis, without ony naye,
> My merchandyse renneth, the sothe for to tell;
>   In Gene & in Jenyse & in Genewaye,
> In Surry & in Saby & in Salerun I sell.[10]

An introduction would initially have been useful, perhaps necessary, as a device for gaining a hearing in circumstances when there were not the formalities of set starting times, trumpet calls or theatre bells. It was open to development as a frame of the kind in which *The Digby Play of the Conversion of St. Paul* (*c*.1500) is set. In this play, the Poet speaks the Prologue, introduces his subject, comments between the parts of the play, and makes his apologies at the end. Glynne Wickham suggests that he might also have remained on the stage to prompt the actors.[11] We have something similar in Bishop Bale's *Temptation of Our Lord* (1538) and we are not far removed from his aptly named Interpreter in his *King John* (1538):

> In this present act we have to you declared,
> As in a mirror, the beginning of King John:
> How he was, of God, a magistrate appointed
> To the governance of this same noble region,
> To see maintained the true faith and religion;
> But Satan the Devil, which that time was at large,
> Had so great a sway that he could it not discharge.[12]

It is then a very short step to the Choruses of *Henry V* (1599) and intermeans of Jonson and Randolph. To what extent, one wonders, were audiences of the time aware of the different planes of reality which were created by these dramatic structures? To what extent did the tradition surprise or confuse an audience accustomed to the cycle tradition which found no need for such mediatory devices? Bearing in mind that cycles and non-cyclical plays co-existed for some 150 years or more, the answer must be that an audience would not be in the least put out. The two traditions could co-exist as readily as could legitimate and illegitimate drama in the nineteenth century without their audiences being perplexed.

This is not to imply that the dramatic illusion in the Middle Ages could withstand *any* degree of disruption. A break directly involving the audience, especially if effected clumsily, might completely and permanently destroy the play-world. Thus, in *Mankind* (1465–70), when the collection is taken up before the appearance of Titivillus, or in *Mind Will, and Understanding* (?1460–3), when the Devil abducts an inattentive member of the audience — this 'fals boy' — and we have the stage direction, 'her he takyt a screwde boy wyth hym, & goth hys wey, cryenge',[13] the possibilities for fatally disruptive horseplay are fairly obvious. Consider, however, the break in the *Ludus Coventriae*, 'Noah and Lamech'. In this, whilst Noah goes off to build the Ark, an 'interlude' is played between the blind Lamech and a young man. This is a 'farce' in the culinary sense of something stuffed into the main course of action. Lamech accidentally kills Cain, blames the boy — 'Thou stynkynge lurdeyn'[14] — and kills him. Compare that with the advertising breaks which occur, several times, stuffed into commercial television plays. It will be realised that even though we now have become accustomed to a tradition of silent, almost religious attention at plays presented in quasi-realism, we can overleap even the grossest intrusions.

How much more readily might a medieval or Tudor audience, not burdened by a tradition of stage realism, take up again the illusion after a 'break'?

I am inclined to think, therefore, that we exaggerate very greatly the disruptive effects of breaks in dramatic continuity, especially in drama seen long before middle-class, plush-seated, warm, darkened auditoria became the norm. It was not that disruption took place but the use to which that disruption might be put that mattered. Far from breaking the illusion, direct address to the audience and the 'special excursions' made by comic characters among the spectators, were means whereby, as T. W. Craik put it, continual contact with the audience was sought and maintained and the spectators encouraged to join in.[15]

The cycles were enjoyed within 'the little tradition'. The plays were not only a means of teaching religious truths, but a manipulation within the little tradition (i.e. without the trappings of the complete theology and dogma understood by those of the great tradition), by which the majority was persuaded to have faith in salvation and learned to understand its process. As soon as plays were written which fell outside that tradition, plays which if not learned (and compare the phrase *commedia erudita*), but which drew on a different range of imaginative experience than that shared by all, some form of introduction, of mediation even, seemed, at least to some authors, to be necessary. The story of *Dux Moraud* is 'imaginative' in this sense. Seduction is early a feature of secular drama — for example, *The Interlude of the Clerk and the Girl* (1290–1330) and the dialogue *Dame Sirith*[16] — but the incest theme of the *Dux Moraud* is rather more surprising (though it is dangerous to make assumptions from such fragmentary evidence as the surviving early secular dramas).

This mediation, by prologue, 'Poet', Interpreter, together with the 'special excursions' of the comic characters, whether only verbal or actually physical, served not only to maintain contact with the audience, but, as the drama developed, helped the unlettered majority to understand what was being offered to them. Shakespeare and his contemporaries were not simply indulging the groundlings in low comedy, but, more subtly than in the moralities, drawing those of the little tradition into the world of the great tradition. And, however learned some dramatists were, such as Chapman and Jonson, they did not entirely abandon those 'special excursions'.

It is possible by an examination of *Fulgens and Lucres* (1497) to summarise much of what has been suggested in this chapter and, at the same time, provide a base for a discussion of Elizabethan drama of the great tradition.

In this play one can see fully evolved the device of the frame and intermean used in *The Taming of a Shrew* (1589, and curtailed in *The Taming of the Shrew*, 1594), *The Old Wives' Tale*, (1590), in several of Jonson's and Randolph's plays, in masques, and in the rehearsal plays of the seventeenth and eighteenth centuries.[17]

The circumstances in which Henry Medwall's *Fulgens and Lucres* was performed, though not absolutely certain, are fairly well agreed. F. S. Boas and A. W. Reed suggested in their 1926 edition that the occasion was the visit of the Flemish and Spanish ambassadors to Cardinal Morton at Lambeth Palaces at Christmas, 1497, and that Morton commissioned his chaplain to write the entertainment.[18] What is known of Tudor staging, and the play itself, suggests that the interlude 'required no setting at all. The banqueting hall was the theatre with architectural features of the room serving in many cases for background.'[19]

The device upon which the play succeeds brilliantly or founders disastrously involves two actors in the guise of Morton's household servants, first discussing whether a play is to take place and then successively attaching themselves as servants to the principals in the play. The subject of the play is a debate. Who is more worthy to marry Lucres, daughter of Fulgens: Publius Cornelius, who is noble by birth, or Gaius Flaminius, ennobled through his own achievements? The servants are comic and continually address remarks to the audience, which cannot (at least at first) know whether they are of the household or in the play. The debate is of a serious issue — not who is a fit husband for Lucres, but wherein lies true nobility. Is nobility inherited or can it be won in this world? In Medwall's source, the Senate makes the choice but its decision is left for the reader to guess. Medwall who was more a teacher than a priest and, as Creeth suggests, a man of some nerve,[20] presented to his audience a significantly different conclusion. First, he allows Lucres the right to make her own decision; secondly, her choice rests upon Flaminius — upon nobility earned through achievement. Medwall has very plainly come down on the side of a new way of looking at nobility and relations between the sexes.

The degree to which Medwall's device has impressed commentators has varied enormously, perhaps because there have been few opportunities to see the play and none to experience it at the kind of occasion on which it was first given, divorced from the knowledge of dramatic developments to come. The first editors, F. S. Boas and A. W. Reed, thought the consequence of intermingling actors and spectators revealed 'an imperfect sense of dramatic objectivity'. Wickham castigates this as 'nonsense in the proper dramatic context of the play in performance' and Thelma

Greenfield considers it to be a denial of the artistry by which the play is adapted to the circumstances of its original production (a very important point). To Boas and Reed, Medwall's understanding of dramatic illusion is naive, but, as Thelma Greenfield points out 'To pretend that the audience was not there, under such intimate circumstances, would have been naïveté indeed.' In this she is surely right, given the kind of playing area which the actors had to use. She goes on: 'Medwall has avoided clumsy pretence on the one hand and confusion on the other. He has controlled the situation by dramatising it with the audience itself given a role — that of being the audience.'[21]

T. W. Craik speaks of Medwall's 'assured accomplishment' that implies an existing tradition[22] and David Bevington describes the interplay of the two modes of illusion as brilliant. However, he is hardly correct in asserting that there is 'a rigorous distinction' between the play's comic and serious scenes, and to say that, in contradistinction to the participants of the comic scenes, 'the disputants of the main action *seldom* [my italics] acknowledge the presence of the spectators' undervalues the importance of their contacts with the audience and thus exaggerates the difference in the relationship between the audience and the serious and comic actions.[23]

Anne Righter, whilst acknowledging a certain charm, is of a mind with Boas and Reed and dashes cold water over Medwall's achievement:

> Despite the fact that there is even less room for them here than in a typical Tudor morality, the Cardinal and his guests appear in virtually every scene of *Fulgens and Lucres*. Made a party to resolutions and plots, asked to open doors and hunt for missing letters, their presence prevents characters more important to the plot from creating a realistic, three-dimensional image of life. The play world is charming, but it can develop neither complexity nor depth. Lucres and her suitors gesture vainly towards their own far-off time and country, but in the end they speak clearly only of the long tables in the Cardinal's hall at Lambeth, the guests, the bustle of servants, and the great fire blazing against the December cold.[24]

Medwall's application of technique to circumstance (occasion and place) and subject matter seems to me nothing less than masterly. We do not know whether he addressed his play to the servitors present as well as the distinguished guests (though it is not beyond the bounds of possibility), but there is little doubt that some of the audience, though not 'common people', would find the burden of the serious part of the play novel and challenging. It is noticeable, therefore, that in addition to using the actor-servants, A and B, as intermediaries to the play-world, ushering in each of the two parts of the play, they ensure that the story is understood, and act as mediators in a very important way in the transmission of the idea that women should choose their husbands and, even more important, the basis upon which that choice should be made: the nature of true nobility, *post* Wars of the Roses.

If one imagines a banquet in a hall without special playing area, it can easily be seen how A and B gradually create space and place for the action. This *must* mean that they address members of the company. What is surprising is the freedom with which, whether as pseudo-house servants or as actors, they speak to those attending the banquet. The very first lines of the play are appropriate to a licensed jester rather than a servile waiting-man:

> *A*:   For Goddes will
> What mean ye, sirs, to stand so still?
> Have ye not eaten and your fill,
> And paid nothing therefore?
> Iwis, sirs, thus dare I say,
> He that shall for the shott pay
> Vouchsafeth that ye largely assay
> Such meat as he hath in store.
> I trow your dishes be not bare
> Nor yet ye do the wine spare;
> Therefore be merry as ye fare,
> Ye are welcome each one
> Unto this house without feigning.
>
> (I.1–13)

Possibly the raillery was designed to ensure attention, eliciting the unspoken question 'Who is this that so addresses us?' The same sort of abuse is offered at the beginning of the second part when, after further feasting in the interval between the two Parts, the play is to continue:

> But now to the matter that I came for!
> You know the cause thereof before:
> Your wits be not so short.
>
> (II.7–9)

Then, when B knocks to be admitted:

> One of you, go look who it is!
> *Intrat B. [Enter B.]*
> B: [*To the member of the audience who opens the door*]
>
> Nay, nay! All the meyney of them, Iwis,
> Cannot so much good!
> A man may rap till his knuckles ache
> Ere any of them will the labour take
> To give him an answer!
>   (II.75–80)

Any assumption that it might be another servant who is called upon to open the door is denied by A's response:

> I have great marvel on thee
> That ever thou wilt take upon thee
> To chide any man here!
> No man is so much to blame as thou
> For long tarrying!
>   (II.81–5)

What one may well have here is the kind of inversion of hierarchy common in the custom of the Boy Bishop and, later, the Boy Admiral, or the Terrae Filius. Just as the officers serve the men at Christmas (or did not so very long ago), so here the servants give the orders. The use of Mummers (II.387 ff.) and the farcical scenes based on Running at Quintain — the jousting 'at fart-prick-in-cule' (I.1165 ff.) — show that Medwall was well aware of folk customs,[25] and it is likely that this raillery of a distinguished audience by actor-servants at Christmas is an example of what Keith Thomas calls inversionary humour (see p. 10 above). The 'confusion', if that be what it is, between A and B's roles as servants and actors may not have been quite so perplexing to the audience of the time, therefore, in that even as servants they might, on such an occasion, be privileged to 'invert their usual positions'.

The audience's attention having been attracted, it is then directed to the serious part of the play as first B and then A attach themselves to the suitors. When Cornelius, the first of the suitors to appear, is left on his own, he directly addresses those in the hall:

> *Cornelius:*   [*To audience*] Now a wise fellow that had
>   somewhat a brain

And of such things had experience
Such one would I with me retain
To give me counsel and assistance,
For I will spare no cost or expense
Nor yet refuse any labour or pain
The love of fair Lucres thereby to attain.
So many good fellows as [be] in this hall,
And is there none, Sirs, among you all
That will enterprise this geare?
But, if you will not, then I must
Go seek a man elsewhere.

Et exeat [*He goes out*] *Deinde loquitur B* [*Then B speaks*]

B: Now have I spied a meet Office for me!
        For I will be of counsel, and I may,
        With yonder man —
A: Peace, let be!
        By God! Thou wilt destroy all the play.
B: Destroy the play, quotha? Nay, nay!
        The play began never till now!
        I will be doing, I make God a vow;
        For there is not in this hundred mile
        A feater bawd than I am one!
A: And what shall I do in the meanwhile?
B: Mary, thou shalt come in anon
        With another pageant!
A: Who? I?
B: Yea, by St John!
A: What? I never used such thing before.
B: But follow my counsel and do no more!

                                    (1.347–72)

Creeth comments interestingly:

The participation of A and B in the lives of ancient Romans constitutes
the most striking feature of Medwall's dramaturgy. He formalizes
what Sir Thomas More, according to Roper's Life, had done
extempore in Morton's household before leaving it in 1492. More
would 'sodenly sometymes slip in among the players and make a parte
of his owne there presently among them'.   (p. 538, n ll)

The conjunction here of contemporary (i.e. 1497) and ancient worlds is something which, even today, when historical perspective is strong and scholars annotate as anachronisms clocks striking in Shakespeare's Rome, passes unremarked in the theatre. In much the same fashion, the Warwickshire constable, Dogberry, can appear in the Messina of Beatrice and Benedict, and Renaissance Rome can co-exist with Ancient Britain in *Cymbeline* (1609). This may nowadays go unremarked because, to the less understanding auditory, it is 'all of the past', whilst those who know 'understand', but in Shakespeare's or Medwall's time, if the two worlds were noticed, an audience's capacity for multiconscious apprehension would enable it to respond without confusion and the device would have the effect of taking the audience into the play-world through its own contemporary representatives. Thus, the disguise of the Mummers as Spaniards and B's imitation Flemish are both compliments to the visiting ambassadors and a way of bringing them into the play-world. That Shakespeare still regularly used this device, though usually more subtly (e.g. through Aumerle, or Octavia, or Enobarbus) suggests how effective it was found to be.

The way that A gets himself recommended to Flaminius is a neat example of the planting of a player in the audience and, simultaneously, an ironic comment on the value of the 'independent referee'. Gaius Flaminius is willing to take on A if he can produce a surety.

> *A*:   Yes, I can have sureties plenty
>   For my truth within this place.
>   Here is a gentleman that would trust me [*i.e. B*]
>   For as much goods as he has!
> *Gaius*: Yea, and that is but little percase!
> *A*:   By my faith, go where he shall,
>   It is as honest a man as any in the [realm]
>   I have no more acquaintance within this hall:
>   (1.623–30)

B, of course, is most willing to oblige and beautifully revealingly assures Gaius Flaminius that A is as true as is B himself:

> He and I dwelled many a fair day
> In one school, and yet I wot well
> From thence he bare never away
> The worth of an half-penny that I can tell.
>   (1.643–6)

As we have been told earlier in the play that A and B do not know each other, in the play-world at any rate [for A mistakes B for an actor, much to B's disgust, making the excuse that nowadays it is difficult to 'know a player from another man!' (I.44–56)], the worth of this reference is plain to the audience. This is a nice irony but more important, the audience shares knowledge with one group of players which the others do not possess. Time after time this device will be used by Elizabethan dramatists, and it is particularly effective in scenes involving multiple staging, as in *Ralph Roister Doister* (1552), *Much Ado about Nothing* (1598) and *Troilus and Cressida* (1602; see below, pp. 63–4).

Although it is A and B who most frequently involve the audience, the characters in the main plot also directly address the company and it is reasonable to ponder why. Anne Righter, in the passage quoted above, thinks A and B's presence 'prevents characters more important to the plot from creating a realistic, three dimensional image of life'. Quite apart from the need for or desirability of creating a *realistic* image of life, it can be maintained that the characters of the main plot are a little rounder than is here suggested but, much more importantly, it is arguable that it is A and B, not Gaius, Cornelius and Lucres, who are the more important to *the plot*. Taking first the matter of the Roman characters' lack of a third dimension, it will be noted that Cornelius, Gaius and Lucres all address the audience directly and inevitably must build up *some* sort of rapport with the audience, so giving these characters greater 'presence'. Lucres's speech is particularly charming. Following the typical clownish mistaking of the word by B — he has told Lucres she kissed Cornelius (or he kissed her) 'On the hole of the arse' instead of saying 'the hollow ash' (II.290 and 299) — she addresses the audience:

Lucres: [*To audience*] Now, forsooth, this was a lewd message
          As ever I heard since I was bore!
          And if his master have therefore knowledge
          He will be angry with him therefore.
          Howbeit, I will speak thereof no more,
          For it hath been my condition alway
          No man to hinder, but to help where I may.

                                             (II.310–16)

But the brief contact with the audience made by each suitor is much more significant to what Medwall has to say. Referring to the boldness of Gaius's attack on the aristocracy, 'so explicit in its details about the

conduct of many of them during the Wars of the Roses', Glynne
Wickham goes on:

> but Medwall has protected himself and his master both by the initial
> appeals of Cornelius and Gaius to the audience not to take their
> speeches too personally, and by distancing both spokesmen into the
> mists of Roman antiquity.   (I.656 n)

This refers back to a passage spoken to the audience by Gaius:

> And whatsoever I shall speak in this audience —
> Either of mine own merits or of his insolence —
> Yet first unto you all, sirs, I make this request;
> That is would like you to construe it to the best.
>   (II.589–92)

The direct address serves here to mediate between performers and
audience and although the characters in the main plot may seldom so
speak as compared with A and B, *their* direct address becomes in contrast
the more significant and, in the context of so much direct address in the
play, 'normal'. In fact, although nineteenth-century conventions of
realism (which can only exist in a critic's mind) are broken, this technique
permits of a very much more realistic — relevant — content to the entertainment than might otherwise be possible. Real issues are dramatised:
the behaviour of the aristocracy in the Wars of the Roses; the out-
datedness of the tournament (dramatised through Running at Quintain
which is entertaining to the whole company, the elite participating in the
little tradition); the matter of true nobility; and woman's choice of a
husband.[26] These last two issues can now be discussed in the light of an
important crux that has puzzled scholars.

Early in Part I, B, having come to terms with A, tells him and the
audience 'somewhat of the matter of the play' (I.62). To do this, Medwall
changes B's rime couée (colloquial verse) to formal rime royal,[27] just as a
century later, Shakespeare's allegorical Gardener in *Richard II* will,
unusually for a 'low' character, speak verse. He tells the story that is to be
dramatised — but he gets it wrong. When it comes to choosing a
husband for Lucres, B says:

> This matter was brought before the Senate
> They to give therein an utter sentence
> Which of these the two men should have pre-eminence.
>   (I.166–18)

This follows the source, Bonaccorso's *De Vera Nobilitate*, translated by Mielot into French in 1449, into English by Tiptoft, and published by Caxton in 1481. In the source, the storyteller affects not to know what the Senate decided and tactfully leaves it to the reader to judge which kind of nobility is preferable.[28] Medwall's B, however, gives the Senate's decision:

> And finally they gave sentence and award
> That Gaius Flaminius was to be commend
> For the more noble man, having no regard
> To his low birth of the which he did descend:
> But only to his virtue they did therein attend,
> Which was so great that of convenience
> All the city of Rome did him honour and reverence.
> (I.119–25)

Two points made by editors of Medwall are here relevant. Glynne Wickham points out that the contemporary frame ensures that the moral is not 'ignored or dismissed as only applicable to Roman times' (p. 39); and Creeth suggests that, as it is in fact Lucres, not the Senate, who chooses Gaius, 'Possibly Medwall has not yet decided how to effect the resolution of the play' (p. 538 n. 6). Wickham is surely right, and Creeth is here, I think, wrong.

Of course, it is possible that Medwall was uncertain as to how he was to end the play, but it is not so long a play and the issue is central to what he (and presumably Cardinal Morton) wanted to put across, that an error is less than likely, especially in so perfectly constructed a play. Might not this 'error' be quite deliberate on Medwall's part? He had a tricky issue to dramatise before very powerful people. He begins his play by suggesting, as did the source, that the Senate — the audience's peers — decided the issue. He then adds to the source what the decision was; at this stage of the play, this is a Senatorial decision in a story of the ancient past. As the play progresses and the contemporary audience (including the Spanish and Flemish Ambassadors) is brought into the play, Medwall goes one stage further: it is Lucres who decides. Then, as a protection, he uses the device already referred to whereby Gaius's condemnation of aristocratic behaviour was distanced, but this time he employs not only Lucres but also A and B. First Lucres begs the audience:

> I pray you all, sirs, as many as be here,
> Take not my words by a sinister way.
> (II.767–8)

B than enters and is aghast:

> B: Yes, by my truth! I shall witness bear,
> Wheresoever I be come another day,
> How such a gentlewoman did openly say
> That by a churl's son she would set more
> Than she would do by a gentleman bore!
>
> (II.769–73)

Lucres carefully and delicately makes plain what really was the substance of her words and, unless the elite members of the audience wish to share the actor/servant's response, they must go along with Lucres's argument. After Lucres has left, A enters and the outcome is crudely explained to him and he asks the women in the audience if that is how they would like husbands to be chosen:

> A: [*to audience*] How say you, good women? Is it your guise
> To choose all your husbands that wise?
> By my truth, then I marvel!
>
> (II.849–51)

Again, would the members of such an audience wish to agree with a common servant? The frame has thus done more than introduce the 'main plot' and provide fun and horseplay. It has served to mediate the important and revolutionary messages of the play to the elite audience. In this sense, it is not unreasonable to suggest that it is A and B who are most important to the 'plot' — a plot which Medwall has devised to put across novel concepts.

Medwall brilliantly manipulates various planes of reality — reality of place, time (the ancient and contemporary worlds), and occasion, and most cleverly of all, uses these to dramatise ideas whilst ensuring his audience enjoys what is put before it. It is also possible to see in the play how the ideas of the great tradition can be married with the popular entertainments of the little tradition, and how these may be mediated so that they may be received by a wide range of people. The breaches of dramatic illusion are not to be interpreted as if the play were a product of the high peak of naturalism at Antoine's *Théâtre Libre*, but with an awareness of how an audience capable of multiconscious apprehension would respond.

It is likely that *Fulgens and Lucres* was not known long into the sixteenth century, but it perfectly epitomises that combination of real-

and play-world which Shakespeare will employ, notably when he, too, is concerned with a similar theme: the nature of true honour. In *1 Henry IV* (1597) Hal must learn for himself the difference between the ancient form of chivalric honour, gloriously but vainly represented by Harry Hotspur, and the expediency grossly embodied in Falstaff:

> What is honour? A word. What is in that word, honour? What is that honour? Air. A trim reckoning! Who hath it? He that died a'Wednesday. Doth he feel it? No. Doth he hear it? No. 'Tis insensible then? Yea, to the dead. But will it not live with the living? No. Why? Detraction will not suffer it. Therefore I'll none of it. Honour is a mere scutcheon — and so ends my catechism.   (v.i.135–43)

Hal must discover for himself an integrity that is as honourable as Hotspur's ideal once was and as human as association with common man can make it. The strength of the dramatic tradition embodied in *Fulgens and Lucres* is to be found in the use Shakespeare made of what he inherited; there was no need for him to have had direct knowledge of Medwall's play.

One final point should be made about *Fulgens and Lucres*. A and B not only serve to introduce the main subject and indicate its significance to the audience, but they provide a genuine sub-plot which, as in the later, more sophisticated drama of Shakespeare's time, reflects and comments upon the main action. Just as Cornelius and Flaminius seek the hand of Lucres, so do A and B court the maid, Joan. Ironically, the nobles debate but the servants resort to what was once the prerogative of the nobility, courtship by tournament, but tournament made to look absurd, out of place in this new, Tudor world. A first offers to play for Joan at quoits, but B dismisses that as only suitable for boys. B proposes that they should sing for Joan, which they do, but he becomes hoarse and, what is more, A accuses him of not keeping time. Joan proposes that they try the matter in some other way and A suggests that they wrestle. This they then set about with Joan acting as judge. She declares that B has not gained a fall when he believes he has and he accuses her of partiality. He implies, of course, that only the prowess of the men, and not the judgement of the woman, shall decide who shall be her husband. B then proposes a tournament in the manner of high chivalry:

> Even here I cast to him my glove
> Or ever I hence go,
> On the condition that in the plain field
> I shall meet him with spear and shield
> My life thereon to jeopard.
> Let me see [if] he dare take it!

> *Tunc proiiciet cirothecam.*
> [*Then he throws down a leather gauntlet*]
> (I.1148–53)

It is at this point that the Running at Quintain occurs, one man in turn bending over whilst the other charges his posterior with a blunt shaft.[29] Although Joan seems to continue to favour A, when he falls howling (despite having asked the audience to fall to prayer to aid his cause), the 'flower of the frying pan', as B has called Joan, offers him little sympathy. Far from being won by either A or B, she says she is 'taken up before' (with *double entendre* presumably). She rewards both with a beating but does promise them each a new pair of breeches for their pains.

A and B are released by Gaius who enters just after Joan has left and who finds them with their hands tied behind their backs. A, just as Falstaff will in *I Henry IV*, then offers an elaborate explanation as to how they came to be bound. They met 'False thieves', in Cornelius's pay, and though A claims he has been left for dead on the ground

> And I have a great [gash] here behind
> Out of which there cometh such a wind
> That if you hold a candle thereto
> It will blow it out — that will it do!
> (I.1259–62)

he, with B's help, slew two or three of the assailants. Having warranted them dead, however, A fears that they may return and take revenge on B:

> A: Yes, so help me God! I warrant them dead.
>   Howbeit, I stand in great dread
>   That if ever he come in their way
>   They will cut off his arm or his head
>   For so I heard them — all three — say.
> Gaius: Which? They that were slain?
> A: Yea, by this day!
>   What needeth me therefore to lie?
>   He heard it himself as well as I.
> Gaius: Well than you lie, both two!
> (I.1276–83)

One cannot but wonder whether *Fulgens and Lucres* was known to Shakespeare but it is probable that he was simply working in the same tradition as Medwall.

The parallelism with the main action is clear and so is the mocking of the idea of jousting. We cannot tell how Joan has been 'taken up' — whether by her own choice or no — but clearly she puts down the two men, so much so that B declares he would rather she had his 'knife' (= 'genitals', according to Wickham) than become his wife. Thus, Lucres and Joan are independent instead of, as in the world of tournament, either merely decorative or prizes to be won whether they will or no. And this, of course, is in accord with the new spirit of humanism. The drama is here clearly emancipated from its religious heritage.

One hundred years later, these fictional planes were to be used in an even more complex form in a play still relatively primitive (in literary terms) when compared to what immediately followed it, but which made considerable demands upon its audiences' imaginative capacities: *The Spanish Tragedy* by Thomas Kyd. Twice Kyd designs no fewer than three planes of action. In III.ii the audience watches whilst Andrea and Revenge observe Balthazar and Lorenzo secretly overhear Horatio and Bel-Imperia, and Kyd risks all (perhaps too much) by having Balthazar and Lorenzo respond antithetically to the lovers' exchanges, the rhyme-words overleaping the two planes of action.

In IV.iv, the play of 'Soliman and Perseda' is watched by the Court; both are observed by Andrea and Revenge; and all three by the theatre audience. As if that were not enough. Hieronimo, at the completion of the play, refers directly to the essential fiction of drama, yet implies that this is not the convention ruling in this fictive act:

> Haply you think, but bootless are your thoughts,
> That this is fabulously counterfeit,
> And that we do as all tragedians do:
> To die today, for fashioning our scene,
> The death of Ajax, or some Roman peer,
> And in a minute starting up again,
> Revive to please tomorrow's audience.
> No, princes, know I am Hieronimo ....
>
> (IV.iv.76–83)

Whether or not the shift from the play being performed, as originally intended, in 'sundry languages' to 'our vulgar tongue', suggests that the complexity of illusion presented problems not readily overcome, there can be no doubt from *The Spanish Tragedy* and the drama it presaged, that Elizabethan audiences were offered, and could cope with, much more than single-planed dramatic illusion.

3 Shakespeare and the Comics

Two contrary tendencies can be found in Shakespeare's treatment of the integrity of dramatic illusion. Despite his audiences' evident ability to overleap breaks in the continuity of the dramatic narrative, he seems, for a time at least, to have concentrated upon controlling the excesses of his clowns; secondly, he developed in a very subtle manner the breaking of illusion in ways that would, under his control, enrich or intensify the dramatic experience and, paradoxically 'stress a deeper reality'.[1] These tendencies have two things in common. First, they reveal the desire of the great artist to hold as much of his art in his control as he can. Second, they are both concerned with the relationship of the play world and the real world and the way that the dramatic illusion is breached. For a clown to overstep the mark when 'some necessary point in the play' is then to be observed *is* vile 'and shows a pitiful ambition in the fool that useth it', said Hamlet and so, I think it can be shown, Shakespeare. Yet in a variety of ways Shakespeare breaks the integrity of the dramatic illusion, either by reminding us of the 'real' world, or that we are in a theatre watching a fiction, or by juxtaposing different kinds of dramatic illusion. Thus, in *As You Like It*, not only the name Jaques, but the reference to Master What-ye-call't directly remind us of the real world, and the Duke's anatomising of Jaques does so indirectly:

> Most mischievous foul sin, in chiding sin.
> For thou thyself hast been a libertine,
> As sensual as the brutish sting itself;
> And all th' embossed sores and headed evils
> That thou with license of free foot hast caught
> Wouldst thou disgorge into the general world.
> (II.vii.64–9)

The joke continues into the Restoration and the eighteenth-century drama, being the title of a play by John Gay (1715), and pinpointing Mirabell's warning to Millament that she should have no commerce with the gentlewoman of What-d'ye-call-it Court, whence various disgusting

34

products, which include the marrow of roasted cat, are derived for use in making cosmetics (*The Way of the World*, IV.i).

We are reminded directly that we are in a theatre so often in Shakespeare that examples are scarcely necessary. But from *As You Like It*, Jaques's reference to the other characters speaking blank verse (IV.i.33-4), so causing him to quit their sight, is worth mentioning because it simultaneously draws attention to the dramatic convention used in so much dialogue (i.e. the unreal mode of expression used to dramatise reality) and, at the same time, its incorrectness, for in the 230-odd lines of IV.i. there is only one iambic pentameter (which is the line to which Jaques immediately responds), Orlando's 'Good day, and happiness, dear Rosalind!'. Had Jaques not described this as blank verse, it would have sounded no different from the rest of the prose of the scene. Shakespeare occasionally makes obvious allusions to modes of acting, in, say Richard III's ability to 'counterfeit the deep tragedian':

> Speak and look back, and pry on every side,
> Tremble and start at wagging of a straw,
> Intending deep suspicion: ghastly looks
> Are at my service, like enforced smiles;
> And both are ready in their offices,
> At any time, to grace my stratagems.
>
> (III.v.6-11)

There is also the description of Wolsey in *Henry VIII* (1613), which recalls the actor:

> he bites his lip, and starts;
> Stops on a sudden, looks upon the ground,
> Then lays his finger on his temple; straight
> Springs out into fast gait; then stops again,
> Strikes his breast hard; and anon he casts
> His eye against the moon. In most strange postures
> We have seen him set himself.
>
> (III.ii.114-20)

Perhaps the most subtle, and one of the most puzzling, allusions to the real world occurs in *As You Like It*. Act V, scene iii consists of a short interlude to provide dramatic time. Two of the Duke's pages entertain Touchstone and Audrey. They sing the famous song, 'It was a lover and his lass' and, when it is finished, Touchstone comments, 'Truly young gentlemen, though there was no great matter in the ditty, yet the note was very untuneable', to which the first page replies 'You are deceived sir. We kept time, we lost not our time'.[2] There is here a curious crux.

As the passage reads in Q/F (and as it is represented in the New Arden edition in 1975), Touchstone comments on pitch whereas the page refers to time. It *could* be that 'time' should twice read 'tune' — the confusion of minims in an Elizabethan hand would be easy enough — but the appeal may be to another dimension of the play not recorded on the printed page: the music accompanying the song. It so happens that Elizabethan music for the song has survived and in the last line there is a seeming irregularity in the time of the penultimate bar.[3] The effect deceives Touchstone (and some modern editors) and the more knowing and more aware members of the audience have to make a judgement as to whether the page or Touchstone is right by reference to the 'external' conventions of music. It is as if in a quasi-realistic film a character within the filmplay appealed to the musical accompaniment to validate what he said.

Perhaps in no plays of Shakespeare are different worlds of dramatic illusion so remarkably juxtaposed as in *The Winter's Tale* and *Cymbeline*, although these are by no means the first occasions on which Shakespeare brings together times and characters which could not have co-existed: Dogberry in Messina has already been mentioned and Bottom and company do not at once strike us as Athenians.

Shakespeare is not alone in his period in seeking to control dramatic illusion and make it more complex. Ford's *The Fancies Chaste and Noble* (1635), much less successful though it is than *The Winter's Tale*, juxtaposes different comic modes in a remarkable manner.[4] However, partly historic accident, partly his own genius, ensured that it was Shakespeare who most brilliantly and effectively came to terms with the problems and opportunities posed by breaches in dramatic illusion. I propose, therefore, to concentrate in this chapter upon Shakespeare, and to begin by discussing the comic material he inherited and some of the uses to which he put it; the tradition of *ad libbing* and Shakespeare's attempt to control that; Shakespeare's use of different planes of dramatic illusion; and to conclude by saying something of the bad pun, to which he was addicted.

In her study, *The Extra-Dramatic Moment in Elizabethan Plays before 1616*, Doris Fenton gives a very large number of examples of 'passages that occur within the play itself, masquerading as of it and yet set apart either in form or in substance' (p. 8). She devotes most attention to direct comic address, noting not only written-out examples but indications for *ad libbing* allowed by the dramatist,[5] and considers also appeals for sympathy, and expository and didactic address. Her study was based on a reading of all Elizabethan plays up to 1616 (excluding Latin plays and masques) and she notes instances of the extra-dramatic moment in over two hundred plays. The practice was, therefore, widespread to say the least. Having read a further fifty plays written after 1616, she noted, as she says in her Preface, 'a decided lessening in the amount of extra-dramatic material' and so her cut-off date neatly, but reasonably, coincides with the death of Shakespeare. It is striking, however, that she was able to conclude that far from being a mark of early composition, there were more instances of the extra-dramatic moment in plays written between 1600 and 1616 than in those of 1580 to 1600 (p. 113; and contrast Anne Righter's assertion that after 1550 direct address to the audience decreases, p. 5 above). Although she found that every dramatist of any note used the device, including Shakespeare and Jonson, some, such as Middleton, Chapman and Heywood, used it more freely than others (p. 114). Although her work is open to modification (by for example, J. A. B. Somerset in his Ph.D. thesis, 'The Comic Turn in English Drama to 1616', University of Birmingham, 1966), and though examples can be added and perhaps removed,[6] there is no question but that she establishes very clearly, and with a wealth of examples, how frequently the integrity of the dramatic illusion was broken in Elizabethan plays, either by design of the dramatist or through the extemporal acts of clowns.

What did the Elizabethan comics actually do on the stage to which Hamlet (and perhaps Shakespeare) objected? Possibly the best guide to this, and certainly the most interesting one, is the little book known as *Tarlton's Jests*. The history of this book is complicated;[7] the earliest edition to survive is that of 1613 but this is incomplete. There was still a demand for the book fifty years after Tarlton's death in 1588 and a copy of the 1638 edition was until recently believed to be the earliest to survive. Like some of Deloney's works, it was probably so popular that editions were read out of existence. As John Feather says, 'There is no reason to suppose that all the anecdotes recounted in the book are authentic to Tarlton and indeed several of them can be traced to French and Italian jest-books of the sixteenth century.' Nevertheless, Tarlton's jests give, in some respects, a pretty fair picture of the way in which the clown *ad libbed* in the course of an Elizabethan play and there is no reason to doubt that, as the title on C2^r states, '*Tarlton* made *Armin* his adopted sonne to succeed him'.

The way in which Tarlton was supposed to have taken over the Lord Chief Justice's role in what was probably *The Famous Victories of Henry V* (1586) has often been reprinted[8] so it might be more profitable here to repeat two other stories of Tarlton's prowess, one because it also illustrates a turn used by Shakespeare and the other because it centres on a joke-word which will be found in a passage quoted later from *Dr Faustus* (1592). The book is in three parts, Court-Witty Jests, City Jests and Country Jests. The first example comes from the City Jests. (The spelling has been modernised.)

> *How Tarlton and one in the gallery fell out.*
> It chanced that in the midst of a play, after long expectation for Tarlton (being much desired of the people), at length he came forth; where, at his entrance, one in the gallery pointed his finger at him, saying to a friend that had never seen him, 'That is he'. Tarlton, to make sport at the least occasion given him, and seeing the man point with one finger, he in love again held up two fingers. The captious fellow, jealous of his wife (for he was married) and because a player did it, took the matter more heinously, and asked him why he made horns at him.
> 'No', quoth Tarlton, 'they be fingers:
>
> > For there is no man, which in love to me,
> > Lends me one finger, but he shall have three.'
>
> 'No, no', says the fellow, 'you gave me the horns.'
> 'True', says Tarlton, 'for my fingers are tipped with nails, which are like horns, and I must make a show of that which you are sure of.' This matter grew so, that the more he meddled the more it was for his disgrace; wherefore the standers-by counselled him to depart, both he and his horns, lest his cause grew desperate. So the poor fellow, plucking his hat over his eyes, went his ways. (B2$^{r/v}$)

It can be seen from this that the euphemistically described 'V-sign' goes back long before Churchill but that its meaning (if not the fact that it was an insult) was a little different then than now. More to the purpose here, however, is the kind of disruption suggested not merely by this incident but by the line 'to make sport at the least occasion given him', which suggests that Tarlton eagerly sought such opportunities. The second example is from the Country Jests.

> *Tarlton's jest of a gridiron.*
> While the Queen's Players lay in Worcester City to get money, it was his custom oft to sing extempore of themes given him amongst which

they were appointed to play the next day. Now one fellow of the city amongst the rest, that seemed quaint of conceit to lead other youths with his fine wit, gave out that the next day he would give him a theme to put him to a *non-plus*. Divers of his friends acquainted with the same expected some rare conceit. Well, the next day came, and my gallant gave him his invention in two lines, which was this:

> Me thinks it is a thing unfit,
> To see a gridiron turn the spit.

The people laughed at this, thinking his wit knew no answer thereunto, which angered Tarlton exceedingly, and presently with a smile looking about, when they expected wonders, he put it off thus:

> Me thinks it is a thing unfit,
> To see an ass have any wit.

The people hooted for joy to see the theme-giver dashed, who, like a dog with his tail between his legs, left the place. But such commendations Tarlton got, that he supped with the bailiff that night, where my themer durst not come, although he were sent for, so much was he vexed at that unlooked-for answer.   (C4$^{r/v}$)

It will be noted that Tarlton's — or the clown's — personality comes through here, particularly his dislike of being worsted, and that his *envoi* does not really complete the theme. It should also be noted how apposite is the reason given for the players performing in Worcester — 'to get money'. There is nothing here about art for art's sake! Metro-Goldwyn-Mayer would surely approve![9]

Whether Tarlton did or did not say this, there is no doubt at all that clowns did engage with members of the audience in such exchanges as this relatively late example from Philip Powell's *Commonplace Book* in Cardiff Central Library cryptically confirms. The manuscript dates from the 1630s.[10]

one Kendal in a stage play in Bristoll being
[newe?] acctinge the part of the vize, spake extempore as foloweth, in dispraise of the noble Brittans,

---

if thou art a Brittane borne, it fitts thee to were the horne

---

John Brittan a prentiz of on Thomas Deane of Bristoll his re-ply to Kendal: twise: as foloweth:

A Brittans name I truly beare, I leaue the horne for thee to were:	
the horne becomes the saxons best I kis^d. thy wife supose the rest:	Kendal the saxon put to silence.

This game, it will be recalled, is played by Armado and Moth (with interjections by Costard) in *Love's Labour's Lost* (III.i.75 ff.). The incident in the play is totally self-contained and one wonders whether it was an attempt by Shakespeare to control a clown's extemporal habits, or whether it was expanded in performance, the clown taking the opportunity for extemporal wit-play with the audience.

Thomas Godwin, in the chapter, 'De Ludis' of his *Romanae Historiae Anthologiae* (Oxford, 1614), describes the actions of English clowns in stage plays in a passage which may either be intended to define Roman clowns, or English clowns in terms of those of Rome:[11]

> Concerning the diverse kindes of stage plaies I read of fowre, called by the *Grecians, Mimicae, Satyrae, Tragoediae, Comoediae*: by the *Romanes Planipedes, Attellanae, Praetextatae, Tabernariae*. In English, **Fables Mimicall, Satyricall, Tragicall, Comicall**. These Mimicall players did much resemble the clowne in many of our English state-plaies, who sometimes would go a tip-toe in derision of the mincing dames; sometimes would speak ful-mouthed to mocke the country clownes; sometimes vpon the top of their tongue to scoffe the citizen. And thus, by their imitation of all ridiculous gestures or speeches, in al kinds of vocations, they provoked laughter; whence both the plaies and plaiers were named *Mimi* . . . (13ᵣ)

This vividly suggests the kind of by-play indulged in by clowns.

Shakespeare's most outspoken comment on clowns is that put into Hamlet's mouth when the young Prince gives the Players the benefit of his advice. It is very dangerous to imagine that what a specific character says in a play represents what the author thinks. Usually scholars are very careful to indicate that this is a speech put into the mouth of a young, inexperienced amateur by a very skilled professional writer. Certainly Hamlet's admiration for the old-fashioned 'rugged Pyrrhus' speech does not lead us to think that he was the most sophisticated of dramatic critics. But it is a convenient protection for a dramatist to guard himself from attack by explaining that it is only his characters who are speaking not he himself. Nevertheless, though one might suspect that this is Shakespeare speaking, suspicion is not proof. There is, however, a curious circumstance attaching to this speech which might suggest that the sentiments about clowns are Shakespeare's. The text in Q2, which was probably set from Shakespeare's completed draft, reads:

> and let those that play your clownes speake no more then is set downe for them, for there be of them that wil themselues laugh, to set on some quantitie of barraine spectators to laugh to, though in the meane time, some necessary question of the play be then to be considered, that's villanous, and shewes a most pittifull ambition in the foole that vses it: goe make you readie. (Q2:G4^r)

Now the Bad Quarto of Hamlet, published in 1603, the year preceding Q2, is *generally* (nothing is universally agreed about Shakespeare) thought to be a reported text and the quality of that reporting varies considerably in different parts of the play. The first part of the speech in Q1 follows fairly closely on that in Q2 (Shakespeare's 'original'). As Q1 almost certainly represents a performance at the Globe prior to the publication of Q2, it indicates — give or take the exactness of the reporting — what was said on the stage. It will at once be noted that it goes on after 'pitiful ambition in the fool that useth it':

> And do you hear? let not your clown speak more than is set down. There be of them, I can tell you, that will laugh themselves to set on some quantity of barren spectators to laugh with them, albeit there is some necessary point in the play then to be observed. O, 'tis vile, and shows a pitiful ambition in the fool that useth it. And then you have some again that keeps one suit of jests, as a man is known by one suit of apparel; and gentlemen quote his jests down in their tables before they come to the play, as thus: 'Cannot you stay till I eat my porridge?' and 'You owe me a quarter's wages', and 'My coat wants a cullison', and 'Your beer is sour', and blabbering with his lips, and thus keeping in his cinquepace of jests, when God knows, the warm clown cannot make a jest unless by chance, as a blind man catcheth a hare. Masters, tell him of it.[12]

The most surprising thing about this *ad lib* — for surely that is what it is — is that it is *not* spoken by the clown but by Hamlet himself, or should one say, by Richard Burbage himself? Why, one asks? An audience might or might not know, then or now, whether a clown was genuinely *ad libbing*. Although good comics can usually engage in repartee, many seeming *ad libs* are carefully positioned and even rehearsed. But an *an lib*, whether placed or genuinely extempore is, of its nature, designed for the audience and intended to be recognised as such by them. The *ad lib* represented in *Hamlet* Q1 would certainly not be recognised as such by the audience. It would seem no more than the continuation of the speech given by the dramatist to Hamlet, especially as it was spoken by 'the deep tragedian', Burbage. What, then, is its function? This *ad lib* would only be recognised by the players of Shakespeare's own company for what it was: an unauthorised addition. It must have been a company 'in-joke' and one surely directed at Shakespeare, presumably for so directing the clowns and delivered, in all likelihood, by the most important member of the company, and an actor not himself a clown. If this theory is correct, it suggests very strongly that Shakespeare was anxious to control his clowns and did not find the habit of extemporal play any more to his taste than did his Cleopatra, who it will be remembered, feared that 'the quick comedians/Extemporally will stage us, and present/Our Alexandrian revels' (v.ii.215–17) — itself an intriguing allusion to what was being presented on the stage at the time.

Catch-phrases are not discussed in detail in this volume but it is worth noting those used here. When the Bad Quarto version is performed, as it occasionally still is, the catch-phrases get little response (unless one breaks the continuity and points out after the second or third that they are *not* raising a laugh — this ensures laughter of sorts after the third or fourth catch-phrase). In their day they presumably sent people into gales of laughter. In *A Yorkshire Tragedy* (1606) one of these four catch-phrases seems to be tucked away and a fifth is possibly suggested. In the first scene, Oliver and Ralph, two serving men, are talking and they are joined by a third, Samuel, 'Furnisht with things from London'.

> Samuel: ... But what haue we heere? I thought twas somwhat puld downe my breeches: I quite forgot my two potingsticks. These came from London; now any thing is good heer that comes from London.
>
> Oliver: I, farre fetcht you know.
>
> Samuel: But speak in your conscience, yfaith, haue not we as good potingsticks ith Cuntry as need to be put ith fire. The mind of a thing is all. The mind of a thing's all, and as thou saidst eene now, farre fetcht is the best thinges for Ladies.
>
> Oliver: I, and for waiting gentle women to.
>
> Samuel: But, Ralph, what, is our beer sower this thunder?
>
> Oliver: No, no, it holds countence yet.

Samuel: Why, then, follow me; Ile teach you the finest humor to be drunk in. I learned it at London last week.[13]

The reference to the beer being sour sounds suspiciously like a catch-phrase mentioned in *Hamlet* (and *A Yorkshire Tragedy* is dated 1606), and it is just possible that the repetition of 'The mind of a thing's all' indicates a catch-phrase. It has the right ring about it.

It is not difficult to see why a dramatist concerned about the integrity of his art should wish to control the extravagances of the comics. But, of course, as the first of Tarlton's jests quoted indicates, the audience waited long in expectation for the clown. It is a puzzle never satisfactorily solved as to why the clowns of *Macbeth* (1606) and *Othello* (1604) have so little to do. Did they extemporise? — for in *Macbeth* it seems inconceivable that after so long a wait an audience would be satisfied with the short routine given to the Porter; this is an act easily open to extension by a clown. Or was the clown's part cut for a shortened performance at Court? But then, why cut the clown and leave IV.iii. so long? Or by the excision of the clown and the retention of IV.iii. was it intended to flatter James I and VI? *Othello* is, in this respect, even more puzzling. Was Shakespeare trying to do without a clown at this period, only to find an ideally integrated part for Lear's Fool (possibly played by Tarlton's protégé, Armin[14]), and relenting in *The Winter's Tale* by writing in Autolycus a part for a clown that might have suited Kempe a dozen or more years earlier? Although Hamlet's advice might well, in the main, be 'his own', I suspect that the advice to the clowns comes from Shakespeare's heart and that the Lord Chamberlain's company recognised this.

It is possible to see, by comparing the 1604 and 1616 editions of *Dr Faustus*, how a part could be expanded by the clowns. As always when working from a printed version back to how that text came to be printed, one has to guess the nature of the underlying manuscript and the best that one can manage is conjecture based upon scholarly expertise. Although the argument has been modified recently, it seems to me that *in the passage discussed here*, the order and manner of composition suggested by Sir Walter Greg holds good.[15] This maintains that the 1604 edition represents a version of the play acted within the preceding decade, after Marlowe's death, reflecting modifications in performance. The 1616 edition, contrariwise, represents a manuscript version from Marlowe's lifetime, and though that edition has been modified in places by the 1604 edition, that does not affect the passage analysed here. I would firmly state two things about this textual problem. One is that the argument is inevitably circular — that is, that the differences we find in the texts suggest how those texts came to be — but the texts are then evaluated according to that conjecture; the other is that so far as this passage is concerned, I have no doubt that the 1604 (A) text represents a performed version and that the 1616 (B) text represents the original manuscript written before performance had taken place. The version below is based on Greg's parallel text, but the spelling has been modernised and the significantly different lines *ad libbed* in A have been printed in italics. The three extracts are taken from A, lines 368–403, and from B, lines 348–69. Only nine or ten lines are omitted but by printing the examples in three separate groups the technique of *ad libbing* from *a dramatist's original* can readily be seen. The first extract shows a very familiar device:

A, *ll.368-73* (representing what was performed):

> Wagner: . . . he would give his soul to the devil for a shoulder of mutton, though it were blood raw.
>
> Clown: *How, my soul to the devil for a shoulder of mutton though 'twere blood raw? Not so good friend, by Our Lady*, I had need have it well roasted, and good sauce to it, if I pay so dear.

B, *ll.348-52* (representing what was in the author's manuscript):

> Wagner: . . . he would give his soul to the devil for a shoulder of mutton, though it were blood raw.
>
> Clown: Not so neither; I had need to have it well roasted, and good sauce to it, if I pay so dear, I can tell you.

The technique the clown uses is identical with that of the music-hall comedy duo in which the second speaker repeats a key part of the first speaker's statement in order that the point be punched home and the audience primed as to just when to laugh. A particularly hackneyed example will serve to illustrate this:

> 1: Who was that lady I saw you with last night?
>
> 2: *Who was that lady you saw me with last night?*
>   That was no lady, that was my wife!

Ad libbing enables the comic to express his individuality; it is part and parcel of the clown's act and to deny the right to *ad lib* is to take away something peculiar to the clown. It is also a means of expanding a play. Arthur Roberts, the very successful nineteenth-century music-hall comedian, wrote illuminatingly about 'gagging'.[16] People, he said, often blamed him for gagging. Somewhat disingenuously he claimed that he had no particular wish to gag but was often 'compelled to put in an extra wheeze or two'. He would never gag in a W. S. Gilbert, Henry Arthur Jones or Arthur Wing Pinero play, but frequently he had been given a sheet of blank paper and told 'This is your part, Mr. Roberts.' He then describes playing in the pantomime, *The Yellow Dwarf*, in Manchester (about 1883 probably). There had been 'a great deal of indiscriminate gagging in the pantomime' and the manager posted a notice to the effect that all gags had to be rigorously excluded. The performers were crestfallen but obeyed. The result was chaos:

> We only spoke the lines that were in the script, and the consequence was that no artiste could change his clothes quickly enough to catch his proper entrance. The ballet was disorganised by being hurried on — laces were bursting, and the dressers flew about like wild-fowl. The carpenters could not change the scenes quickly enough, and the orchestra had to scamp half the music. A Manchester pantomime generally starts about seven o'clock and is over shortly before eleven. On this occasion the whole pantomime, including the harlequinade, was over by a quarter to ten! There was not a light outside the theatre at ten o'clock, and the talk of the town was:
>
> 'What is wrong with the Royal? Have they 'bust up'? Have they run out of gas?'
>
> The following evening the manager politely waited upon us.
>
> 'Gentlemen,' he said, 'will you please reinstate the gags?'
>
> We did, successfully, and lived happy ever afterwards.

Roberts makes a particular point of the harshness of this ruling on the Brothers Raynor, 'clever original comedians, and full of quaint notions and ideas of stage business'. Without their 'business' they were simply not an act, and the Brothers Raynor were behaving in no different way than the actors given the parts of Wagner and the Clown three hundred years earlier.

The second extract from *Dr Faustus* is an example of one of the oldest verbal devices open to the clown. The device was old in Shakespeare's day and well known to him. Thus, in *The Two Gentlemen Of Verona* (1593), Speed asks Launce how it is that his master has become 'a notable lover'. 'A notable lubber', answers Launce and Speed replies, 'Why, thou whoreson ass, thou mistakest me' (II.v.43–50). Then, in the next act, Launce plays the same trick and Speed comments, 'Well, your old vice still; mistake the word' (III.i.285–6), and one suspects a play on 'vice/the Vice'.

A, ll.376-83 (as performed):

Clown: How, in verse?
Wagner: No sirrah, in beaten silk and stavesacre.
Clown: *How, how, knavesacre? Aye, I thought that was all the land his father left him. Do y'hear, I would be sorry to rob you of your living.*
Wagner: *Sirrah, I say in stavesacre.*
Clown: *Oho, oho,* stavesacre, why then belike, if I were your man, I should be full of vermin.

B, ll.354-7 (as written):

Clown: What, in verse?
Wagner: No slave, in beaten silk and stavesacre.
Clown: Stavesacre? That's good to kill vermin. Then belike if I serve you, I shall be lousy.

The joke is not now one that will have an audience rolling in the aisles, but the technique is obvious enough.[17] The third example shows considerably greater expansion:[18]

A, ll.392-403 (as performed):

Wagner: Well, do you hear sirrah? Hold, take these guilders.
Clown: *Gridirons, what be they?*
Wagner: *Why French crowns.*
Clown: *Mass, but for the name of French crowns a man were as good have as many English counters. And what should I do with these?*
Wagner: Why, now sirrah, thou art at an hour's warning whensoever or wheresoever the devil shall fetch thee.
Clown: *No, no, here, take your gridirons again.*
Wagner: *Truly I'll none of them.*
Clown: *Truly but you shall.*
Wagner: *Bear witness I gave them him.*
Clown: *Bear witness I give them you again.*

B, ll.365-9 (as written):

Wagner: Well sirrah, leave your jesting and take these guilders.
Clown: Yes, marry sir, and I thank you too.
Wagner: So, now thou art to be at an hour's warning, whensoever and wheresover the devil shall fetch thee.
Clown: Here, take your guilders, I'll none of 'em.

The joke about French crowns probably dates from some time in or after 1595, well after the play was written. Again it means nothing to a modern audience. Two things are noteworthy about this extension. One is that *both* clowns are involved and the second is the appeal to the audience — there is no one else on the stage — to bear witness who has the money. This appeal to the audience to bear witness is also to be found in *Fulgens and Lucres* when B has persuaded Joan to kiss him and at that moment A enters. He is suspicious of Joan and B being together alone — for then 'all is wrong'. B points out that there is an audience present to bear witness that all is well and Joan also appeals directly to the audience:

B: Nay, nay! Here be too many witnesses
        For to make any such business
        As thou weenest hardily!
Joan: [*to the audience*] Why? What is the man's
        thought?
        [*to B*] Suppose you that I would be nought
        If no man were by?

                                        (I.1016–21)

What is immediately apparent from this short sequence from *Dr Faustus* is the way the two clowns built up the material provided for them. The result (though it cannot amuse a modern audience much because of the topical basis of the jokes) is a much better routine than Marlowe and his co-author provided. Whereas the taking over of a play in the manner described in Tarlton's jests could clearly ruin a play, even allowing for the audience's capacity for multiconscious apprehension, it is also clear that the clowns needed to be free to work up material within the main structure which the dramatist provided, as Arthur Roberts argued late in the nineteenth century. What we cannot know is the extent to which Shakespeare's clowns did this. It does seem that he provided them with monologues and cross-talk acts. As these were close to the traditions he inherited, it looks very much as if he was trying to integrate the tradition into his drama, providing his clowns (and his company had the best clowns of the day) with material that would not disappoint the audiences' expectations. His problem was rather as if comedians of the stature of Frankie Howerd, Bob Hope, and Morecambe and Wise were to be fitted into every 'straight' play today. Nothing is more illustrative of the restriction placed upon such comedians than the recording in which Frankie Howerd 'plays' Launce. He simply acts the words as best he may in the legitimate tradition whereas he should be able to work them up with an audience in his own style. It is possible to gauge the effect of this if Frankie Howerd's recording is compared with one of Stanley Holloway playing Bottom. Holloway, in fact, adds virtually nothing except slight repetitions, but this gives a much freer effect. Such an approach, bearing in mind Shakespeare's advice to the clowns, would seem to be truer to the spirit of the plays.

It is quite easy to see how many of the monologues given to clowns stand apart from the plays of which they are a part, although Shakespeare being what he was, manages to make them 'fit' in place and theme. The Porter's speech in *Macbeth* may stand out in a particularly isolated way because his other entries have been cut, but taking the play as we have it, this scene invariably elicits special explanation from commentators: 'comic relief', 'reminder of the real world of plain bread and butter', and so on. But, in truth, it *is* isolated, linked though it may be thematically with the theme of equivocation by courtesy of many Notes and Queries. Launce and his dog Crab (and the clown and his dog were traditional, as Richard Axton points out in his comments on *Dame Sirith*[19]), and Launcelot Gobbo can give their soliloquies without their seeming so isolated. This is partly because the characters have more to do in their plays, but partly because one suspects they owe something to lost clown acts. I have on occasion found it quite easy to convince an audience of students who have never come across *The Two Gentlemen of Verona* (1593) that a performance of the monologue that opens IV.iv (the adventure of Crab under the Duke's table), set within a programme of nineteenth- and twentieth-century music-hall acts, is exactly of that later tradition. It comes as a surprise that 'this is Shakespeare'. This is just as it should be. If the sixteenth-century diction is modified, this is as splendid and effective a routine as any to be heard in Dan Leno's day. The tradition is age-old and, as the comparison of Launcelot Gobbo's monologue with a sermon (suggested on pp. 14–15 above) indicates, goes back to pre-dramatic times.

Shakespeare also makes use of a kind of cross-talk act that is not dissimilar in manner, and sometimes in quality, from that associated with the end and middle men of a nineteenth-century minstrel show. Contrast, for example, these two short 'cross-fires' from the nineteenth century with the *kind of act* and elementary language play of early Shakespeare, two examples of which follow. The italicisation appears in the original.[20]

He Died Lying

Mid: When does a young lady go into the lumber business? When she *pines* for her sweetheart, who is a *spruce* young man with *ebony* face, and of whom she thinks a great *deal*. Now don't say that this is a *chestnut*.

End: No Sir!

Mid: While I remember it, I wish to call you to account. You told certain people that I was a famous liar.

End: No; I didn't say that. I never made use of such an expression. I said you were an *infamous* liar. Speaking of liars, how's your father? There is the greatest old liar that ever lived.

Mid: Don't dare to call my father a falsifier!

End: He's not a falsifier, he's just a plain old liar. He'd rather lie than eat. He'd lie all the time.

Mid: Don't speak of him in that manner; he's dead.

End: You don't say so. What was the complaint?

Mid: *There was no complaint.*

End: *Everybody was satisfied, I s'pose.* Where did he die?

Mid: He died in the house.

End: Did he die standing up?

Mid: Certainly not. He died *lying*!

End: *He kept it up to the last didn't he?*

(p. 65)

All About Cards

End: When you are playing cards, you don't realise what every card means, do you?

Mid: I did not know that cards had any significance beyond their merit in the game or their face value.

End: Of course not; because you never think of these things. Now, let me tell you about the cards: England's best card is the *Queen*. Uncle Sam has just turned down a *King*, a Spanish one. A policeman's best card is a *club*. The politician's best card is a *knave*.

Mid: How about a society actress' card?

End: *Diamonds*! Have them stolen.

Mid: The grave-diggers best card?

End: *Spades.*

Mid: Lover's best cards?

End: *Hearts*!

Mid: A waiter's best card?

End: *The tray.*

Mid: How about a photographer's best cards?

End: Face cards of course. Wives give bad husbands the *deuce*.

Foxhunters want *the whole pack*. Barbers get *edges*. Dancers get the *shuffle*. Rejected lovers get *cut*. Parents of triplets get *three of a kind*. Merchants get the *deal*. Actors get the *play*, but butchers always get the *steaks*.

Mid: I'll remember all that.

End: And if you play, get a chimney sweep and a cornet player for partners.

Mid: Why?

End: The chimney sweep will always follow *soot*, and a cornet player will *trumpet*.

(p. 51)

Brief extracts from two of Shakespeare's plays will serve to remind readers of the routines he provides for his clowns. The first is from *Two Gentlemen of Verona*:

Speed: ... What news then, in your paper?

Launce: The blackest news that ever thou heardest.

Speed: Why, man, how black?

Launce: Why, as black as ink.

Speed: Let me read them.

Launce: Fie on thee, jolthead! thou canst not read.

Speed: Thou liest; I can.

Launce: I will try thee. Tell me this: who begot thee?

Speed: Marry, the son of my grandfather.

Launce: O, illiterate loiterer! it was the son of thy grandmother. This proves that thou canst not read.

Speed: Come, fool, come: try me in thy paper.

Launce: There; and Saint Nicholas be thy speed!

Speed: *Imprimis, She can milk.*

Launce: Ay, that she can.

Speed: *Item, She brews good ale.*

Launce: And thereof comes the proverb, 'Blessing of your heart, you brew good ale'.

Speed: *Item, She can sew.*

Launce: That's as much as to say, 'Can she so?'

Speed: *Item, She can knit.*

Launce: What need a man care for a stock with a wench, when she can knit him a stock?

Speed: *Item, She can wash and scour.*

Launce: A special virtue; for then she need not be washed and scoured.

Speed: *Item, She can spin.*

Launce: Then may I set the world on wheels, when she can spin for
her living.

(III.i.286–321)

This routine continues for a further sixty lines.

The routine from *Comedy of Errors* includes one of the hoariest of jokes,
which was still being used by Flanagan and Allen in the 1930s:
'heir/hair'.[21] Dromio of Syracuse is describing his kitchen-wench, Nell,
to his master, Antipholus:

Antipholus: What's her name?

Dromio: Nell, sir; but her name and three quarters, — that is, an ell
and three quarters, — will not measure her from hip to
hip.

Antipholus: Then she bears some breadth?

Dromio: No longer from head to foot than from hip to hip: she is
spherical, like a globe; I could find out countries in her.

Antipholus: In what part of her body stands Ireland?

Dromio: Marry, sir, in her buttocks: I found it out by the bogs.

Antipholus: Where Scotland?

Dromio: I found it by the barrenness; hard in the palm of the hand.

Antipholus: Where France?

Dromio: In her forehead; armed and reverted, making war against
her *heir*.

Antipholus: Where England?

Dromio: I looked for the chalky cliffs, but I could find no whiteness in
them: but I guess it stood in her chin, by the salt rheum
that ran between France and it.

Antipholus: Where Spain?

Dromio: Faith, I saw it not; but I felt it hot in her breath.

Antipholus: Where America, the Indies?

Dromio: O, sir upon her nose, all o'er embellished with rubies,
carbuncles, sapphires, declining their rich aspect to the hot
breath of Spain, who sent whole armadoes of carracks to be
ballast at her nose.

Antipholus: Where stood Belgia, the Nethlands?

Dromio: O, sir! I did not look so low.

(III.ii.111–44)

Shakespeare makes use of formulaic parodies on a number of occasions.
For example, Falstaff, at the end of his speech on honour, specifically

describes it as his catechism. In *As You Like It*, a quasi-litany begins at
v.ii.92 (with the responses, 'And so am I for Phebe/And I for
Ganymede/And I for Rosalind/And I for no woman'). Shortly after,
Touchstone gives the formula for quarrelling on a lie seven times
removed and its degrees (v.iv.7 ff.). As far back at least as the Townley
Mactatio Abel (1435-50) one can see a formula so parodied when Cain
reads out a pseudo-royal proclamation announcing he is guiltless of Abel's
murder. As Cain reads out each sentence, his boy, instead of crying
'Oyez, Oyez' as he has been instructed, subverts what Cain has said,
until he has to climb a tree to escape his master's wrath. A few lines will
give an impression of this routine:

> *Cayn*: I commaund you in the kyngis nayme,
> *Boy*: And in my masteres, fals Cayme —
> *Cayn*: That no man at thame fynd fawt ne blame.
> *Boy*: Yey, cold rost is at my masteres hame.
> *Cayn*: Nowther with hym nor with his knafe,
> *Boy*: What! I hope my master rafe —
> *Cayn*: For thay ar trew, full manyfold;
> *Boy*: My master suppys no coyle bot cold.
> *Cayn*: The kyng wrytys you untill.
> *Boy*: Yit ete I neuer half my fill.[22]

Wager uses the same routine in *The Longer Thou Livest* (1559), Moros
crying 'Gay gear', 'good stuff', 'very well' and 'fin-ado', 'with such
mockish terms' after each sentence of Discipline's litany (lines 433-48).

Shakespeare is by no means alone in his period in using this tradition.
Jonson makes play with the 'four choice and principal weapons' of the
subtle science of courtship: the Bare Accost, the Better Regard, the
Solemn Address and the Perfect Close in *Cynthia's Revels* (1601)[23] and the
play concludes with a Palinode that takes off the litany:

> *Amorphus*: From spanish *shrugs*, french *faces, smirks, irps*, and all *affected*
>   *humours:*
> *Chorus*: Good MERCURY defend vs.

And so on for ten more exchanges. Chapman, in the fourth act of *All
Fools* (1604), has a long parody of a legal formula (possibly not so far from
the genuine article), and this sort of thing will, in our time, be utilised by
Harold Pinter in the second act of *The Caretaker* (1960).[24] Although the

traditions of such routines go back for centuries, they still have life in them.

Another routine used by Shakespeare with a long tradition before and since is the insistent use of the same rhyme-syllable. Once again this is to be found in *As You Like It*, a play which, though so courtly and looking back to the origins of drama in tournament, yet has so many popular elements, from wrestling (compare *Fulgens and Lucres*) to language games. In III.ii, Rosalind enters reading a poem addressed to her, alternate lines of which end in 'Rosalind'. Thus, all the rhyme syllables require the '-ind' sound (with the comic variation of long — and short — sounding 'i'). Touchstone immediately parodies this, for, as he explains, it is his basic stock-in-trade to be able to rhyme like that 'eight years together':

> If a heart do lack a hind,
> Let him seek out Rosalind.
> If the cat will after kind,
> So be sure will Rosalind . . . and so on.

Jacob and Esau (1554) — 'a new, merry, and witty Comedy or Interlude', possibly by Hunnis or Udall — makes use of the same device. Mido, the boy, imitates for Ragau the way Esau ate up his potage. Again the first dozen of twenty-one lines will indicate the nature of the routine:

Mido: . . . Oh I thanke you Jacob: with all my hart Jacob.
Gently done Jacob: A frendely parte Jacob.
[*Here he counterfaiteth supping out of the potte*]
I can suppe so Jacob.
Yea than wyll I suppe too Jacob.
Here is good meate Jacob.
Ragau: As ere was eate Jacob.
Mido: As ere I sawe Jacob.
Ragau: Esau a dawe Jacob.
Mido: Swete rice pottage Jacob.
Ragau: By Esaus dotage Jacob.
Mido: Joily good cheere Jacob.
Ragau: But bought full deere Jacob.[25]

This kind of routine, however simple, reveals that delight in the sound of words which is a feature of popular drama. It was very common in the radio show *ITMA*. This example, from the show number 172 of the series of 310, broadcast on 10 May 1945, was chosen at random. 'Mer' stands for 'Mayor' and is quasi-Liverpudlian.

The Mer:	This isn't fer, it isn't fer.
Tommy Handley:	Who are you?
The Mer:	The Mer.
Tommy Handley:	The Mer? I don't ker if you are the Mer — take a cher, Mer.
The Mer:	Wher?
Tommy Handley:	Ther. Now, what's the trouble?
The Mer:	All this worry, I cannot ber —
Tommy Handley:	Ooh, you're suffering from wer and ter. Did such things happen when *I* was Mer?
Sam:	Yeah —
Tommy Handley:	Quiet cur. Now, Mr Mer, sign this and pull that chain off your neck.
The Mer:	I protest, I decler.
Tommy Handley:	But it's après la guer —
The Mer:	Oh, but sper my grey hers.
Tommy Handley:	Oh get up them sters —
	[*Door closes*]
Tommy Handley:	Well now, Sam, I'll make my speech. Now sound a fanfer.
	[*Trumpet: comic flourish*]
Tommy Handley:	That's all fan and no fur. Give me that trumpet and I'll show you how to blow it.[26]

Pistol, it will be remembered, has similar fun with this sound when he takes Monsieur le Fer prisoner in *Henry V*, IV.iv.

It would be wrong to give the impression that play with words, and particularly the way they may be tossed from one character to another, picked up, turned round, misunderstood, capped, and in every way delighted in, is peculiar to any period or even to English. What is suggested is that although wit is a mark of sophisticated society, sheer delight in words for their own sake, and for their sound, is often 'popular' (hence the love of the bad pun, so pervasive in English). One example quoted by Kate Lea from *commedia dell' arte* will serve to make plain that the possibilities of language play are not restricted to English. The example she gives of a *Dialogue of Mutual Disdain* is, of course, translated from Italian, and the Skelton-like opening followed by a short, later extract will prove adequate.

Dialogue of Mutual Disdain

She: The bonds

He: The chains
She: that bind
He: that fetter
She: this soul
He: my heart
She: crack
He: burst
She: If faith
He: If love
She: constrain you
He: entangle you
She: anger
He: scorn
She: annihilates you
He: disperses you . . . .

She: I say I detest you
He: I say I abhor you
She: and that I cannot endure the sight of you anymore
He: and that I cannot bear to be with you anymore.
She: Do you not know, these bonds . . . .
He: Do you not know, these shackles
She: which you call gold
He: which you said were of diamond
She: are proved false
He: were only of glass
She: They were gilded fetters
He: They were counterfeit stones
She: Therefore they are burst
He: For this I shattered them.[27]

The last routine I would mention is that based on the lesson. This also is a long-lasting act. One of the most entertaining from before Shakespeare's time comes from John Redford's *Wit and Science* (1539). It still works well today and it is surprising the anonymous adaption *The Marriage of Wit and Science* (1568) and Francis Merbury's adaption, *The Marriage of Wit and Wisdom* (1579), should have omitted it, especially as Ignorance and Idleness both appear in the 1568 play and Merbury calls his Vice, Idleness. The text here is modernised and slightly abbreviated. It will be noted that Renaissance domestic animals spoke a rather different language than do ours, though it is accurately imitative.

Idleness:	Say thy lesson, fool.
Ignorance:	Upon my thumbs?
Idleness:	Yes, upon thy thumbs. Is not there thy name? Where wast thou born?
Ignorance:	I was born in England, mother said.
Idleness:	In England?
Ignorance:	Yes.
Idleness:	And what's half 'England'? Here's 'ing' [*points to Idleness's thumb*] and here's 'land' [*and to finger*]. What's this [*pointing to thumb*]?
Ignorance:	What's this?
Idleness:	What's this, whoreson? What's this? Here's 'ing' and here's 'land'. What's this?
Ignorance:	'Tis my thumb.
Idleness:	Thy thumb! 'Ing,' whoreson, 'ing,' 'ing'!
Ignorance:	Ing, ing, ing, ing.
Idleness:	Forth! Shall I beat thy arse, now?
Ignorance:	Um-m-m-m-
Idleness:	Shall I not beat they arse, now?
Ignorance:	Um-m-m-
Idleness:	Say 'no,' fool, say 'no.'
Ignorance:	Noo, noo, noo, noo, noo!
Idleness:	Go to, put together; 'Ing'
Ignorance:	'Ing.'
Idleness:	'No.'
Ignorance:	'Noo'
Idleness:	Forth now! What says the dog?
Ignorance:	Dog bark.
Idleness:	Dog bark? Dog ran, whoreson, dog ran!
Ignorance:	Dog ran, whoreson, dog ran, dog ran.
Idleness:	Put together: 'Ing.'
Ignorance:	'Ing.'
Idleness:	'No.'
Ignorance:	'Noo.'
Idleness:	'Ran.'
Ignorance:	'Ran.'
Idleness:	Foorth now! What saith the goose?
Ignorance:	Lag! Lag!
Idleness:	'Hiss, whoreson, hiss'!
Ignorance:	Hiss, his-s-s-s.
Idleness:	Go to, put together: 'Ing.'

Ignorance:	'Ing.'
Idleness:	'No.'
Ignorance:	'Noo.'
Idleness:	'Ran.'
Ignorance:	'Ran.'
Idleness:	'Hys.'
Ignorance:	'His-s-s-s-s-s.'
Idleness:	Now, who is a good boy?
Ignorance:	I, I, I, I, I, I.
Idleness:	Go to, put together: 'Ing.'
Ignorance:	'Ing.'
Idleness:	'No.'
Ignorance:	'Noo.'
Idleness:	'Ran.'
Ignorance:	'Ran.'
Idleness:	'Hiss.'
Ignorance:	'His-s-s-s-s.'
Idleness:	'I.'
Ignorance:	'I.'
Idleness:	'Ing-no-ran-hiss-I.'
Ignorance:	'Ing-no-ran-his-s-s-s.'
Idleness:	'I.'
Ignorance:	'I.'

They rehearse the whole lesson again and then comes the test:

Idleness:	How saist, now, fool? Is not there thy name?
Ignorance:	Yea.
Idleness:	Well then! What has thou learned? Tell me the same!
Ignorance:	[*lamely*] I don't know.[28]

What we have here, even thought it is a school play, is a fully worked example of a clown act which, appropriately for a school, shows the more stupid clown being taught something. One clown teaching another is still a common routine in this century, from Harry Tate in 'Motoring' being taught the intricacies of π before the First World War,[29] to Laurel and Hardy, and Morecambe and Wise. Chapman's *The Gentleman Usher* (1602) has a letter-dictating act of this kind in III.ii, but possibly the most interesting variant is teaching the clown to woo. This routine has attracted 'learned' dramatists such as Chapman, Jonson and Ford, and it is still a fertile source of popular comedy.

In *The Yeoman of the Guard* (1888), Colonel Fairfax, having taught the fool, Point, to woo tells him to apply his new-learnt knowledge to someone other than Elsie Maynard. Possibly the very best act of this kind, however, at least in this century, happily preserved in a recording made before an audience of soldiers in the early part of the Second World War, was 'The Proposal' by Arthur Askey and Richard Murdoch. The section reproduced below cannot give all the nuances, nor represent the stage business, but it may indicate the character of this routine. Askey wishes to learn how to propose to Miss Nausea Bagwash and Murdoch first gives him a demonstration, he taking Askey's role and Askey pretending to be Nausea. They then reverse roles. It is particularly interesting how fully the setting can be pictured in the mind — the big sixth step, the fact that Askey is very small, the wicket gate, the dog, and so on. These have all been 'placed' earlier in the sketch, of course. It is also possible to get, even from a transcript, some idea of the way in which the illegitimate performer can assume a role, change that role, and simultaneously maintain his or her own personality. Some indications are given of the way lines are spoken and when laughter comes.[30] Even more intriguing is the way *another* comedian, Cyril Fletcher, can be 'taken into the world of the act' by imitation.

Murdoch: I'm coming up to the front door. I'm knocking at the front door, knock-knock.

Askey: [*coy*] Come in.

Murdoch: You can't hear me.

Askey: Why, am I deaf as well as blind?

Murdoch: You're up in the boudoir.

Askey: Oh yes, I keep forgetting that, yes.

Murdoch: Now, I'm knocking at the front door, knock-knock. Ah! Good morning! Opened by the butler.

Askey: Mrs. Bagwash got a butler?! Oh, she's sold the jam jars, I'd no ... [*audience laughter*]

Murdoch: Ah, good morning Blenkinsop. Is Miss Nausea Bagwash at home? She is? And she'll see me? I'm delighted. Now watch me closely.

Askey: Yes [*though he is 'up in the boudoir'*]

Murdoch: I'm hanging my hat in the hall.

Askey: M'm.

Murdoch: Now I'm coming up the stairs

Askey: [*excited*] He's coming up the stairs [*much running*]. Whoa, she doesn't live in a lighthouse!

Murdoch: Well, how many stairs are there?

Askey: Six.

Murdoch: Six.

Askey: Mind the top one, it's a big one. Be careful.

Murdoch: One, two, three, four, five, big one. Now I'm outside your boudoir.

Askey: [*coy excitement*] I know it [*audience laughter*].

Murdoch: Are you ready now [*to control laughter*]. Now I'm knocking at the boudoir door — knock-knock.

Askey: [*falsetto*] Come in.

Murdoch: I'm inside your boudoir.

Askey: [*with meaning*] I know [*big laugh*].

Murdoch: Oh Nausea, do you know what I'm here for?

Askey: I've got a damn good idea [*big laugh*].

Murdoch: Nausea darling, I want to ask you a question.

Askey: Well the answer's 'No' [*big laugh*].

Murdoch: Nausea, I've had something trembling on my lips for weeks.

Askey: Well, why don't you shave it off? [*laugh*].

Murdoch: Nausea, I kneel before you. I am intoxicated by your beauty. The perfume of your presence, those beautiful eyes, those beautiful lips, those pearly white teeth [*laugh*]. Nausea, darling, I come to press my suit.

Askey: Mary, put the iron on.

Richard Murdoch then tells Arthur Askey that he must now show what he has learned and they exchange roles. Murdoch is supposed to go into the boudoir and Askey to the garden gate (though they remain standing side-by-side in front of a microphone). Askey gets his thumb caught in the gate, is threatened by Murdoch's dog (all to be imagined by the listener) and finally the little man reaches the front door:

Askey: Now I'm kicking at the front door.

Murdoch: What are you kicking it for?

Askey: Well I can't reach the knocker, it's too high [*laughter*]. I'm coming up the stairs. Now I'm going down the stairs.

Murdoch: What y'doing that for?

Askey: Hang me hat in the hall. Coming up the stairs. Knock-knock.

Murdoch: Come in [*own voice*].

Askey: Don't be so anxious. Here I come. Nausea. I've got something hanging on my face.

Murdoch: Trembling on your lip you fool.

Askey:	Ah, trembling on your lip you fool. Nausea [*very firmly*], I'm drunk.
Murdoch:	Oooh.
Askey:	I'm plastered.
Murdoch:	I'm intox-[*both*] icated by your beauty.
Askey:	Nausea, you smell like a pheasant.
Both:	The perfume of your presence ...
Askey:	[*in style of Cyril Fletcher*] I've been dreaming of my darling love of thee. Nausea, what lovely eye.
Murdoch:	Eyes.
Askey:	I can only see one from here. Those lovely lips, just like petals,
Murdoch:	Ah, rose petals.
Askey:	[*malicious glee*] No, bicycle pedals.

Shakespeare has a number of scenes in which the art of wooing is taught. Possibly the two most famous are in *As You Like It* and *Henry V*. In *As You Like It*, Rosalind — a boy playing a girl's role, but dressed as a boy — teaches Orlando how to woo. Thus, Orlando has to 'woo' a boy, acting a girl's part but pretending to be a boy, whom he will later 'wed' when he/she resumes the role of Rosalind. The shifts in planes of make-believe and reality shimmer throughout the whole scene (as the all-male National Theatre production suggested) and the lesson is leavened with highly sophisticated wit. This is a clown scene completely transmogrified.

The 'teach me to woo' scene in *Henry V* also, but more directly, owes something to the popular tradition. The King explaining he is but a mere, tongue-tied soldier, begs Katharine to teach him what to say; but he never stops talking. The scene must have struck the first audiences as funny in part because of the way it parodies the clown tradition — an inversion of the usual practice of clowns parodying the wooers of the main action (as in *Fulgens and Lucres*). In *Henry V*, Shakespeare also makes use of another routine, the school lesson (see above, p. 55) in which Katharine is taught a kind of English.

What has so far been said does not purport to cover every kind of comic routine — nothing has been said, for example, of the absurdist monologue of which there is a beautiful example in Wager's *Enough is as Good as a Feast* (1540).[31] The intention has been to show the context in which Shakespearean routines were set with, lightly sketched-in, suggestions that many characteristics of these routines continued into the nineteenth and twentieth centuries. In *Contemporary Drama and the Popular Dramatic Tradition* modern routines are discussed in detail and comparison with what has been shown here will indicate something of the continuity of the illegitimate dramatic tradition, even though its relationship with the legitimate tradition was broken in the mid-nineteenth century.

The late F. P. Wilson beautifully summed up Shakespeare's relationship to the clown tradition in his British Academy lecture of 1941, 'The Diction of Common Life':

> Shakespeare inherited a ripe tradition of clowning — it was Tarlton's legacy to the English stage — and in ripe clowning, in 'merry fooling', there is little to choose between his early work and his late. As his art matures, he may bring everything more and more into a unity — Dogberry and Stephano are essential to the action, while Launce is a music-hall turn — but the humour of Launce's talk with his dog is already ripe, as nothing else in that play is ripe.[32]

It is the way that Shakespeare brings these routines into unity with his high poetic art that is one manifestation of his genius. Why, one then asks, does he invert a popular comic wooing scene tradition in *Henry V*? It is not possible to know for certain but may it not perhaps be that he wants to suggest, by implication, the *human* nature of God's deputy on earth? This is not only Great Harry, but the human being whose touch in the night meant so much to the common soldiers before Agincourt, whose human follies we have seen in *1 Henry IV*, and whose growing pains we witnessed in *2 Henry IV* (1597). Just as beneath Richard III lies the comic Vice, to be laughed at but rejected, so, but the other way about, the clown (suitably disguised) underlies Henry V at this point in the play. This suggests not only the humanity inherent within this king, but, more significantly, allows Shakespeare to present *simultaneously* the epic hero dear to Elizabethan (and later) tradition, and a subtle critique thereof. King Henry's rough wooing of Kate — his volubility which runs so absurdly counter to his request that Kate 'teach a soldier terms' (v.ii.99) — is immediately followed by the return of the French court and Burgundy's 'frank mirth', which, with its incessant use of the 'con-' prefix, recalls the 'la robe — de coun' indecency at the end of Kate's English lesson in III.iv. Henry's 'English lesson' for France has entailed the rape of her cities — their forcible entry — with which Kate is now equated:

King Henry: ... you may, some of you, thank love for my blindness, who cannot see many a fair French city for one fair French maid that stands in my way.

French King: Yes, my lord, you see them perspectively, the cities

	turned into a maid: for they are all girdled with maiden
	walls that war hath never entered.
King Henry:	Shall Kate be my wife?
French King:	So please you.
King Henry:	I am content; so the maiden cities you talk of may wait
	on her: so the maid that stood in the way for my wish
	shall show me the way to my will.

(v.ii.343–56)

Shakespeare's use of comic routines and clowns goes far beyond verbal links and contrasts of tone — comic relief, for example. What he does most subtly is use the low comic's ability to present things on more than one plane simultaneously, and the audiences' capacity to respond thereto, in ways that do not show *direct* debts to the popular comic tradition. Three well-known examples will suffice to show how this can be effected by a single character and through the interplay of characters, and then it will be practicable to suggest how the technique can be adapted to complete plays — *The Winter's Tale* and *Cymbeline*.

It has been pointed out that 'It is difficult to determine how much consciousness of the presence of an audience is implied by an Elizabethan soliloquy like the one with which *Richard III* begins.'[33] It can be argued that Richard *does* here appeal directly to the audience, getting it on his side, as it were, in much the same manner as did the old Vice, such as Ambidexter, with whom Richard III and Iago have much in common. As Richard says to the audience,

> Thus, like the formal Vice, Iniquity,
> I moralize two meanings in one word
> (III.i.82–3)

But the relationship with the audience holds good in other circumstances. It would apply, for example, to the stichomythic exchanges between Richard Gloucester and the Lady Anne in I, ii. The repartee, for that is what it is, has much in common in style and structure with popular dramatic technique. Furthermore, one of the characters, like the Vice, is 'determined to prove a villain' (I.i.30). Richard builds up — like a partner in a music-hall duo — a special relationship with the audience. The comic element, and the low comic tradition are obtrusive, and the result is a nicely judged 'embarrassment' of the audience. It does not know *quite* where it stands and that makes it the more emotionally open to the dramatist's art. O'Casey will use the same technique of 'embarrassment' in *Juno and the Paycock* (1924) and *The Plough and the Stars* (1926). It is not only low comedy that can be used in this way, for Shakespeare uses the verbal wit, so at home in *Love's Labour's Lost* (1595), in *Richard II* (1595) where a sick man plays so nicely with his name. This again permits the dramatist to control the audience's unease to a nicety for dramatic effect.

Much Ado About Nothing and *Troilus and Cressida* both include scenes in which characters overhear other characters and there is, simultaneously, direct address to the audience. The technique is an expansion of the comic routine in which two or more clowns will address each other, being 'overheard' by the audience, and will in the same routine address the audience directly. The use of this technique is not confined to Shakespeare. In *Ralph Roister Doister* (1552) I,iii, the audience overhears Tib and Marjorie talking to one another. Simultaneously, Ralph overhears them and comments to the audience, so building up a special relationship with the audience. After a little while, Marjorie says she knows that she has all the time been overheard. This has the effect of undercutting Ralph's position of superiority, but it also must affect the audience, making *its* relationship with Ralph uncertain and challenging its point of view.

In *Much Ado About Nothing*, II,iii, Benedick overhears (as is intended) Don Pedro and Leonato as they talk of how much Beatrice is allegedly in love with Benedick. As they talk, Claudio watches Benedick to ensure that he is getting the message and, at the same time, joins in their conversation and tells them 'the fowl sits' and 'this fish will bite'. At the same time as this complex of overhearings is going on — all of which the audience 'overhears', of course — Benedick comments three times to the audience; Don Pedro and Leonato as well as Claudio have 'asides' not intended for Benedick; and finally Benedick addresses the audience directly, analysing from his point of view what has just been played out to the audience.

The result is richly comic, but is, at base, no more structurally complex than the common duo-act of the music hall in which at various times the audience will be asked to 'Bear witness' of this or that. Falstaff, when he recounts in *I Henry IV*, II.iv, his version of what happened at Gad's Hill, uses the same technique. At first the audience is 'in the know' with Hal and Poins, but as Falstaff's story becomes more and more exaggerated, he must win the audience to him, if the full effect of his punch line is to be realised: 'By the Lord, I knew ye as well as he that made ye. Why, hear you, my masters: was it for me to kill the heir apparent?' (II.iv.299–301). At the same time, Hal and Poins become more and more involved in the stage action, loosening their direct link with the audience. The result is that the tables are turned on Hal and Poins. Falstaff, like the Vice in whom he originates, has seduced the audience to his point of view with the result that *even an audience which knows what is to happen* will laugh at the Prince's discomfiture. This is nothing to do with the lines written. It stems from the contrast between the relationships on-stage and those made directly by the characters with the audience, just as in the popular comic tradition.

It is one thing to do this in comedy, and the three examples so far given are firmly in that mode, especially in the scenes discussed. It is, however, also possible to use these relationships in, if not tragedy, a 'serious' moment in drama. In *Troilus and Cressida* v.ii, Cressida has been returned to the Greeks. She is seen by Troilus and Ulysses as she and Diomedes engage in talk of love. The audience therefore sees simultaneously two actions, and one character, Troilus, commenting on what he sees whilst his companion tries to calm him. At the same time, Thersites comments to the audience on both activities, 'How the devil Luxury, with his fat rump and potato finger, tickles these together! Fry, lechery, fry!' (v.ii.53–5). When Diomedes and Cressida leave (she after speaking what is, within her action, a short soliloquy), Thersites continues to comment to the audience on Troilus: 'Will he swagger himself out on's own eyes?' Diagrammatic representation of the direction of the speeches in these scenes of *Much Ado* and *Troilus and Cressida* clearly shows up the complexity of performer-audience relationships.

Direct address by Benedick and Thersites, and Falstaff's building up of a special relationship with the audience, never breaks the dramatic integrity of these plays, even though they are so different in tone. This is dramatic control of the very highest order and it stems from a thorough, perhaps implicit, understanding of the relationships on-stage and between stage and audience. Here Shakespeare is doing with superb artistry, with genius, what Medwall, for all his ingenuity, cannot quite achieve. And it is essentially a theatrical skill and one that is natural to the good music-hall performer.

In some of the late plays, Shakespeare extends the limits of theatricality still further, yet at the same time reverts to earlier techniques. Autolycus has something in common with the earlier clowns. In *Henry VIII* (1613) one suspects Shakespeare has the actors invade the area occupied by the groundlings around the stage. Just before the christening procession for the future Queen Elizabeth is to pass by, the Lord Chamberlain enters and is appalled that the way is not clear. What, he asks, have the Porters been up to to permit the assembly of such a crowd?

> Where are these porters,
> These lazy knaves? Ye have made a fine hand, fellows!
> There's a trim rabble let in. Are all these
> Your faithful friends o' the suburbs?
>
> (V.iv.75–8)

To whom does he point as the 'faithful friends o' the suburbs'? The groundlings? And does the procesion then make its way through a *real* crowd — the audience?[34]

Cymbeline comes near to being an ill-sorted heterogeneous mixture of styles, times and genres. The play is an extreme example of that 'multiplicity' described by G. K. Hunter (see pp. 15–16 above). Ancient Britain and Renaissance Italy; a representative Frenchman, Dutchman and Spaniard, two of whom are mute; and a plot right out of the Italian *novella* tradition; a glorious song ('Hark! hark! the lark') sung by perhaps the most boorish character in all Shakespeare; the headless trunk of Cloten whom the disguised Imogen (who has ever by mischance suffered the wrong name, as if to suggest how ill-placed she finds herself!) takes to be her husband's body; apparitions; and a descending Jupiter, would, in any other dramatist's hands, be regarded as impossibly mixed. Indeed, one suspects that it is only the name Shakespeare that has won the play the attention it requires.

Cymbeline, like *The Winter's Tale*, though less successfully, operates on several planes simultaneously. If the scenes described from *Much Ado About Nothing* and *Troilus and Cressida* are extensions of the clowns technique of complex address, these two plays are further extensions of the technique developed for those scenes. The capacity of the audience to apprehend so much that is diverse is strained to the uttermost in *Cymbeline*, but in *The Winter's Tale* the various planes of fancy and reality work together like a charm. Possibly the idea of a winter's tale (an improvement on Peele's *The Old Wives' Tale*, 1593) provides the fundamental element of illusion which helps a company and an audience to come to terms with the play and to respond to it in its parts as a whole. There is a sense of life suspended at various points in the play, and not only as this affects Hermione. Her re-awakening is the symbol of Perdita's recovery of what she has been denied, and her renewing grace is itself symbolic of natural renewal. The restoration of Hermione to Leontes rewards the self-awareness to which he has struggled. The union of Sicilia and Bohemia through Perdita and Florizel reaffirms political renewal. The manner in which Shakespeare holds over the various actions of the play so that the eventual fulfilment of each reflects one upon another in part explains the success of the play in performance. There *are* creaky joints. Shakespeare does resort to various gentlemen meeting with news more often than one would ideally wish in *The Winter's Tale* (and in *Henry VIII*), but the effect of a multi-faceted jewel which suddenly comes into our view as a whole does work.

We cannot be sure whether Hermione's coming alive in that most moving of *coups-de-théâtre* was in the original version of the play. It is incredible, if it were in the play from the first, that Simon Forman should not have mentioned it.[35] It seems as if this was the afterthought that enabled the whole play to be brought into focus. As we acknowledge each plane of the story, we yet need some point of focus to relate them all. But, if the coming to life of the statue is not to seem an absurd fantasy, we must be raised through one world of wonder to another — that jealousy can be like this; that its effects can be as they are dramatised; that a son should die, and a wife seemingly also; a daughter cast away; that we should, through Time, be transported to a pastoral world; and that, despite all opposition, love should triumph — until only a wonder out-doing all others will perform the stage magic that unites and resolves all.

The outstanding problem — carefully omitted from the catalogue above — is that of poor good-hearted Antigonus, eaten by the bear. Of course, the very popular *Mucedorus* (1590) rejoiced in a bear.[36] Mouse, the Clown, is sure it cannot be a real bear, but 'some Devil in a beare's doublet' (I.ii.4). It is strange that Shakespeare should have repeated this device, and that the eating of Antigonus by the bear should have been the subject of black humour. It is also a little odd that the child Mamillius should die. It is, perhaps, an attempt by Shakespeare to present his audience with the whole gamut of experience and emotion, so that we can realise that reconciliation is meaningless unless it comprehends not only real loss but the awful grotesquerie sometimes attendant upon death.

There is one final aspect of low comedy to which reference must be made. The antiquity of the pun is well known and although this is not the place to write its history, the pun is so important in popular comedy and in Shakespeare, and arouses such strong feelings amongst literary critics, that it cannot be passed over in silence. It is not, of course, a solely English characteristic and in the ancient world similarities of sound served to link words in unintentionally false etymologies.

The chief objection to the pun in English arises from its being considered too easy to make — 'a Sound, and nothing but a Sound' according to Addison[37] — so that it lacks intellectual or aesthetic quality. Worse, there is a delight in the bad pun. James Brown recognises two kinds of bad pun: one that makes use of a forced or false lexical ambiguity and another that brutally manipulates contexts so as to utilise ambiguities fetched from afar.[38] The difficulty for the literary critic, especially in evaluating Shakespeare, is that there is an obvious delight in bad puns by even this greatest of authors. How can high literary aestheticism — the great tradition of Redfield or Leavis — come to terms with literary badness? Why *does* the bad pun attract the greatest literary minds — Shakespeare, Swift, Joyce, to name but three — *and* the most common burlesque writers? There is an undoubted irony in the fact that these lines (which Brown selects as an example of the use of the bad pun by Shakespeare) might easily have come out of a nineteenth-century burlesque of *Hamlet*:

> *Polonius*: I did enact Julius Caesar; I was killed i' the Capitol; Brutus killed me.
> *Hamlet*: It was a brute part of him to kill so capital a calf there.
>
> (III.ii.108–11)

The really intriguing thing about this exchange is that Shakespeare 'sets up' Polonius's speech so that it attracts just such a reply. The splitting of 'I enacted Julius Caesar and was killed by Brutus in the Capitol' into three sections ensures that the audience has the vital words separated and emphasised so that the puns will easily be recognised in the theatre. Compare this delight in bad punning with that from three nineteenth-century burlesques.[39] Thus *A Thin Slice of Ham let* (*c.* 1863, anonymous); referring to the play in which Hamlet hopes to trap the king:

> *King*: What kind of trap? A mouse-trap
> *Hamlet*:   Right you are;
>
> But an anony*mouse* trap, for no bar
> Or bait you'll see.
>
> (p. 68)

Hamlet! The Ravin' Prince of Denmark!! (1866, anonymous): Hamlet's advice to the Players — given in The Back Kitchen, which, in Thackeray's *Pendennis* (1848–50) represents the disreputable Cyder Cellars, an early form of music hall (ch. 30):

> *Hamlet*: Now, then, you duffers, do you know your parts?
> Let's have no speaking them by fits and starts;
> But look at me and get them all quite *pat*.
>   [*To* Player Queen, *who appears decidedly stout*]
> I've anti*pathy* to a gal so *fat*

I wish I 'ad a leaner *Patti* here
To act *as prima donna* — never fear.
I'll play *a spree mad on her* — meaning Ma.
Pa would approve it — *pas si mauvais pas.*
But, to *pass* on; that pun's not up to *par.*
(pp. 110–11)

Even in burlesque attention can be drawn to language and continuity can be broken. The speech continues with a passage of direct address to the audience in which the decline of the Thespian art is deplored: 'there animates the nation/One taste, one passion, one desire — Sensation!' A trifle ironic in a burlesque! In the third example, from *Hamlet, or, Not Such a Fool as He Looks* (1882) by A. C. Hilton, Polonius is picking up chessmen which the king has thrown on the floor:

Polonius: ... One wretched *piece* is missing still, confound it,
             And I shall have no *peace* until I've found it.
                 Enter *Hamlet*, who falls over *Polonius*.
Hamlet: Ha, crawling on the floor! Just like your slyness.
Polonius: Picking up chessmen, please your royal highness,
             A knight is missing. Would you hold the light?
Hamlet: No, wait for *day*, and never mind the *knight*.
             Observe, Polonius, I have made a pun.
Polonius: Your royal highness is so full of fun.

(p. 305)

Again, attention is drawn to a characteristic of the dialogue, obvious though it is.

Although Shakespeare's puns are the most infamous in his time, Jonson was not above such word-play.

Marian: You are a wanton. *Robin Hood.* One I doe confesse
           I wanted till you came, but now I have you,
           Ile growe to your embraces, till two soules
           Distilled into kisses, through your lips,
           Doe make one spirit of love.[40]

The earliest pun associated with the English is that made by Pope Gregory on seeing Angles brought to Rome as slaves in the sixth century. It was told by Aelfric and repeated by Bede — in Latin. There are, in fact, three puns.

Again therefore he enquired what was the name of that people. Answer was given that they were called Angles. Whereon he said: 'Well are they so called, for they have too an angel's face, and it is meet such men were inheritors with the angels in heaven. What is the name of the particular province from which those boys of yours were brought?' The merchants answered that the people of that same province were called Deirans. 'Marry!' quoth he, 'well are they called Deirans, being plucked from the ire of God and called to the mercy of Christ. How is the king of that province called?' It was answered that his name was Aella. Whereupon Gregory playing upon the name saith: 'Alleluia! the praise of God the Creator must be sounded in those parts.'

Notice Bede's 'playing upon the name' — 'adludens ad nomen'.[41]

Puns are suggested in Anglo-Saxon and although some scholars are conservative as to the dozen or so they would admit in Chaucer, others have, with some justification, found the pun more commonly used by him. Paull B. Baum, for example, lists well over a hundred. He demonstrates (as have others) that Chaucer would have read Geoffrey of Vinsauf's *Poetria Nova* in which the pun on *malum* (with long and short 'a', respectively meaning 'apple' and 'evil') summarises Eve's fall in the Garden of Eden: 'O malum! miserum malum! miserabile malum!'[42]

Milton employs puns with a high degree of intellectual wit in *Paradise Lost* and, interestingly in the light of Vinsauf's example, there are many on 'fruit', meaning the apple and the fruit, or result, of eating that apple; and on 'fruitless' — so that Adam and Eve, after the fall, spend 'fruitless hours' in mutual accusation.[43] A brilliant example of Milton's punning — the kind of punning that has nothing to do with laughter (as Sir Walter Raleigh pointed out in 1900) — is to be found in these lines from *Paradise Lost*:

> Their song was partial, but the harmony
> (What could it less when Spirits immortal sing?)
> Suspended Hell ...
>
> (II.552-4)

'Partial' means prejudiced and singing in parts; 'Suspended' is physical and musical — as in a suspended chord — but Milton goes one better, actually suspending the resolution of his sentence (as if a musical suspension) by interpolating a parenthetical question.

In the eighteenth century the pun lost favour in most high literary circles and its practitioners were savagely attacked, though there was at least one significant exception. In *The Dunciad*, the Goddess Dulness sees a King (Theobald) 'Who leads my chosen sons / To lands that flow with clenches and with puns' (A.1.251). Nevertheless Pope, in that same poem, brings off one of the best of all bad puns — on taking the 'high priori road' — and he also uses the pun with the subtlety of Milton. Thus there is a pair of triple puns in *An Essay on Criticism* (1711): 'Wit's Titans braved the skies / And the Press groaned with licensed blasphemies'. The Press is the printing press, the institution THE PRESS, and the mob; and 'licensed' means simultaneously liberty to do something, formal permission and licentiousness — thus, a public saddled with follies of the media and blasphemies publicly attacked, but surreptitiously approved, by Church and State.

The pun, and particularly the bad pun, never went out of fashion, however. Many of the cross-fires created by Dumont (see pp. 48–50 above) depended upon them. For example:

Mid: Where should poultry dealers spend their vacation?
End: *Egg Harbor*! That's easy!
Mid: Bike riders?
End: *Wheeling*
Mid: Surgeons?
End: *Lansing*
Mid: Cowards?
End: *Cape Fear*! You're a cinch for me.
Mid: People who bet, but never win?
End: *Luzon*! (lose one.)
Mid: Gluttons?
End: *Samoa*! (Some more.)
Mid: Dudes?
End: *Scilly Islands*!

In the 1930s, the popular comedian Tommy Handley (of *ITMA*, see pp. 53–4) and the Eton-educated Gilbert Frankau had a variety act known as Murgatroyd and Winterbottom, of which this is a brief, typical example:

Murga: Well I hear you went away on a cruise.
Winter: Yes, but I came back.
Murga: Where did you go, Norway?
Winter: No, I went the other way.
Murga: I went on a cruise too.

Winter: Oh, two crews?

Murga: Yes, Oxford and Cambridge.

Winter: Oh, we went much further than that. We went to the Scilly Isles.

Murga: Aren't they stupid? Did you go to Greece?

Winter: Only in the hot weather. Did you have a nice trip?

Murga: I fell down once or twice. Did you have a good berth?

Winter: Well, it's so long ago. You'd better ask my mother.

Murga: I mean, what was your cabin like?

Winter: It was on the starboard side. Did you sleep on the starboard side?

Murga: I slept on my chest. I suppose you had lots of deck games?

Winter: Oh, quoit, quoit. Where did you go ashore?

Murga: Mar-sales.

Winter: When?

Murga: Thursday.

Winter: I was very disappointed with Florence.

Murga: Why?

Winter: She didn't turn up. Did you strike the Nile?

Murga: Yes ... I hit the nile on the head.

Winter: How irrigating. Did you go to Jamaica?

Murga: Yes.

Winter: What didja-make-a Jamaica?

Murga: Oh, dearer than Madeira.

Winter: But nicer than Nice.

Murga: Brighter than Brighton.

Winter: More pop'lar than Poplar.

Murga: Coarser than Corsica.

Winter: Father than Mother.

Murga: Oh much.

The Scilly Isles, it will be noted, appear in both the last two examples. A variation of the form was much practised by Flanagan and Allen, also in the 1930s. This extract is from their routine called 'Cl''OI''sters'. (The 'OI', as in 'Digging H''OI''les' mentioned in note 21, refers to their frequently interjecting 'Oi' in unison at a particularly 'bad' line.)

Flanagan: Had a marvellous time. Went up West. Past Young William.

Allen: Past where?

Flanagan: Young William.

Allen: Young William — Old Bailey

Both: Old Bailey.
Flanagan: Right through Jekyll Park
Allen: Jekyll Park — Hyde Park.
Both: Hyde Park.
Flanagan: Hide at night, Jekyll in the daytime; saw bad fish.
Allen: You saw what?
Flanagan: Bad Fish.
Allen: Bad Fish — Rotten Row.
Flanagan: Yes, Rotten Row. And I been down to the docks.
Allen: Oh, you saw the ships?
Flanagan: Oh yes, saw all the ships coming into whiskey.
Allen: Coming into port.
Flanagan: Into port. Oh, its a marvellous sight. Have you seen it?
Allen: Never.
Flanagan: It's avaricious, really. See all the labradors at work.
Allen: The what?
Flanagan: The labradors.
Allen: The labradors — the salvadors.
Flanagan: The stevedores y'fool. I've got a marvellous house.
Allen: I bet it's marvellous.
Flanagan: All your lifetimes — you should have such a house as I've
             got — I got a wonderful gate.
Allen: Have you really?
Flanagan: And from the gate to the door I've got a putt.
Allen: A putt?
Flanagan: An approach.
Allen: An approach? A drive.
Both: A drive.
Flanagan: Come on, I'll show you round the house — I've got
             beautiful salad work all round.
Allen: Beautiful what?
Flanagan: Salad work.
Allen: Salad work?
Flanagan: Radishes.
Allen: Radishes? Lettuce work
Both: Lattice work.
Flanagan: And I've got a Labour Party.
Allen: A Labour Party?
Flanagan: Liberal?
Allen: Liberal — Conservatory.
Both: Conservatory ... and so on.

Notice the reversal at 'salvadors / stevedores' where the ostensibly less knowledgeable of the two (Flanagàn), corrects his cleverer partner, a frequent characteristic of this act but also representative of the turn-round in relationships in such duos as Laurel and Hardy and Abbot and Costello.

This does not represent high intellectual activity of course, but it is a play with, and a delight in, language that has much in common with Shakespeare and with that great exception to those who in the eighteenth century condemned the pun, Swift. Nor is the habit unknown today in pseudo-intellectual circles. Thus, the *Guardian*, reporting not butter from Brittany, but a statement made at the annual conference of Plaid Cymru in 1975 that Bretons were 'languishing without charges or trial in the prisons of France', headed the story with as bad a pun as any, 'Breton butter', the more tactless because of the way it distorted the implication of the message to be conveyed.

This brief account will suffice to provide a context for Johnson's very well-known condemnation of Shakespeare's addiction to the pun:

A quibble is to Shakespeare, what luminous vapours are to the traveller; he follows it at all adventures, it is sure to lead him out of his way, and sure to engulf him in the mire. It has some malignant power over his mind, and its fascinations are irresistible. Whatever be the dignity or profundity of his disquisition, whether he be enlarging knowledge or exalting affection, whether he be amusing attention with incidents, or enchaining it in suspense, let but a quibble spring up before him, and he leaves his work unfinished. A quibble is the golden apple for which he will always turn aside from his career, or stoop from his elevation. A quibble, poor and barren as it is, gave him such delight, that he was content to purchase it, by the sacrifice of reason, propriety and truth. A quibble was to him the fatal Cleopatra for which he lost the world, and was content to lose it.[44]

In brief: a pun was to Shakespeare as was an *ad lib* to his clowns.

Boswell told Johnson that he only so condemned Shakespeare because Johnson himself lacked facility in punning, to which Johnson replied:

> If I were punished for every pun-I-shed,
> There would not be left a puny-shed
> For my punnish head.

Charles Lamb made a defence of the bad pun, almost equally well known, in 1826:

This species of wit is the better for not being perfect in all its parts. What is gains in completeness, it loses in naturalness. The more exactly it satisfies the critical, the less hold it has upon some other faculties. The puns which are most entertaining are those which will least bear analysis.[45]

It is illuminating to contrast the use of the pun by two of its most famous literary practitioners, Shakespeare and Swift, in the light of these statements. Swift wrote whole tracts in punning mock-Latin and mock-Spanish, included puns in his *Journal to Stella*, and wrote a 'Modest Defence of Punning' in reply to 'God's Revenge against Punning'. That he did not publish his defence may be due to his discovering that the pseudonymously published 'God's Revenge' was written by Pope. He also wrote outrageous etymologies based on puns to 'assert the antiquity of the English Tongue'. Thus, Latin *'turpis'* (filthy, nasty), is really two English words, the letter 'd' having been omitted by syncope — 'tur(d)-pis'. These extracts from Swift's 'Dying Speech of Tom Ash' show his exuberant word-play in a more sustained manner:

> MY FRIENDS,
>   It is time for a man to look *grave*, when he has one foot there. I once had only a *pun*nick fear of death, but of late, I have *pun*dered it more seriously. Every fit of *coffing* hath put me in mind of my *coffin*.... I, that supported myself with good *wine*, must now be myself supported by a *small bier*.... But, as the *mole* crumbles the *mold* about her, so a man of my small *mold*, before I a*m old*, may *molder* away ... whatever doctors *may design* by their *medicines*, a man in a *dropsy drops he* not.... I do confess I have let many a *pun go* which did never *pungo*.... But, I am going; my *wind in* lungs is turning to a *winding* sheet. The thoughts of a *pall* begin to a-*pall* me ... .[46]

Shakespeare's use of the pun is, in fact, very varied. It can be as deplorable as Johnson suggests, so much so that one might suspect puns where none are intended, as in *Titus Andronicus*, on 'barbarous':

> *Aaron*: ... They cut thy sister's tongue and ravish'd her,
>   And cut her hands and trimm'd her as thou saw'st.
> *Lucius*: O detestable villain! call'st thou that trimming?
> *Aaron*: Why, she was wash'd, and cut, and trimm'd, and 'twas
>   Trim sport for them that had the doing of it.
> *Lucius*: O barbarous, beastly villains, like thyself!

                                                          (V.i.92–7)

Three puns on the word 'grave' may succinctly suggest something of the variety of Shakespeare's technique. In *Antony and Cleopatra*, at IV.x.38, Antony calls Cleopatra his 'grave charm', at once solemnly charming and one who will bewitch him to his grave. The effect is not comic and the word-play dramatises their equivocal relationship. Mercutio, in *Romeo and Juliet*, on the point of death, reveals a notable courage when he says 'Ask for me tomorrow and you shall find me a grave man' (III.i.103–4). Here the purist might consider that Shakespeare is bordering on the indecorous. He will have no doubt that Shakespeare has overstepped the mark when Hamlet, lugging Polonius's dead guts to the neighbour room, speaks of the old counsellor as 'most still, most secret, and most grave / Who was in life a foolish prating knave' (III.iv.214–15), and the jingling rhyme accentuates the grotesquerie.

Although it is possible to show that there is a lexically fruitful side to punning in some languages, and that it can be used, as by Milton, in an extraordinarily subtle manner, there is no doubt that it is also the despised product of the low comedian, and in the great writer is to be deplored as a regrettable aberration. When, as literary critics, we can speak of ambivalence or ambiguity, we are content — Hamlet's mother, for example, 'posting with dexterity to incestuous sheets'. We have then, as one critic puts it, 'a symbolic device which can force us from the pragmatic realm of direct experience into the complex realm of abstractions, the magnificent realm of fantasy'.[47] It is not just the matter of the goodness or badness of a pun, or of the worst being best, as Lamb would ingeniously seem to suggest; or the easy coincidence of mere sound. There are those of quick wit and serious mind, such as Swift, who took delight in the worst of puns; there are those, as great literary figures, and just as moral, like Pope and Dr Johnson, who seem to deplore the whole business. As Pope puts it 'The Father of Lies [Satan] was also the Father of Puns.'[48] Why is this?

In a local Elizabethan sense F. P. Wilson offered a sound explanation:

> To an Elizabethan the play upon words was not merely an elegance of style and a display of wit; it was also a means of emphasis and an instrument of persuasion. An argument might be conducted from step to step — and in the pamphleteers it often is — by a series of puns. The genius of the language encouraged them.[49]

This can, I think, be taken a little further. W. B. Stanford has argued that the significance of what was implied in a name was strong in Greek literature and goes far beyond amateurish philological speculation.

Lurking behind [such etymological ambiguities] was the shadow of a profound superstitious belief in the principle of ὄνομα ὄρνις or *nomen omen*, a conviction that in some supernatural way a man's name might, if properly interpreted, contain the secret of his destiny or reveal his true character.[50]

The influence of real or suspected etymological relationships was not restricted to such words. Thus Pliny and Martial both express a Roman belief that eating the animal, the hare, promoted beauty because of a supposed relationship between *lepus*, a hare, and *lepos*, beauty.[51] It has been argued that Aeschylus goes so far as to use a Doric form, ἑλένας (for 'destroyer of ships'), instead of the usual Attic form, ἑλέναυς, in order to make more pointed the pun on Helen's name (within which there is an element in Greek implying destruction), which appears in the preceding line.[52] There is no more famous example in English literature of a play on the significance of a man's name than that by John of Gaunt in *Richard II* (II.i.72 ff.). Well might Richard ask, 'Can sick men play so nicely with their names?' In this play there is almost an obsession with the relationship of the word to the thing which it describes. When Bolingbroke returns illegally from banishment he claims, 'I was banished Hereford, / But as I come, I come for Lancaster' (II.iii.113–14). That is, with his father's death, the Duke of Hereford becomes Duke of Lancaster. But has he changed himself with his name? Is the man no longer subject to banishment because of the change of title? Of course not. Central to the play is Gaunt's titling of Richard II as 'landlord' instead of 'king' — for as landlord of England he is no longer the lord of the land, but a mere disposer of tenantries. It is this that strikes Richard on the raw — for there is evidently much in a name.

From the *Mabinogion* to Rudyard Kipling,[53] names can be given a significance which is interpreted as being present in the words themselves. (The practice of nicknaming suggests a carry-over of the supposed relationship of name to person.) Often this relationship of name to person was taken with deadly seriousness, though there were comic usages and sometimes comic and deadly combine. *The Leeds Courier* published an announcement that John, son of Henry and Rachel Longbottom had died on 13 April 1895, aged two and a half. A London paper, in the unfeeling way of the south, commented: 'Vita brevis est arse(e) longa'.[54]

The idea of a power within the word itself, of a special relationship between the word and that to which it refers, the relation of 'the word' — the 'logos' — to 'god', 'providence', 'Christ incarnate', the 'soul of the universe', is played upon in St John's Gospel. The tradition was used by Christ himself when he renamed the apostle Simon, Peter, and then punned upon the word: 'Thou art Peter and upon this rock I will build my church' (Matt. 16:18). The intention of the pun is made the more certain because, in Aramaic, Paul uses the equivalent word in that language to name Peter — Cephas (1 Cor. 1:12). Such attitudes to the word, whether they be Christian or Stoic, imply a reverence for the sanctity of the word as word. To tamper with that relationship, to play on words, must seem almost sacrilege to some people. Yet, perhaps the most sensitive critic and poet of the twentieth century, T. S. Eliot, does not forbear using the pun, the ambiguity, dependent upon 'the Word' in its Christian and poetic senses. In 'Burnt Norton' he writes:

> The Word in the desert
> Is most attacked by voices of temptation.[55]

Here it is at once the temptation of Christ and the vulnerability of language in its struggle against unreason (just as at the conclusion of the fourth book of *The Dunciad*) which Eliot simultaneously invokes.

To the idea that the word actually encapsulates its own significance, is the possessor as it were of its own meaning, there have been two responses: that which tends to take the word as quasi-divine; and that which seeks to force alternative meanings upon words. For those for whom the mystique of the word is paramount, punning is to be deplored; the implication must be that the word dominates man. Alternatively, man can seek to control the word, to impose his will upon the word, and therefore he will play upon meaning. Thus, in about 1400, the Celtic *Red Book of Hergest* said it was the duty of the minstrel to mock, to imitate and to play on words.[56]

It is well know that some contemporary writers find that language dictates what they say, and that they must devise strategies to avoid this. Beckett, therefore, has written first in French on a number of occasions and then translated and adapted what he has written for an English-speaking audience. At a more modest level, in the ordinary discourse of daily life, the pun, and perhaps most especially the bad pun, is one way in which we can refresh our spirits and assert our independence as human beings *vis-à-vis* the word.[57] By demanding that a word means what we wish it to mean, we can subvert due order and rational expectation, but if we gain response from those who hear us — a laugh or a groan — we not merely assert our individuality but gain the acceptance of the group for our independence. The response is important for without that acknowledgement, however grudging, we are failing to get societal agreement for our attempt to dominate the word, and so to assert our right to individuality. The appeal of the punster in these circumstances is not to the literary critic but to that society of which we are a part.

The pun — and again, the bad pun especially — as used by Shakespeare, plays not only upon the word but upon the individual's relationship with the community, within the play-world and the real-world. It epitomises both our individuality and, through the response, that we have a place in the community. Of all literary devices it is the one that, in an hierarchical community, can most readily transcend class. It epitomises, as Shakespeare and the comics recognise, doubtless unwittingly, the dramatic experience at its best, in which the individual member of an audience shares in a communal experience whilst retaining his or her individuality. Perhaps, most curiously in such a society, what is thus shared across class boundaries is essentially subversive and it may be that, paradoxically, this plays a part in the stabilisation of such a society.

Perhaps in nothing so much as in his affection for the quibble did Shakespeare reveal his association with the popular comic tradition. And in nowhere can we see the continuance and life of that tradition so readily as in its use to the present day. The bad pun may be said to be the epitome of 'popular appeal', demanding of an audience to a play conscious awareness of, and response to, extra-dramatic, social, relationships.

4 Jonson and his Contemporaries

Although Shakespeare's use of the overheard drama and the drama of direct audience address not only pervaded his work but was developed in particularly subtle ways, it will be apparent from the references made to other dramatists of his time that he was not alone in drawing on the popular tradition. Although the influence of the popular comedic tradition is most easily recognised in the clown acts of Shakespeare and his contemporaries, often what had originated in the comedy of direct address was transmuted into something more complex. The debt that Aaron, Richard III, Iago and Falstaff owe to the Vice has frequently been commented upon. This is not just a matter of Aaron's comic thrusts such as his response to Chiron's 'Thou hast undone our mother', when the blackamoor Child is revealed: 'Villain', says Aaron, 'I have done thy mother' (*Titus Andronicus*, IV.ii.76–7). Nor direct allusions to the Vice, such as Hal's description of Falstaff as 'that reverend vice, that grey iniquity, that father ruffian, that vanity in years' (*I Henry IV*, IV.ii.505–7). Nor Richard III moralising two meanings in one word like the formal Vice, Iniquity (III.i. 82–3). Iago, even when he speaks of pluming up his will in double knavery (*Othello*, I.iii.400), is not as patently based on the Vice as is *Richard III* when he explains in the soliloquies which open and close I.i the *way* in which he will prove a villain by setting Clarence against the king, for example, 'In deadly hate the one against the other' (l.35). Nevertheless it is not difficult to see Ambidexter of Thomas Preston's *Cambises* (1561) beneath Iago as well as Richard. When he first appears, absurdly accoutred, like A in *Fulgens and Lucres*, he maintains that he does not know his name (and, of course, we never learn of names for either A or B). When he does remember, he explains for those without Latin what his name means and, in outlining what he will do, lays the crude foundations for Shakespeare's Richard and Iago.

> Ha, ha, ha, now ye wil make me to smile
> To see if I can all men beguile.
> Ha! my name, my name would you so faine knowe?

79

Yea, iwis, shal ye, and that with all speed —
I have forgot it, therefore I cannot showe.
A, a, now I have it. I have it indeed!
   My name is Ambidexter. I signifie one
That with bothe hands finely can play,
Now with king Cambises and by and by gone.
Thus doo I run this way and that way.
   For awhile I meane with a souldier to be,
Then give I a leape to Sisamnes the judge.
I dare avouch you shall his destruction see.
To all kinde of estates I meane for to trudge.
   Ambidexter? Nay, he is a fellow, if ye knew all![1]

The similarity with Shakespeare's characters is not simply a matter of
direct address, nor the satirical humour that Shakespeare develops from
that of the clownish Ambidexter. Perhaps most important in an age
which seeks psychological motivation in its characters (and motive
hunting in Iago antecedes 'The Method'), is the *donnée* of evil found in
Aaron, Richard and Iago. No more than the Vice do they need the
motivation that would be essential to a psychologically-based character of
drama written since Strindberg. That Shakespeare makes his characters of
this kind so much more complex and interesting should not disguise that
from us. J. A. B. Somerset, in writing of the way the Vice operates,
accurately and succinctly describes what happens in *Othello* (1604) and
Richard III (1592–3). He is concerned specifically with the Vice in such
plays as *1. Nature* (1495) and *The Four Elements* (1517).

As an audience, we would probably begin by sharing the hero's
virtuous, albeit untried, principles of right living. Following the hero
into his seduction we credit the methods of the vices (who always
present a better case *dramatically*) and therefore we allow that evil can
operate. This perhaps disturbs our moral sensibility, because the great
contrast between the vices and the straightlaced virtues affects us, and
the vices do appeal to us by making us laugh. Further, the vices
succeed at times in detaching us from our moral attitudes and making
us relax, momentarily suspending our moral judgments....

As the vices amuse us, we can be said to share the hero's seduction.
We have believed in it, have felt the springs of sympathetic laughter,
and have perhaps even been called upon to assist in seduction.

Somerset also gives explanations for the Vice not being able to keep his council, telling us through asides and direct address, in play after play, how evil he is; 'Direct revelation and the arousal of laughter result'.[2] Needless to say, these characteristics are not presented by Shakespeare and his contemporaries (in Vindice, Flamineo and Bosola, for example), as crudely as they are by Preston, but the *donnée* of evil for its own sake, the direct address, the humour (which with the Jacobeans becomes irony and bitter satire), and above all, the seduction *of the audience*, are ever present. It is in *Othello* that the Vice-like Iago most intriguingly seduces the audience and the critics — the critics especially. Iago does not only deceive Othello, Desdemona, Roderigo, Cassio, Brabantio and even his wife, Emilia (a rich haul, surely!) but those critics who, forgetting the experience of the theatre, are surprised 'how easily Othello is deceived'. In much the same way, because Falstaff is not seen as deriving from the Vice, surprise can be expressed that he is rejected by Hal. A Poet Laureate, John Masefield, went so far as to describe Hal as a prig, but no Elizabethan audience would have been surprised by what happened, for not only did they know from experience that the Vice was rejected, but they knew that that was how it should be. All the Vice-like characters of Shakespeare, Tourneur and Webster *must* be expelled, and those more wicked than Falstaff will die. It should be borne in mind that Falstaff's colleague, Bardolph, will be hanged (with Nym) in *Henry V*. Only Pistol is left, like the 'roaring devil i'the old play' so his wooden dagger may serve to pare everyone's nails (IV.iv.76–8). Falstaff — and the audience — is plainly told that Hal will reject his former companion, but critics and producers have a habit of forgetting this, and the reasons therefor, when the moment of rejection comes.[3]

In addition to comedy, it is also possible to find traces of direct moral address in Shakespeare. For example, *Richard III* not only owes much to the Vice tradition, but Richmond's speech which concludes the play has much in common with Barnabas's address to the audience at the end of *A Nice Wanton* (1550). Barnabas is the good son of parents who have spared the rod and so spoiled his brother and sister so that one ends on the gallows and the other dies of the pox. At the end of the play he preaches a little sermon to his mother, Xantippe, and then sends her in to comfort his father. He will follow on, he tells her, but first he has something to say to the audience. He then addresses the audience — and there can be no mistake about this because he begins, 'Right gentle audience ...' — and in a speech of twenty-two lines tells those assembled what they have seen in 'thys interlude' and what the moral is. Then he kneels down and, in the text we have,[4] asks all to join with him in a prayer for the Queen.

Presumably audiences knelt at this point. At the end of his prayer, which concludes with 'God saue the Quene, the Realme, and Cominalitie!', he makes a curtsey and goes out. There is then a somewhat puzzling indication for a song — perhaps some form of jig. The ending is a good example of that 'multiplicity' which G. K. Hunter describes in the work of Lyly. *Nice Wanton* is not alone in ending in a prayer. Both Wager's plays, for example, *The Longer Thou Livest* and *Enough is as Good as a Feast*, end in prayer and both do so calling attention to the presence of the audiences — those we have troubled, as Enough says (l.1536). Prayer also ends the Catholic Interlude, *Respublica*, performed in the first year of Queen Mary's reign, 1553 (in which the Vice, Avarice, represents the Protestant Church), but the audience is not specifically mentioned.

The end of *Richard III* does not so blatantly call for the audience to join in prayer but, especially bearing in mind the play's links with the earlier drama, there is little doubt whence Shakespeare drew his inspiration. Although the presence of an audience is implied in Richard's first soliloquy (see p. 79 above), this is less certain for the last speech of the play, given by Richmond. It could quite easily have been addressed to those on stage in Shakespeare's day, as it will be in most proscenium-arch productions, but, as the speech progresses, surely it is intended to unite performers and audience:

> Abate the edge of traitors, gracious Lord,
> That would reduce these bloody days again,
> And make poor England weep in streams of blood!
> Let them not live to taste this land's increase,
> That would with treason wound this fair land's peace!
> Now civil wounds are stopp'd, peace lives again:
> That she may long live here, God say amen!
> (v.iv.48–54)

What audience of the 1590s could forbear to echo that amen!

Although she does not mention *Richard III* in her section devoted to the didactic address (pp. 101–12), Doris Fenton does list many examples of this tradition. These are taken from plays by such dramatists as Beaumont, Chapman, Dekker, Heywood, Jonson, Marlowe, Middleton, Shakespeare and Webster. It is plain that the tradition of direct moral address was frequently practised throughout Shakespeare's lifetime.[5]

Though it falls outside the concern of the tradition of direct address, there is one aspect of the popular dramatic tradition that should never-theless be mentioned briefly. The cycles, and moralities such as *Everyman*,

were, in their grand design, like Dante's *Comedy*. Man passes through
many tribulations but, given that he does certain things and avoids
others, he will eventually enjoy eternal peace. This comedic frame was
not the only format known to Tudor dramatists: the tragic fall,
epitomised by Thomas Watson's *Absalom* (*c*.1540) and the verse
biographies in *A Mirror for Magistrates* and *Gorboduc* (1562), was also
important. Nevertheless, the persistence and the appeal of that comedic
frame has been a tremendously powerful influence on English drama,
especially at the more popular end of the scale. The traditional Hollywood
Western (not the pseudo-intellectual variety), and American television
'private eye' and legal-counsellor dramas, are the tail-end of a tradition
that begins in English in the cycles. The *deus ex machina*, whether the
Seventh Cavalry, the cowboy who rides in from the plains to accomplish
some demi-god-like task before journeying on into the sunset, or the
lawyer in a wheel-chair (the very epitome of a god in a machine!), who
never fails to get his client off, ensures that all problems are solved — and
will from the start be known to be solved — in the play-world of such
drama. This pattern has been extraordinarily pervasive and it is not being
too fanciful to trace it back to the pattern of the cycles, which are centred
on a *deus ex machina* who can solve every human problem.

It is not possible to know all the ways in which the traditions of direct
address and popular clowning were used by Elizabethan dramatists. This
is not merely because so many plays have not survived (and one suspects
that the cruder work has, in the main, either been lost or was not thought
worth printing), but because the clown's routines are sometimes omitted
from the published play, just as they were earlier in this century from 'the
book' of the Drury Lane pantomimes which could be bought at the
theatre. One well-known Elizabethan example of this practice occurs in
A Knack to Know a Knave (1592). The title-page advertises that is contains
'Kemps applauded Merrimentes of the men of Goteham, in receiving the
King into Goteham' but, as Doris Fenton says, this is 'actually
represented by a very meagre page and a third of text' (p. 23).

Much more puzzling, and disappointing, is *The History of the Two
Maids of Moreclack* (1608) written by Robert Armin, Tarlton's protégé
and the clown who succeeded Kempe in Shakespeare's company. It was
originally written about 1597–8, revised for the Children of the King's
Revels in 1606–7, and published in 1609.[6] Apart from not being out-
standingly comic, the part originally played by Armin (according to his
own statement in his address 'To the friendly peruser'), that of John of
the Hospital,[7] is very short indeed. He makes three brief appearances and
has only twenty-five lines in the first two and is silent in the third; yet the

sub-title states 'With the life and simple maner of Iohn in the Hospitall'. This John, an 'innocent Idiot', as Armin calls him, is discussed much more fully in Armin's *Fool upon Fool* (and *Nest of Ninnies*), and the few lines in the revised version cannot possibly represent Armin's act. It is possible that the same clown played John and Tutch, for Tutch only appears after John's two speaking parts. He has some 113 lines, but even these do little to suggest Armin's reputation. What happens so often is what the printer of Marlowe's *Tamburlaine* (1587) ingenuously explains to his customers:

> *I haue (purposely) omitted and left out some fond and friuolous Iestures, digressing (and in my poore opinion) far vnmeet for the matter, which I thought, might seeme more tedious vnto the wise, than any way els to be regarded, though (happly) they haue bene of some vaine conceited fondlings greatly gaped at, what times they were shewed vpon the stage in their graced deformities: neuertheles now, to be mixtured in print with such matter of worth, it wuld prooue a great disgrace to so honorable & stately a historie.*[8]

Shakespeare did not exhaust the possibilities for using the popular comedic tradition. Two instances will suffice to show how Jacobean dramatists used what they had inherited.

There is in Middleton and Rowley's *The Changeling* (1622) a very interesting use of multiple direct address. Act II, scene i begins with five lines of dialogue between Beatrice and Jasperino before the latter exits. Beatrice then has a 21-line soliloquy. De Flores enters, refers to her and, as she stands silent, speaks an even longer 'aside' of twenty-six lines (a technique which anticipates that used by O'Neill in *Strange Interlude*). The following exchange then ensues, of which only one line — 'Thy business? What's thy business?' — is not an aside, until dialogue commences in the last two speeches reproduced here.

Beatrice:	[*aside*]
	Again!
	This ominous, ill fac'd fellow more disturbs me
	Than all my other passions.
De Flores:	[*aside*]
	Now't begins again;
	I'll stand this storm of hail though the stones pelt me.
Beatrice:	Thy business? What's thy business?

De Flores: [aside]
                    Soft and fair!
            I cannot part so soon now.
Beatrice: [aside]
                    The villain's fix'd. —
            Thou standing toadpool!
De Flores: [aside]
            The shower falls amain now.
Beatrice: Who sent thee? What's thy errand? leave my sight.
De Flores: My lord your father charg'd me to deliver
            A message to you.[9]

The same routine is used again in II.ii.57–100, though with a number of lines which are not asides, between the same characters, and between Beatrice and Alsemero in IV.ii.123–32. The play is hardly a comedy. What Middleton and Rowley are doing is using the technique of direct address found in the comedy of intrigue for dramatising deception that will have a tragic outcome. The comedic mode has the effect of creating uncertainly for the audience. As with the mixture of evil and comedy found in the Vice's direct address, or Richard III's soliloquies, the audience is 'taken into' the villain's plot.[10]

The death of clowns in plays is unexpected. They should have at least the licence to jest in drama that they do in a royal court. The hanging of Bardolph has already been mentioned and there is at the end of *King Lear* a notable crux which some interpret as referring to the king's clown — 'And my poor fool is hanged' (V.iii.307). The poor clown in *Titus Andronicus* suffers an unexpected and untimely end, but this reflects more on those who order his execution, Saturninus and Tamora, than on him (IV.iv.45 and 47). The central character of Wager's *The Longer Thou Livest, the More Fool Thou Art*, to give the play its full title, is a fool, Moros (the word derives from the Latin 'moror' [I am a fool]; Piety, at line 271, states that 'Moros a fool doth signify'.[11]) Moros is shown as a boy, a young man and as an old man receiving judgement from God, who strikes him with his sword of vengeance:

> That he is a God of power, mighty and strong,
> The fools shall know by experience.
> (ll. 1789–90)

He is punished because he has never learnt to be other than a fool but though we may accept that he should be stripped of his 'godly gear' and learn that he is 'now a peasant of all peasants', his end comes as something of a shock. Moros refuses to go with Confusion to receive his reward:

> Confusion, poverty, sickness and punishment;
> And after this life, eternal fire
> Due for fools that be impenitent.
>
> (II. 1848–50)

Moros would prefer that the devil carry him away on his back and so he goes, to give the devil his due. Although Moros is not simply the clown of the play, but a flawed hero, that this should be the end for such a character still takes us aback. Benbow comments: 'The grotesque humour of the play is perhaps in a direct descent from the judgment plays of the mystery cycles and looks ahead to the fortunes of Faustus' (p. xvi).

The play which, less than a decade before the closing of the theatres, provides an even greater surprise of this kind is Ford's *'Tis Pity She's a Whore* (1633). Here a clown-character, Bergetto, is accidentally killed and his death is as great a surprise to him as it is to us.

> *Bergetto:* O help, help! Here's a stitch fallen in my guts, O for a flesh-tailor quickly! — Poggio!
> *Philotis:* What ails my love?
> *Bergetto:* I am sure I cannot piss forward and backward, and yet I am wet before and behind. — Lights, Lights! ho, lights!
> *Philotis:* Alas, some villain here has slain my love! ...
> *Bergetto:* O my belly seethes like a porridge-pot, some cold water, I shall boil over else; my whole body is in a sweat, that you may wring my shirt; feel here — Why, Poggio! ...
> *Bergetto:* Is this all mine own blood? Nay, then good night with me. Poggio, commend me to my uncle, dost hear? Bid him for my sake make much of this wench. O! — I am going the wrong way sure, my belly aches so. — O, farewell, Poggio! O! — O! —. [*Dies*][12]

Bergetto's language, especially the reference to his belly seething like a porridge-pot, and the graphic description of pissing forwards and backwards simultaneously, strip his death of any shred of dignity. The humour is ridiculously comic, yet this is a moment also of pathos, as Poggio's grief for him underlies. This conjunction of death and comedy goes right back to the Middle Ages.

These highly individual uses of the popular comic tradition must not be allowed to give the impression that there was always a near-magical transformation of base materials by the Elizabethan dramatists into something remarkable and still theatrical. There cannot by any such thing as 'the typical Elizabethan play', but a glance at a good workmanlike drama, by a dramatist able enough to work with Ben Jonson and Harry Chettle, may *suggest* what the norm might have been like.

Henry Porter's *The Two Angry Women of Abingdon* (1588) was evidently successful enough to demand a second part (though that has not survived) for Henslowe records payments to Porter for work thereon.[13] Doris Fenton neatly summarises the play and simultaneously indicates its relationship to the popular tradition of direct address.

> *The Two Angry Women of Abingdon* is a play two acts of which proceed largely by monologues, as the angry women, their husbands, sons, daughter and serving-men, blunder about in the dark fields, trying either to help or to hinder the elopement of Mall and Francis. A few of these speeches show definitely that they are addressed to the audience and the tone of the rest is so much the same, that one may assume them to be likewise. The majority combine information as to the progress of affairs with matter of mirth, in such proportion that one can hardly say which predominates. (p. 51)

The play includes a drunken clown, Dick Coomes, who engages in cross-talk acts of this kind:

Francis: Sirrah, be quiet, or I do protest —
Coomes: Come, come, what do you protest?
Francis: By heaven, to crack your crown.
Coomes: To crack my crown! I lay ye a crown of that, lay it down, an ye dare; nay, 'sblood, I'll venture a quarter's wages of that. Crack my crown, quotha!
Francis: Will ye not be quiet? will ye urge me?
Coomes: Urge ye, with a pox! who urges ye? You might have said so much to a clown, or one that had not been o'er the sea to see fashions: I have, I tell ye true; and I know what belongs to a man. Crack my crown, an ye can.
Francis: An I can, ye rascal!
Philip: Hold, hair-brain, hold! dost thou not see he's drunk?

(I.ii. p. 111)

The old joke about the angel (punning on the heavenly and monetary kind), beloved of Shakespeare, appears in one of Coomes's monologue-like speeches:

> *Mrs Goursey*:   Art thou resolved, Dick? wilt thou do this for me? And if thou wilt, here is an earnest-penny of that rich guerdon I do mean to give thee.
> [*Gives money*]
> *Coomes*:   An angel, mistress! let me see. Stand you on my left hand, and let the angel lie on my buckler on my right hand, for fear of losing. Now, here stand I to be tempted. They say, every man hath two spirits attending on him, either good or bad; now, I say, a man hath no other spirits but either his wealth or his wife: now, which is the better of them?
>
> (II.iv. p. 142)

Shakespeare can be seen working in the same clown tradition. The likeness to Launcelot Gobbo's first speech in *The Merchant of Venice* (1596) is obvious. Costard will play on 'guerdon' and on 'remuneration' in *Love's Labour's Lost* (1595), one being a shilling and one a mere three-farthings (III.i). There is also possibly an anticipation of the clown's attempt to get money from Viola in *Twelfth Night* (1600, III.i).

Act IV, scene iii of *The Two Angry Women of Abingdon* takes place in the dark. As much of the point of the humour depends upon darkness — falling over molehills and into ponds, the clown trying to kiss a man who is pretending to be a woman, and two actions taking place on-stage simultaneously unbeknownst each to the other — one can only think that the Admiral's Men, who performed the play, had audiences with vivid imaginations and a remarkable capacity for suspending disbelief if, as we must suppose, the play was performed in the full light of the afternoon. Even more demanding of the ability to suspend disbelief is the scene in Act V in which the two angry women struggle for the single torch that 'lights' the scene. In addition to monologues and monologue-like speeches, there is much use of the aside (by the two angry women in the last act, for example), and what is one of the most unusual of all breaches of continuity in any play. When Hodge is pretending to be a woman in IV.iii, and Coomes is blundering about in the dark trying to kiss 'her', Hodge begins to show acquiescence, 'if I thought nobody would see'. Coomes assures him 'they must have cat's eyes' to be able to see, so dark is it (even though the stage would be open to the afternoon sky). Coomes continues to blunder about, eventually to fall into a pond off-stage, and on the way he bumps into one of the stage posts holding up the heavens — although the scene is in the open fields. 'A plague on this post!', he says, 'I would the carpenter had been hanged, that set it up, for me. Where are ye now?' (p. 173) — and off he goes into the pond.

It is impossible to know whether this stretched the audience's suspension of disbelief to breaking point, but we do know that Porter was paid to write a second part to the play. It does illustrate in what a crude form the comedic tradition inherited by the dramatists of the period might be used with 'box-office success' and it illustrates what a practical dramatist believed he could demand of the imagination of his audience.

There is one important form of the tradition in which the actors share with the audience the knowledge that they were all in a theatre together (implicit in direct address) that has not been discussed. This is the induction with which may be associated the interman. It is interesting to compare Shakespeare's use of the induction, or the preliminary chorus, with that of other dramatists, and especially with Jonson. As had been done for *The Taming of a Shrew*, Shakespeare provides an induction for *The Taming of the Shrew*, but he forgets the device and Christopher Sly slips out of the play. And although the choruses of *Henry V* are prominent, Shakespeare is at pains that the audience shall use its imagination. Jonson's inductions and intermeans, however, do not work like this.

In *The Induction in Elizabethan Drama*, Thelma Greenfield distinguishes between dumb-show inductions, of which she lists sixteen; occasional inductions (25); critical inductions (25); and frame plays (7). The dramatist most frequently represented is Jonson with no less than seven plays with inductions, all but one critical: *Every Man Out of His Humour* (1599), *Cynthia's Revel's* (1601), *Poetaster* (1601), *Bartholomew Fair* (1614), *The Staple of News* (1626) and *The Magnetic Lady* (1632). She lists *The Devil is an Ass* (1616) as an occasional induction. The next most common users of the induction are Marston with four (three critical and one dumb-show)[14] and, very interestingly as the next chapter will indicate, Thomas Randolph, one of the 'Tribe of Ben', also has four. As she points out there are difficulties in classification of the inductions and one of Randolph's four listed as a frame might well be included with the critical inductions 'By virtue of containing a realistic and critical representation of play spectators' (p. 67). Beaumont's *The Knight of the Burning Pestle* (1607) likewise spans both categories.[15]

Although in its so obviously being a burlesque, *The Knight of the Burning Pestle* anticipates the burlesques of the Restoration and eighteenth century, it was probably less influential on later drama than were the critical inductions and the masques (which Thelma Greenfield does not discuss). *The Knight of the Burning Pestle* does, of course, make play with the stage and supposedly real worlds, principally through the intervention of the Citizen and his Wife and their insistence that their apprentice, Ralph, shall not only play a part and be provided with suitable 'reparrel', but that the play being presented should be distorted to meet the Citizen's request that Ralph make an immediate appearance:

> Citizen: ... but *Nel* I will have *Raph* doe a very notable matter now, to the eternall honour and glory of all *Grocers*, sirrah you there boy, can none of you heare?
>
> Boy: Sir, your pleasure.
>
> Citizen: Let *Raph* come out on May-day in the morning and speake upon a Conduit with all his Scarfes about him, and his fethers and his rings and his knacks.
>
> Boy: Why sir you do not thinke of our plot, what will become of that then?
>
> Citizen: Why sir, I care not what become on't. I'le have him come out, or I'le fetch him out my selfe, I'le have something done in honor of the Citty, besides, he hath bene long enough upon Adventures bring him out quickly or if I come in amongst you —
>
> Boy: Well sir hee shall come out, but if our play miscarry, sir you are like to pay for't. [*Exit* Boy]
>
> Citizen: Bring him away then.
>
> (IV.iv.4–19)

Ralph enters and has a lengthy speech in fourteeners with such splendidly irrelevant lines as:

Now little fish on tender stone, beginne to cast their bellies,
And sluggish snails, that erst were mute, do creep out of their shelies.

> (IV.iv.43–4)

He also, as a sort of audition piece, recites a huffing part. This implicitly draws attention to the theatre as theatre, and is rather loosely remembered from *1 Henry IV*:

> Wife: ... Hold up thy head, Rafe shew the Gentlemen what thou canst doe, speake a huffing part, I warrant you the Gentlemen will accept of it.

Citizen: Do, Rafe do.
Rafe: By heaven me thinks it were an easie leap
           To plucke bright honour from the pale-fac'd Moone,
           Or dive into the bottome of the sea,
           Where never fathame line touch't any ground,
           And plucke up drowned honor from the lake of hell.
                                                    (Ind. 70–8)[16]

The main target of the burlesque, however, is of the romance tradition, the play being written only a few years after the publication in 1605 of the first part of *Don Quixote*, although before the first appearance of Cervantes's work in English (1612). It was certainly written after *Every Man Out of His Humour*, which therefore anticipates its use of interjectory comment throughout the play.[17]

Thelma Greenfield has shown very clearly how the induction developed, how it was used 'to represent in a more realistic way the actual process of presenting a play'; how it evolved directly 'from a practice generally regarded as naive and crude, from the habit of addressing the audience directly from the stage'; and how it had its origins in classical drama, especially Plautus and Terence.[18] It will be apparent that I do not regard direct address as always naive and crude (nor from her comments on *Fulgens and Lucres* does she), and I am sure that she is right in disagreeing with those 'modern critics' who simply find the induction a breaking of the dramatic illusion, rather than 'exploiting the actual situation in the theater for an effect different from that which we, at the present time, ordinarily consider dramatic' (p. 69).

Although, as so often with Jonson, there are classical origins to his work (and Aristophanes as well as Plautus and Terence), the idea cannot but have been prompted at the end of the sixteenth century by Chettle and Munday's induction and interjections to *The Downfall of Robert Earl of Huntingdon* (1598), which seems to have appeared a little before *Every Man Out of His Humour* (1599). Jonson and Marston, who quickly took up the induction for *Antonio and Mellida* (1599/1600), use the induction for satiric and, directly or indirectly, educational ends. These first three inductions contain between them most of the significant elements that are to be found in the rehearsal plays of the eighteenth century: the use of the rehearsal mode itself (by Chettle and Munday); the deliberate awareness of the problems faced by the actor and writer (notably Marston, who not only has the actors of the main play enter the induction 'with parts in their hands: having cloakes cast over their apparell', i.e. their stage costumes, but who also discusses the difficulties faced by an actor in doubling a part, and, as Thelma Greenfield puts it, 'the poet's problem of molding the language into character patterns', p. 85); and, in Jonson, there is a concern for the education of the audience. It is this last characteristic which prompts so much of the satire of the inductions. Educating the audience is also a constant theme of the masques, from laying hold on the 'more removed mysteries' of *Hymenaei* (1606), to making 'the Spectators Understanders' of *Love's Triumph through Callipolis*, a quarter of a century later (1631). Thelma Greenfield succinctly describes Jonson's aim in his inductions as the bridge of proper criticism between the auditor and the play, 'in short, understanding'.[19] One amusing throwback to the past, incidentally, is William Sly's simulated astonishment in Webster's induction to *The Malcontent* (1604): 'Ile holde my life thou took'st me for one of the plaiers', which is reminiscent of A's similar surprise in *Fulgens and Lucres*.

In his essay, 'Ben Jonson: the Makings of the Dramatist (1596–1602)', Edward B. Partridge shows how Jonson endeavours to educate his audience in the opening Grex of *Every Man Out of His Humour*, but 'in a way that not even a more tactful playwright than he could have made palatable'.[20] Jonson's concern with 'proper criticism', his own didacticism, and what James D. Redwine Jr. has called the 'real subject of Jonson's theory of humours ... neither psychology nor asthetics, but moral goodness',[21] are very closely interwoven. They have a rather obvious similarity to certain twentieth-century schools of 'proper criticism' (which also have strong educational interests), but more important is the way they reflect the past and suggest the more immediate future. Redwine quotes part of Asper's challenge:

> Let him not dare to challenge me of wrong,
> For, if he shame to haue his follies knowne,
> First he should shame to act 'hem: my strict hand
> Was made to ceaze on vice, and with a gripe
> Squeeze out the humour of such spongie natures,
> As licke vp euery idle vanitie.
>
> (ll. 141–6)

One is immediately taken back a generation to the treatment of Moros in *The Longer Thou Livest* and the proposed treatment of Avarice by Nemesis in *Respublica* (1553):

> That he maie bee pressed, as men doo presse a spounge,
> That he maie droppe ought teuerye man hys lotte,

To the utmooste ferthing that he hath falslie gotte.

(v.x.90-2)

Looking to the eighteenth century one can see, in Fielding for example, damaging political satire in his rehearsal plays and burlesques which nevertheless has the general good of the commonwealth very much to the fore. The aim is, as in Jonson, the scourging of fools, but dramatised through the falsities and follies of the stage — the stage world being taken to be the very epitome of the real world.

Partridge also points to the way that *Every Man Out of His Humour* 'unfolds in a series of layers'. By the introduction of his characters in these separate groups, 'Jonson makes possible a complicated scene of reciprocal commenting' (p. 231). This originates in 'the habit of addressing the audience directly from the stage', as Thelma Greenfield noted, and it is not dissimilar from the techniques found in *Much Ado About Nothing*, *Troilus and Cressida* and *The Winter's Tale* described above. One result of Jonson's technique, because it was rooted in satire and was didactic, was that, as Partridge says anent *Cynthia's Revels*: 'Once again we see Jonson moving his auditors gradually into a complex action, and here even exposing the whole argument so that they can then watch the whole action unroll in detachment' (p. 234).[22]

It is this 'detachment', conveyed through the induction-plus-intermean technique, which will later prove of enormous importance. Although that will be the concern of the next chapter, it is as well here to note in outline how this complex action derives from the direct address of the popular comedic tradition; is inherited by the eighteenth-century satirical and burlesque dramatists such as Gay, Fielding and Foote; is taken up by Tieck and thence passes to Pirandello; having departed the English stage after Planché, is brought back to it through Brecht (via Pirandello and Gay). But first more attention must be paid to another form of drama much, though not exclusively, associated with Jonson: the masque.

It is a curious paradox of the masque that this most removed of all drama should, through its staging, have proved so influential in public theatres from the Restoration to the present time. Furthermore, in Jonson's masques, one finds references to popular, even folk, drama, and the use of extremely 'realistic' dialogue. It is not difficult to see how Jonson adapts the technique used in writing *Cynthia's Revels* to the masque. Partridge points to this when he says that this play 'marks the road down which Jonson was to move only in the masques — the road of mythological allegory with a burlesque antimasque' (p. 237). What Jonson often does, as Stephen Orgel points out in his discussion of

Neptune's Triumph (1624), is to present his masque 'both literally and figuratively in the court of King James'.[23] Instead of the lavish setting of so many of the masques, as the initial direction states, 'All, that is discovered of a *Scene*, are two erected *Pillars*, dedicated to *Neptune*'. The contrast must have been striking. The poet enters to distribute copies of the argument of the masque and he is engaged in discussion with the Master Cook, whose 'room, and region too' is the Banqueting Hall where the masque is to take place. As the discussion proceeds it is 'the cook, not the poet, who begins to sound most like the Jonson who was King James's masque writer . . . the cook is insisting that an appeal to the mind properly involves an appeal to all senses as well, that poetry cannot be intellectualized, that every resource at the poet's command is to be explored in order to reach the spectator's understanding' (pp. 92–3). As Davenant was one of the few dramatists to be active before the theatres closed and after they re-opened (becoming one of the two Patentees), and as he was also the author of several masques, one being particularly important,[24] it will be realised how significant was this further development of Jonson's dramatic art.

The relationship of the audience of a masque to what it saw was quite different in certain respects from that of a performance at the Globe or Blackfriars.[25] This was not because the audience was powerful and distinguished (though Jonson did curb his tongue before the monarch), but because a number of members of the royal household (or, as in Milton's *Comus* (1634) a distinguished lord's household) 'acted' in the same masque and, perhaps most important, symbolically at least, because at the end of the masque, masquers and audience joined together in dancing. The evolution of the antimasque, which involved professional actors, could modify this relationship, as could the inductions (for so they were in kind if not in name) which also developed, but this essential difference remained. It is intriguing that the attempt to involve audiences in direct participation with the players should now be a left-wing theatre cult.

From his earliest masques, Jonson had been concerned with explaining his meaning. In the preliminary statement to *Hymenaei*, he comes near to insulting even the greatest persons who were not concerned to pursue the 'more removed mysteries':

> . . . And, howsoeuer some may squeamishly crie out, that all endeuour of *learning*, and *sharpnesse* in these transitorie deuices especially, where it steps beyond their little, or (let me wrong 'hem) no braine at all, is superfluous; I am contented, these fastidious *stomachs* should leaue my

full tables, and enioy at home, their cleane emptie trenchers, fittest for such ayrie tasts; where perhaps a few *Italian* herbs, pick'd vp, and made into a *sallade*, may find sweeter acceptance, than all, the most nourishing, and sound meates of the world. (ll. 19–28)

But for James, and those with no brain, he provided a learned apparatus. When, in 1609, he was asked by the Queen 'to think on some dance or show, that might precede hers, and have the place of a foil, or a false masque', he evolved more fully what he had devised for the masque for Lord Haddington's wedding, *The Hue and Cry after Cupid* (1608). It was for Jonson a very useful means whereby he might, as Stephen Orgel explains: 'set up a problem for which the masque was a solution. In a very real sense, then, for Jonson it was the antimasque that served to give meaning to the masque, to explain it, to make the audience understand' (p. 93). He puts it slightly differently in one of his editions of Jonson's masques:

> through the antimasque we comprehend in what way the masque's ideal world is real ... the antimasque is not a simple antithesis of the world of the revels, but essentially ... another aspect of it, a world that can be accommodated to, and even included in the ideals of the main masque.[26]

The masque is here being used by Jonson as a mode of education and instruction and its similarities, *in these respects*, to propaganda drama such as The Living Newspaper, is illuminating.

The masques preserve in a very interesting manner some of the elements of medieval life and present, in the liveliest fashion, certain characteristics of popular drama. It has been argued that two of the origins of English drama are to be found in the tournament and the sermon, especially its debate form. Jonson, wittingly or not, resuscitates these sources and relates them. Thus, for the marriage of Robert Devereux and Frances Howard in 1606, Jonson wrote *Hymenaei* and on the following night, *The Barriers* was performed. This began with a debate between Truth and Opinion as to whether, as Truth averred, 'the most honor'd state of *man* and *wife*, / Doth farre exceede th'insociate *virgin*-life' (ll. 711–12). After a formal debate, two troops of sixteen richly accoutred knights were led out by the Lord High Constable and the Earl Marshal, and, after exhortations by Truth and Opinion, they fought at the Bar, first singly, then three by three, until the last six having scarcely ended, and Angel appeared out of '*a striking light*' (l. 877) and announced Truth, who, perhaps not surprisingly, proved triumphant (at least in the masque: the marriage ended in divorce seven years later). It is possible to see Jonson here uniting in a solemn manner, the debate, the tournament, the symbolic, the classical and the Christian. In that the union of a man and a woman is being celebrated, this is appropriate. More significant is the way these aspects are reconciled, the word 'reconciled' even appearing in the final stage direction as the thirty-two knights are '*led forth, hand in hand, reconciled, as in triumph*' (ll. 945–6).

Barriers also preceded *The Masque of Oberon* (1611), written for Henry, Prince of Wales, and appropriately therefore including Merlin as well as King Arthur. Like the first barriers, this proved not to augur well for the future for Prince Henry died of typhoid when he was only nineteen. The most interesting of the entertainments in this context is without doubt *A Challenge at Tilt* (1613). This was designed for the day after a marriage and it is the only such masque by Jonson to include colloquial language and material appropriate to the public stage. The opening direction and dialogue are in a very different tone from that of the formal style of earlier masques.

Two Cvpids striuing the day after the Marriage

   1 Cupid: It is my right, and I will haue it.

   2 Cupid: By what law or necessitie? Pray you come back.

   1 Cupid: I serue the man, and the nobler creature.

   2 Cupid: But I the woman, and the purer; and therefore the worthier: because you are a handfull aboue mee, doe you thinke to get a foot afore mee, sir? No, I appeale to you ladies.

   1 Cupid: You are too rude, boy, in this presence.

   2 Cupid: That cannot put modestie into me, to make me come behind you though, I will stand for mine inches with you, as peremptorie as an Ambassador; ladies, your soueraignties are concern'd in me, I am the wives page.

   1 Cupid: And I the husbands.

   2 Cupid: How!

   1 Cupid: Ha!

(ll. 2–16)

The appeal to members of the audience — direct address — will be noted and the device of the quarrelling Cupids has, of course, been already used by Jonson to open *Cynthia's Revels*.

Love Restored, presented in January 1612, was the first of Jonson's masques to be largely in prose. It featured direct address by Masquerado in which there is a pretence of there being no masque at all:

I would, I could make 'hem a shew my self. In troth, Ladies, I pittie you all. You are here in expectation of a deuice to night, and I am afraid you can doe little else but expect it. Though I dare not shew my face, I can speake truth, vnder a vizard. Good faith, and't please your Maiestie, Your Masquers are all at a stand; I cannot thinke your Maiestie will see any shew to night, at least worth your patience. Some two houres since, we were in that forwardnesse, our dances learnid, our masquing attire on and attired. A prettie fine speech was taken vp o'the Poet too, which if hee neuer be paide for, now, it's no matter; His wit costs him nothing. Vnlesse we should come in like a Morrice-dance, and whistle our ballat our selues, I know not what we should doe . . .   (ll. 2–15)

A folk-character, Robin Goodfellow, is introduced, the first such which Jonson will use, and he makes a direct allusion to the world outside the masque and the court, referring to the hoax production, *England's Joy* (1602).[27] Continuity is broken and, in Robin Goodfellow, there is a different 'plane of reality'.

This is even more obvious in the delightful *Irish Masque* (1613) and the masque, *For the Honour of Wales* (1618). It may be that there is con-descension here (it is noticeable that the King's accent is not made the medium for a masque), but it seems rather that Jonson is writing in the tradition of everyone participating in 'the little tradition', as did Medwall in *Fulgens and Lucres*. The opening of *The Irish Masque*, especially bearing in mind the setting, suggests a remarkable union of King with his people, symbolic perhaps, but more directly perceived than the removed mysteries of the earlier masques, and uniting also the public stage (the actors were from Shakespeare's company) and the private world of the masque.

> *The King being set in expectation, out ranne a fellow attir'd like a citizen: after him, three or four foot-men:* Dennise. Donnell. Dermock. Patrick

Patrick: For chreeshes sayk, phair ish te king? Phich ish he, an't be? show me te shweet faish, quickly. By got, o'my conshence, tish he! Ant tou bee king *Yamish*, me name is *Dennish*, I sherue ti mayesties owne cashtermonger, bee mee trote; ant cry peep'sh, ant pomwater'sh i'ty mayesties sheruice, 'tis fiue yeere now. An't tou vilt not trush me now, cal vp ti clarke o' ti kitchin, be ant be, shall giue hish wort, vpon hish booke, ish true.

Donnell:	Ish it te fashion, to beate te Imbasheters here? ant knocke 'hem o'te heads, phit te phoit stick?
Dermock:	Ant make ter meshage runne out at ter mouthsh, before tey shpeake vit te King?
Dennise:	Peash *Dermock*, here ish te king.
Dermock:	Phair ish te king?
Donnell:	Phich ish te king?
Dennise:	Tat ish te king.
Dermock:	Ish tat te king? got blesh him.

(ll. 1–17)

For the Honour of Wales, which in addition to the popular fun made of the Welsh accent,[28] also features a little Welsh, including the same question as Dermock's 'Phair ish te king?': '*Ble mae yr Brenin?*' (l. 208). These two masques, and *The Masque of Christmas* (performed on Twelfth Night, 1617 and again on 19 January, and including such 'characters' as Misrule, Minced-Pie and Mumming, showing Jonson's lively awareness of the folk traditions) are all, or virtually all, antimasque. *For the Honour of Wales* was written, in fact, to precede a repeat performance of *Pleasure Reconciled to Virtue* on Shrove Tuesday 1618. Orgel reproduces a very interesting letter about this repeat performance and adds a comment pertinent to this study. John Chamberlain wrote of the Shrove Tuesday performance that the masque was 'much better liked than the twelveth night by reason of the newe Conceites and Antemaskes, and pleasant merry speeches ... by such as counterfeited Welse men'. Orgel is surely right in suggesting that 'their low comedy could make the difference between failure and success',[29] for low comedy, like the bad pun, is in that little tradition in which all can participate.

The logical outcome of these masques is to be found in *The Masque of Augurs*, performed on Twelfth Night in 1622 and on 6 May of that year. This concludes with a genuine masque of augurs, with singing and dancing (and copious footnotes in Latin by Jonson for the printed version), but that is preceded by what is called the second antimasque ('*Which was a perplex'd Dance of straying, and deform'd Pilgrims, taking seuerall pathes ...*'), into which Apollo descends '*and the Maine Masque begun*' (ll. 271–4). Prior to that second antimasque is what has all the appearance of being an induction. Into this is set a dance of bears (an old Christmas custom, still kept about this time at Christmas in the household of the Percies, for example[30]), accompanied by a ballad sung by John Urson, by his name the bearward. This includes such down-to-earth stanzas as:

> *The Wives of Wapping,*
> *They trudge to our tapping,*
>   *And still our Ale desire;*
> *And there sit and drinke,*
> *Till the[y] spue, and stinke,*
>   *And often pisse out our fire.*
>
> *From morning to night,*
> *And about to day-light,*
>   *They sit and never grudge it;*
> *Till the Fish-wives joyne*
> *Their single coyne,*
>   *And the Tinker pawnes his budget.*
>
> *If their braines be not well,*
> *Or their bladders doe swell,*
>   *To ease them of their burden;*
> *My Ladie will come*
> *With a bowle and a broome,*
>   *And her Hand-mayd with a Iorden.*
>   (ll. 202–19)

Just before Urson enters, Notch has introduced a distressed Lady, with her two women. They are, in fact, a tavern-keeper and two barmaids who, with the bears, will be part of the masque which Notch and his colleague Slug, and a comic pseudo-Dutchman Vangoose (whose accent is even presented typographically, in Black Letter!), have brought 'to make a little merry with his Majesty' in order 'to show our loves':

> ... we should all come from the three dancing Beares in Saint *Katherines* (you may hap know it, sir) hard by where the Priest fell in, which Alehouse is kept by a distressed Lady; whose name (for the honour of Knighthood) will not bee knowne; yet she is come in person here Errant, to fill up the adventure with her two women that draw drinke under her, Gentlewomen borne all three, I assure you.
>   (ll. 115–21)

The element of mock-romance in the style of *The Knight of the Burning Pestle* will be apparent. No wonder, in the light of what they present — and at court — the Groom of the Revels complains: 'why you stincke like so many bloat-herrings newly taken out of the chimney!' (ll. 66–7). In this quasi-induction, Jonson makes an interesting link that takes the masque back to the time of Henry VIII and even Richard II.[31]

Notch: ... our desire is only to know whether the Kings Majesty,
            and the Court expect any disguise here to night.

Groom: Disguise! what meane you by that? doe you thinke that his
            Majesty sits here to expect drunkards?

Notch: No, if hee did, I beleeve you would supply that place better
            then you do this: Disguise was the old English word for
            a Masque, sir, before you were an implement belonging to the
            Revels.

Groom: There is no such word in the Office now, I assure you, sir, I
            have serv'd here, man, and boy, a Prentiship or twaine, and I
            should know. But, by what name so ever you call it, here will
            be a Masque, and shall be a Masque, when you and the rest of
            your Comrogues shall sit disguis'd in the stocks.

Notch: Sure, by your language you were never meant for a Courtier,
            howsoever it hath beene your ill fortune to be taken out of
            the nest young; you are some Constables egg, some such
            Widgin of Authoritie, you are so easily offended!

                                                              (ll. 43–62)

Does one detect in this touch of asperity towards the Groom of the
Revels, something of the troubles Jonson experienced at Court, but
which are usually concealed by a deference in marked distinction to his
attitude to the audiences of the public and private theatres?

Time Vindicated (1623) likewise has an antimasque that is akin to an
induction (the 'characters' of which anticipate by centuries Tristan
Tzara's Dadaist play, *The Gas Heart*, of 1920). In *Neptune's Triumph*
(1624), the idea of an induction is even more obvious for the antimasque
is danced by the persons the Cook has put into his olla podrida, 'the
persons describ'd, comming out of the pot' (ll. 330–1), as the stage
direction puts it.

   Thus, although the antimasque is a device which Jonson is plainly
conscious of using, at times it has much in common with the induction
and it would be not unreasonable to add to the seven inductions to the
plays, a further eight instances of quasi-inductions which show awareness
of the setting and circumstance; make reference to the world outside the
play-world; and in which there is sometimes direct acknowledgement of
the audience.[32] The importance of this cannot be overstressed, if only
because some of those, such as Davenant, who would reintroduce the
drama after the Restoration of Charles II, would not only have
knowledge of such forms of entertainment, but would be *temperamentally*
inclined to the world of the court. That this use of induction and the

breaking of dramatic illusion was not restricted to Jonson, can be seen in the very costly masque by James Shirley, *The Triumph of Peace*, presented by the four Inns of Court to Charles I and Henrietta Maria at the Banqueting House in Whitehall in February 1634.[33]

The masque has no less than thirteen antimasques. Its twenty-three speaking parts are divided into three groups. In the first are such characters as Opinion, Fancy and Laughter who introduce and comment upon (as in Jonson's inductions and intermeans) a complex series of antimasques. These require several changes of scenery, including a tavern 'with a flaming red lattice, several drinking-rooms, and a back door, but especially, a conceited sign, and an eminent bush'; a woody landscape; another landscape (evidently), with a windmill — which, of course, a mute antimasquer knight and his squire vainly assault. Then follows the masque proper, which Irene opens, singing from a cloud. This also has complicated and elaborate scene changes and in addition to the classical 'characters' who speak or sing (and a chorus), there are sixteen masquers, sons of Peace, Law and Justice. This masque proper is interrupted by the violent incursion of the third group of characters. These are ordinary people: a carpenter, a painter, a tailor and his wife, a feather-maker's wife,[34] a property man's wife, and various guards, one being black:

> *The song ended, and the Musicians returned, the Masquers dance their main dance, after which they again retire to the Scene; at which they no sooner arrive, but there is heard a great noise and confusion of voices within, some crying 'They will come in', others 'Knock 'em down, call the rest of the guard'; then a crack is heard in the works, as if there were some danger by some piece of the machines falling; this continued a little time, there rush in —*

[Anti-masque xiii]

A Carpenter,	The Tailor's Wife,	[Two Guards]
A Painter,	An Embroiderer's Wife,	
One of the Black Guard,	A Feather-Maker's Wife,	
A Tailor,	A Property Man's Wife,	

Carpenter:	D'ye think to keep us out?
1 Guard:	Knock her down.
Tailor:	Knock down my wife! I'd see the tallest beef-eater on you all, but hold up his halbert in the way of knocking my wife down, and I'll bring him a button-hole lower.
Tailor's Wife:	Nay, let 'em, let 'em husband, at their peril.
2 Guard:	Complain to my Lord Chamberlain.

Property	My husband is somewhere in the works; I'm sure I
Man's	helped to make him an Owl and a Hobby-horse, and I
Wife:	see no reason but his wife may be admitted *in forma*
	paperis, to see as good a Masque as this.

(ll. 667–89)

There is no more certain breaking of dramatic illusion than the collapse of the scenery and it is used to great comic effect in burlesque. It was notably used in Sir Laurence Olivier's production of *The Critic* in 1945,[35] but possibly the closest parallel to Shirley's use, which avoids outright burlesque, is in Thorton Wilder's *The Skin of Our Teeth* (1942), where scenery disconcertingly falls about the performers. What it suggests in Shirley is that no sooner had a fully scenic set been evolved, mainly (in England) through the work of Inigo Jones (who designed the scenery for this masque), but that its 'lath and plaster' pretensions were immediately and comically made apparent.

The similarity of the opening of the masque to an induction is nowhere more apparent than in the mock horror that there is to be no antimasque (compare Masquerado's speech above) and the appeal to Fancy to address his nimble brain to its invention.

Fancy:	How many Anti-masques ha' they? Of what nature?
	For these are fancies that take most; your dull
	And phlegmatic inventions are exploded;
	Give me a nimble Anti-masque.
Opinion:	They have none, sir.
Laughter:	No Anti-masque? I'd laugh at that, i'faith.
Jollity:	What make we here? No Jollity?
Fancy:	No Anti-masque!
	Bid 'em down with the Scene, and sell the timber,
	Send Jupiter to grass, and bid Apollo
	Keep cows again, take all their gods and goddesses
	(For these must farce up this night's entertainment),
	And pray the Court may have some mercy on 'em,
	They will be jeer'd to death else for their ignorance.
	The soul of wit moves here, yet there be some,
	If my intelligence fail not, mean to show
	Themselves jeer-majors; some tall critics have
	Planted artillery and wit-murderers.
	No Anti-masque! Let 'em look to 't.
Opinion:	I have heard, sir.

Confidence made them trust you'd furnish 'em.
I fear they should have made their address earlier
To your invention, but your brain's nimble.

(ll. 224–46)

Shirley, though credited with no inductions in the drama, can be seen as fully aware of the technique and capable of using it to good effect in the masque. Further, the sense of improvisation, though obviously simulated, helps suggest the kind of 'rehearsal' to be found in Davenant's *The Play-House to be Let* (1663) performed very soon after the theatres reopened.

Jonson's use of the induction, therefore, not only developed the tradition of direct address in the theatre, whence it was taken up by his 'sons', Thomas Randolph especially (who will be discussed in the next chapter), and Shackerley Marmion (in *A Fine Companion*, 1633), but it was used, if in a slightly disguised form, in the masque. It was then easily transmitted, via Davenant for example, to the theatre of the Restoration. Jonson's influence is to be seen, therefore, not only in the characterisation favoured by the Restoration and eighteenth-century dramatists (and still found in nineteenth-century melodrama) but, much more significantly, in the planes of illusion of a stage performance. This is particularly to be seen in that awareness of the theatre as theatre which was to prove so fruitful in developing a theatrical experience which combined involvement and detachment (the antecedent of Brecht's alienation).

It is very well known, of course, that Jonson found the increasing dominance of scenery and machinery repugnant.[36] Yet, well known though it is, it is worth repeating two short sections from his 'An Expostulation with Inigo Jones' because not only do his feelings come through, but the shallowness of thought he found in lath-and-paint drama are apparent in his desire to 'pierce into the mysteries' — to educate his audience.

Your trappings will not change you: change your mind.
No velvet sheath your wear will alter kind;
A wooden dagger is a dagger of wood,
Though gold or ivory hafts would make it good.
What is the cause you pomp it so? (I ask)
And all men echo, You have made a masque.

... O shows! Shows! Mighty shows!
The eloquence of masques! What need of prose,

Or verse, or sense, to express immortal you?
You are the spectacles of state! 'Tis true
Court hieroglyphics, and all arts afford
In the mere perspective of an inch-board.
You ask no more than certain politic eyes,
Eyes that can pierce into the mysteries
Of many colours, read them, and reveal
Mythology there painted on slit deal.
Oh, to make boards to speak! There is a task!
Painting and carpentry are the soul of masque.
Pack with your peddling poetry to the stage:
This is the money-get, mechanic age![37]

Richard Ford drew to my attention a similar, if less bitter, passage in Sir Walter Scott's *An Essay on the Drama* in the 1819 Supplement to the *Encyclopaedia Britannica*: 'Show and machinery ... usurped the place of tragic poetry; and the author is compelled to address to the eyes, not to the understanding or feelings of the spectators.' There is truth in Jonson's and Scott's attitude, but it is not a complete statement of the facts. First of all, one should say that the lack of tragic dramatists as such is not entirely to be put down to the development of the scenic arts. Secondly, it can be argued, as I have tried to suggest, that the stage sets themselves could, in certain circumstances, be directly involved in distinguishing various levels of reality. Thirdly, Jonson's own work shows that, without certain artificial barriers inevitably dividing off audience and performers in some rigid and intrusive manner, the performance might be wrecked. The obvious examples of this are to be found in *The Entertainment at Althorpe* (or *The Satyr*, or *Masque of Fairies*, or *Masque of Oriana*, 1603). This Entertainment was performed out of doors, during the progress of the Queen to be crowned. It took place near Nottingham whilst she was the guest of Sir Robert Spencer at Althorpe and began as the Queen and the young Prince Henry passed through '*a little Spinet*' — a copse. This first night's show seems to have passed off satisfactorily, but, as the accounts printed by Jonson with the second parts of the entertainment indicate, these could not be adequately, if at all, presented in the dining hall because of the crush of people.

The next day being Sunday, the Queen rested, and on Monday, till after dinner; where there was a speech sodainly thought on, to induce a morrise of the clownes thereabout, who most officiously presented themselues, but by reason of the throng of the countrey that came in, their speaker could not be heard, who

was in the person of No-body, to deliuer this following speech, and attyred in
a pair of breeches which were made to come up to his neck, with his armes out
at his pockets, and a cap drowning his face.

(ll. 232–41)

There was also another parting Speech; which was to haue beene presented
in the person of a youth, and accompanied with diuers gentlemens younger
sonnes of the countrey: but by reason of the multitudinous presse, was also
hindred. And which we haue here adioyned.

(ll. 292–6)

The crush of those attempting to see a masque in the Whitehall
Banqueting Room was such that space could sometimes scarcely be found
for the performers. The attempts to gatecrash by those not invited is
admirably described by Robin Goodfellow, at some length, in Jonson's
Love Restored (1612), as these short extracts will indicate. After being
refused admittance, he climbed over the wall

. . . and in by the wood-yard, so to the terras, where when I came, I
found the okes of the guard more vnmou'd, and one of 'hem, vpon
whose arme I hung, shou'd me off o' the ladder, and dropt me downe
like an acorne. 'Twas well there was not a sow in the verge, I had
beene eaten vp else. Then I heard some talke o' the carpenters way,
and I attempted that, but there the woodden rogues let a huge trap-
dore fall o'my head. If I had not beene a spirit, I had beene mazarded
. . .

(ll. 73–82)

Therefore I tooke another course. I watch'd what kind of persons
the dore most open'd to, and one of their shapes I would belie to get in
with. First, I came with authoritie, and said, I was an ingineer, and
belong'd to the motions. They ask'd me if I were the fighting beare of
last yeere, and laught me out of that, and said, the motions were
ceas'd. Then I tooke another figure of an old tyre-woman . . . .

(ll. 87–93)

The 'fighting beare' presumably refers to *The Masque of Oberon* (see p. 182).
Shirley, in *The Triumph of Peace*, is clearly dramatising attempts to
gatecrash by the Carpenter and his friends.

Inevitably there had to be some means of controlling such a press and
the proscenium arch was the answer. This, of course, fitted well with

what Inigo Jones was designing. H. A. Evans notes that Campion's *The Squire's Masque* (1613), had a proscenium consisting of 'an arch triumphal passing beautiful' (which suggests how this intrusion was made to seem natural), but says that 'commonly it was a frieze resting on two pillars, and bearing the name of the masque'.[38] By the time Shirley was writing the elaborate masque, *The Triumph of Peace*, it is plain from the directions that there were several changes of set, but the lengthy initial description records what is virtually the nineteenth/twentieth-century, fourth-wall-removed type of theatre with the audience sitting on raked steps ('degrees').[39]

> This Masque was presented in the Banqueting House at Whitehall before the King and Queen's Majesties and a great assembly of Lords and Ladies and other persons of quality, whose aspect, sitting on the degrees prepared for that purpose, gave a great grace to this spectacle, especially being all richly attired.
>
> At the lower end of the room, opposite the State, was raised a stage with a descent of stairs in two branches landing into the room. This basement was painted in rustic work.
>
> The border of the front and sides that enclosed all the Scene had first a ground of arbour-work intermixed with loose branches and leaves, and in this was two niches, and in them two great figures standing in easy postures in their natural colours, and much bigger than the life.
> . . .
> *A curtain being suddenly drawn up, the Scene was discovered, representing a large street with sumptuous palaces, lodges, porticos, and other noble pieces of architecture, with pleasant trees and grounds. This, going far from the eye, opens itself into a spacious place adorned with public and private buildings seen afar off, representing the Forum or Piazza of Peace. Over all was a clear sky with transparent clouds which enlightened all the Scene.*
> *The spectators having entertained their eyes awhile with the beauty and variety of this scene, from one of the sides of the street enters Opinion, etc.*
> (ll. 124–35; 160–9)

Paradoxically, perhaps an entertainment designed for the most exclusive of audiences transmitted a variety of devices and techniques, for good or ill, which were greatly to influence the theatres when they re-opened after the Commonwealth. It was beside the point that in the masque the effect of the proscenium could be overleaped by masquers and audience joining together at the end in dance; the proscenium, and the sets behind it, had come to stay. Until a few decades ago, there would be only two further really important changes: to make the scenery look 'real' — i.e. in the later nineteenth century Robertson with his cups-and-saucers and Antoine with his mother's kitchen furniture; and to light the stage brilliantly and darken the auditorium.

Behind the proscenium arch dramatists would develop the induction, particularly in the rehearsal form, when the stage-world would be presented for what it was — a theatre — and the satire inherent in Jonson's and Marston's inductions would be developed for specific political purposes. Thus the masque was to shape the nature of theatrical presentation for most eighteenth- and nineteenth-century drama, and its literary content and educative concerns (at least in Jonson's masques) would profoundly influence what was performed. If this was to be curtailed by the Licensing Act of 1737, it was to find a new life via Tieck's *Puss in Boots* (1797). From Tieck Pirandello gained a new conception of the nature of the stage-world, which found expression in his *Six Characters in Search of an Author* (1921). And it was working on Reinhardt's production of that play in 1924 which was so to influence Brecht. So Jonsonian detachment became Brechtian alienation. These later developments are discussed in detail in *Contemporary Drama and the Popular Dramatic Tradition in England*.

5 The Muse's Looking-Glass

From the time when the theatres were closed in 1642 until the end of the nineteenth century, when Shaw and Wilde appear on the scene, there are few dramatists writing in English who gain much attention. Those that do attract critics are associated with the Restoration — Wycherley, Farquhar and Congreve especially — and a handful of their plays are still regularly performed. Goldsmith's *She Stoops to Conquer* (1773) is at least put on by amateurs (particularly schools), and Sheridan, though rather looked down upon in academic circles, still attracts audiences: *A Trip to Scarborough* (1777) does not only mean Ayckbourn. The outstanding exception is not strictly a play at all: *The Beggar's Opera* (1728). It is, apart from a number of Shakespeare's plays, the most continuously successful dramatic work in English. Tate Wilkinson, for example, performed it regularly in his Yorkshire tours between 1772 and 1792, and Cecil Price discovered in rather scanty records that performance had been given in Wales in 1741, 1766 (in Wrexham) and in the 1820s (in Swansea). It has had a tremendous amount of attention since Nigel Playfair revived it in London in 1920, and Brecht refashioned it as *The Threepenny Opera* in 1928. Since then it has come in for some close study — notably by William Empson in *Some Versions of Pastoral* in 1935 (where the essential process behind it is seen as 'a resolution of heroic and pastoral into a cult of independence'); and more recently, in 1970, by Ian Donaldson in *The World Turned Upside-Down*.

Despite *The Way of the World* (1700), *The Recruiting Officer* (1706), *The Country Wife* (1675), *The Plain Dealer* (1676) and *Love for Love* (1693), which have not, of course, won universal acclaim from critics, and admitting *All for Love* (1678) and *The Beggar's Opera*, and perhaps even *The School for Scandal* (1777) and *The Rivals* (1775), it is not a very rich haul for some 250 years. (*The Plain Dealer*, it will be recalled, deliberately draws attention to its theatrical nature through its extensive references to *The Country Wife*.) Of course, other plays can be added — *The Rehearsal* (1671) and *The Critic* (1779) are both great fun and *Caste* (1867) is more than merely 'worthy', but no one would argue that those two-and-a-half centuries have been rich in dramatic *writing*. Paradoxically, however, as *The Beggar's Opera*, *The Rehearsal* and *The Critic* may have suggested, these centuries were full of theatrical vigour. Furthermore, from 1663, shortly after the theatres were reopened, until 1844, when Planché's *The Drama at Home* was performed, audiences were constantly being reminded, in stage performances, that they were in the theatre. Frequently they were looking into the dramatic muse's own looking-glass. It is this characteristic — not the dramatic literature, not the great actors, nor the theatrical squabbles — that I wish to sketch. The awareness of the theatrical art, consciously made manifest, was extraordinarily pervasive in this period; it could be a great deal of fun and it coexisted with drama requiring an audience's total involvement in what was being performed — drama that demanded the complete suspension of disbelief.

From the earliest times, drama has burlesqued itself. As Simon Trussler has pointed out 'Theatrical burlesque is almost as old as the theatre itself. Aristophanes made incidental use of it in several of his own comedies, notably in that histrionic tug-of-war between Aeschylus and Euripides in *The Frogs*.'[1] He refers to Shakespeare's burlesquing of folk-drama in *Love's Labour's Lost* and his travesty of his own *Romeo and Juliet* theme in *A Midsummer Night's Dream* (1595); and he says Shakespeare 'even introduced a rehearsal-play of sorts into *Hamlet*'. He might also, had he wished to enlarge upon this, have mentioned the mocking of *Cambises* in *1 Henry IV*. But the point he wishes to make is that in Shakespeare the burlesque element is no more than incidental. He goes on to argue that:

> the backbiting between Jonson, Marston, and Dekker, which took dramatic shape in such plays as *Every Man Out of His Humour*, *Satiromastix*, and *The Poetaster*, had not really to do with burlesque at all, but with 'comical satire'. The tradition of dramatic satire, as Fielding more satisfactorily dubbed it, is, of course, closely related to that of burlesque, and occasionally overlaps it — but it is, I think, convenient to attempt a rule-of-thumb distinction between the two. (pp. vii-viii)

Trussler distinguishes between burlesque as 'essentially *formal* parody' which 'makes fun of artistic pretensions — whereas dramatic satire hits at faults and foibles in real life' (p. viii). As he rightly says, such a distinction cannot be applied either prescriptively or absolutely. His concern in his volume and its introduction is with burlesque. Dramatic satire, therefore, commands no further attention from him.

This distinction seems just to me but I wish to use it in a slightly different way. As Trussler says, the rehearsal formula was 'a convenient vehicle for an attack on actual, governmental corruption' (p. viii), but I am interested not in the way such drama attacked the government, but in the way that it drew attention to its medium, to the theatre *per se*. To that extent I ignore burlesque (as Trussler does dramatic satire) which, though it mocks excesses in, say, heroic tragedy, does so in the main in a form consonant with the terms of 'overheard drama'. Thus, *Tom Thumb* (1730), though it is burlesquing eighteenth-century tragedy, is 'entirely self-contained', unlike Fielding's other plays which use the rehearsal formula — a distinction made by Trussler (p. 143). I am concerned with plays that are *not* self-contained; that is, plays which break the dramatic illusion by commenting either in direct speech to the audience, or through a frame-play, on what is being done in the drama enclosed, or rehearsed. The appearance of so many such plays, and their remarkable success, from *The Play-House to be Let* of 1663 to Planché's *The Drama at Home* in 1844, suggests that, especially in a theatre in which the lighting of stage and auditorium was not too dissimilar, and in which an audience was likely to be, shall I say, 'participant', *awareness* of the theatrical experience was constantly being drawn to the attention of audiences. It is this aspect I wish to concentrate upon and although I ignore self-contained burlesques such as Fielding's *Tom Thumb* and *The Covent-Garden Tragedy* (1732), it will be realised that in their own way they also drew attention to theatrical absurdity.

When the theatres reopened in 1660 after the restoration of the monarchy, one of the plays which early found favour was Beaumont's burlesque, *The Knight of the Burning Pestle*. It was performed at least twice in 1662, though when Pepys saw it, it 'pleased him not at all'.[2] It seems to have been revived a few years later and Langbaine, writing in 1691, says 'it was in vogue some years since', but it soon disappeared from the repertoire.[3] In 1672 Francis Kirkman's *The Wits, or, Sport upon Sport* was published and this contained, as no. 16, a droll adapted from III.iv.8ff. of *The Knight of the Burning Pestle*. The play was readily available in printed versions. The *Works* was published in 1647 and the folio *Fifty Comedies and Tragedies* appeared in 1679. An octavo Beaumont and Fletcher was published in 1711 — described by Sprague as 'in general a mere scrap-book' (p. 187), and a ten-volume octavo edition in 1750. Further editions appeared in 1778, 1811, 1812 and 1840, and then we begin to get 'modern' editions. *The Knight of the Burning Pestle* was first published on its own in 1613 and then twice in 1635, although the second of these editions was probably published some years later. But although the text was available, at least in collected works, the play was not much performed, it would seem, after about 1670. This is not to say that it was completely lost from sight on the stage. In 1711 an adaption called *The City Ramble: or, A Playhouse Wedding* was made by Elkanah Settle, and this was printed in the following year. However, as Allardyce Nicoll explains, 'because of the author's unpopularity', it ran for only a few nights.[4] Nicoll also suggests that the coffin scene in Steele's *The Funeral* (1702) might have been suggested by *The Knight of the Burning Pestle*.[5] It may not, therefore, be to *The Knight of the Burning Pestle* in particular that we should look in order to seek the source of the burlesque tradition in the theatre, so active in the eighteenth century.

One likely influence was the rise of burlesque poetry, particularly the burlesquing of near-sacrosanct classics. The first part of Scarron's *Virgile Travesti* was published in France in 1648 and it was translated by Charles Cotton in 1664-5. The first part of Butler's *Hudibras* was published in 1662 and the second part appeared two years later; both parts were reprinted together in 1674. In 1681, Dryden's *Absalom and Achitophel* appeared and in the following year his *MacFlecknoe*. *The Rape of the Lock* was published in 1712 and 1714 and the first three books of *The Dunciad* in 1728 (the year *The Beggar's Opera* and *Peri Bathous: The Art of Sinking in Poetry*, originally written about 1713-14, were published). Burlesque and satire were obviously very much in the air so that the atmosphere was conducive to burlesque in the theatre. Nevertheless we must look elsewhere for the particular form it took.

The outstanding burlesque play of the Restoration (and, indeed, of any period) was George Villiers's *The Rehearsal* (1671). This, however, was preceded by a play that, to a certain degree anticipated all these English works: Davenant's *The Play-House to be Let* (1663).

The Play-House to be Let is in five acts.[6] The first is of the nature of an induction in the Jonsonian tradition. The scene opens to discover a Tirewoman and a Chairwoman sitting on two stools, one shelling beans and the other sewing. A Player and the Housekeeper enter and remonstrate with them — shelling beans is 'a proper work / For the Long Vacation' (p. 67) when the theatre is closed. There then enter a series of visitors in answer to a bill advertising the play-house to be let. The first applicant is a French Monsieur and he is followed by Fencers, wishing to demonstrate duelling, a Musician, a Dancer, and a Poet. The Housekeeper explains 'we must like your Trade / Before we let our Shop' (p. 70), but the Poet advises the Player on what they must do if they mean 'to get money':

> You must have something of a newer stamp to make your
> Coyn current. Your old great Images of
> Love and Honour are esteem'd but by some
> Antiquaries now. You should set up with that
> Which is meer new. What think you
> Of Romances travesti

Player: Explain yourself

Poet: The Garments of our Fathers you must wear
                 The wrong side outward, and in time it may
                 Become a fashion.

Housekeeper: It will be strange, and then 'tis sure to take.

Poet: You shall present the actions of the Heroes,
                 (Which are the chiefest Theams of Tragedy)
                 In Verse Burlesque.

Player: Burlesque and Travesti? These are hard words,
                 And may be *French*, but not Law-*French*.

                                                        (p. 75)

The Player and Housekeeper conclude the first act by deciding to sit in judgement on what their applicants have to offer, the Poet electing to come last. Act II features a French farce; Act III, the musician's contribution; Act IV, that of the dancer; and Act V is a travesty of the story of Julius Caesar, Antony and Cleopatra. The tone of the travesty is well represented by this short passage from near the end of Act V:

> *Caesar*:   Call in the Fidlers but heark ye friend *Tony*
>   Whilst now I think on't, have you any money?
>   For though in War I did bear all before me,
>   Cash stays behind, and I'm fain to cry score me!
>
> *Anthony*: *Caesar*, my plunder (I speak it with sorrow)
>   Is squander'd with Girles, and I'm forc't to borrow....
>
>   (p. 119)

Caesar decides that they had best be off to the alehouse where the tapsters known him and the fat hostess will trust him.

The Player and Housekeeper have very little to do after the first act, making only the most cursory appearances but the conclusion is interesting. As soon as the last play has concluded, the Housekeeper asks, 'What is all done?'. The Player replies, in the last speech of the play:

I, and we are undone, some body has let
Our neighbours in — 'slight the House is e'en full,
Stop 'em! they're like to hear, if they will stay
An *Epilogue*, since they have seen a Play.

An epilogue follows (which makes some play with the word 'Mermaid'). This belated recognition that an actual audience is present is also to be found in a number of plays discussed in earlier chapters, both of Wager's plays, for example, and *A Nice Wanton*, and it has been used more recently, by Terence Rattigan in *Harlequinade* (1948, see pp. 162–3).

The Play-house to be Let deserves a little more than 'a small niche in the gallery of true burlesque' as Trussler puts it (p. ix). It may be true that between its fifth act and *The Rehearsal* (1671) 'lies the essential difference between travesty and truly *critical* burlesque' (though Davenant's play is not without its critical awareness of the stage), that Trussler defines as 'the difference between a mere vulgarizing of an elevated or classical theme, and satire purposefully directed against the striking of false tragical attitudes' (p. ix), but there is much more to *The Play-house to be Let* than the fifth act.

Act II is a straight but shortened version of Molière's farce, *Sganarelle; ou, Le Cocu Imaginaire* (1660), which was first performed in Paris the day before Charles II entered London at the Restoration. Davenant presents his version of the play in English with a French accent — as if by a visiting French troupe. The Tirewoman takes fright on hearing the word 'Troop', thinking only of a troop of soldiers, presumably Commonwealth men. There is a curious coincidence about this 'visiting French troupe'. Two summers before, in 1661, a French troupe played in the Cockpit Theatre (which Davenant had used in 1658 and 1659). This visit may have suggested to Davenant the idea for his troupe's 'visit' to play *Sganarelle*. However, more intriguing is the permit 'dated 25 August 1663, for a French company to bring over their scenes and stage decorations'. Eleanor Boswell says that 'nothing further is known of this visit, if, indeed, it took place'.[7] *Annals of English Drama* dates *The Play-house to be Let* as *c*. August 1663 and one wonders if there is a link of some kind here.

Acts III and IV are two of Davenant's own plays as first performed in the last years of the Commonwealth, *before* the theatres were officially re-opened. Act III is his *The History of Sir Francis Drake* (1659), 'Exprest by Instrumentall and Vocall Musick, and by Art of Perspective in Scenes, &c.'. This is the play the Musician describes in Act I as an 'Heroique story / In *Stilo Recitativo*'. Act IV presents in song and dance Davenant's *The

Cruelty of the Spaniards in Peru, expressed in the same manner, according to the title-page of the original quarto and first performed, with great success, at the newly re-opened Cockpit Theatre on 25 July 1658. According to the title-pages of both quartos, published in 1659 and 1658 respectively, they were represented daily at three in the afternoon — punctually. Their presentation despite the official closure of the theatres was probably facilitated by their not being 'straight' plays. Thus they might be said to be examples, some eighty or ninety years in advance, of drama made illegitimate by Walpole's Licensing Act (see pp. 143–4 below). Like Davenant's *The Siege of Rhodes* (1656), often called the first English opera, they escaped the full rigour of the law affecting 'straight' plays.

The Play-house to be Let looks back to the compendium plays of the late sixteenth and early seventeenth centuries (e.g. *Four Plays in One*, 1592, and *Five Plays in One*, 1585)[8] and forward to Planché's revues of 150 years later (see p. 158ff.). Though its importance in introducing burlesque into English theatre is clear,[9] it is also significant because of the part it played in introducing the conscious stage into Restoration theatre. As Arthur Nethercot says:

> though to some critics *The Play-house* was a 'damnable farce' which Apollo could never forgive, it was nevertheless, a play which was the real English father of the innumerable progeny of dramatic 'rehearsals' which have infected the stage, to the general delight of the spectators, ever since.[10]

There is a critical element in this embryonic rehearsal play, lightly presented though it is. Thus, the Housekeeper is concerned with what is proper to be presented in the Playhouse: 'We must like your Trade / Before we let our shop' (p. 68). The discussion with the Dancing Master is a delightful example of dramatic satire, the more so because the reference is to Davenant's own *Cruelty of the Spaniards*:

Dancing Master:	Fie no, Sir; I'm for down-right plain history
	Exprest in figures on the floor, a kind
	Of morals in dumb shows by Men and Beasts.
Player:	Without any Interpreter?
Dancing Master:	Pardon me, Sir; the Audience now and then
	Must be inform'd by Chorus's in Rhime.
Player:	O, dumb-shows with speeches?
Dancing Master:	Yes, Sir, the same: but very short.

(p. 73)

The inspiration for *The Play-house to be Let* has been variously explained. Howard S. Collins puts it down to Davenant finding something to attract to the theatre 'the less sophisticated and less financially fortunate' left in London during the particularly hot summer of 1663.[11] 'Undoubtedly', he says, it was 'the structure of the later *Four Plays in One* by Beaumont and Fletcher that directly influenced Davenant' (pp. 70–1). *Four Plays, or Moral Representations, in One* (c. 1608–13), was probably written by Field and Fletcher.[12] It has an induction and some very slight intermeans, which feature those participating in the celebrations attendant upon the marriage of Emanuel, King of Portugal and Castile. The plays are four 'Triumphs' — of Honour, Love, Death and Time. The first three have characters and the last gods and symbolic figures such as Vain Delight, Poverty, Fame and Honesty. Within the plays are several dumb shows.

Three of Molière's plays have also been suggested as possible sources of *The Play-house to be Let*, though one of them, *L'Impromptu de Versailles*, Davenant can scarcely have known in time. Much more interesting is the suggestion that Philippe Quinault's five-act play, *La Comédie sans comédie*, is a possible source.[13] This play deserves a note in its own right, even if its relationship to the English theatre is tenuous.

La comédie sans comédie (1655)[14] has an introductory act in which a rich merchant expresses his distaste for the theatre and his opposition to his daughters marrying actors. The following four acts present for him a pastoral, *Clomire*; a comedy, *Le Docteur de Verre*; a tragedy, *Clorinde*; and a tragicomedy 'en machines' (for which the Théâtre du Marais, where the play was performed, was famous), *Armide et Renaud*. This last play, Act v, starts with Armide suspended in mid-air. The merchant, La Fleur, watches the plays 'sur un siège au coin du théâtre' (p. 72). He doesn't speak until Act V, Scene x, though his presence is indicated in each scene of Act II, the first of the four plays. At the end of the play, as the stage direction puts it: 'La Fleur, sortant de la place en désordre, où il a été assis depuis le second acte' (p. 125). As a result of what he has seen (which he has taken as 'reality') he is converted to the belief that the art of the theatre is 'noble et doux' (p. 126) and consents to the weddings.

The *structure* of this play is certainly not unlike that of *Four Plays in One* and *Play-house to be Let*, but it is a 'conversion' play, which *Play-house to be Let* is not, and it is by no means certain that Davenant knew the play. The precise date of the first performance of *La comédie sans comédie* is unknown. W. S. Brooks has recently argued that it was put on for the reopening of the Théâtre du Marais in April 1655.[15] At that time, Davenant was in England. He was released from the Tower on 4 August 1654 and, though he applied to go to Paris in the following year, it was not until August 1655 that he was able to leave. It is improbable, therefore, that Quinault's play is the source for *The Play-house to be Let* and this will be even more unlikely if an alternative nearer home can be found.

There is, however, a further aspect to *La comédie sans comédie* that requires mention. Its *characters* include Hauteroche, Chevalier, La Fleur and La Roque. These are the characters named in the play's *dramatis personae*. But these are also the *names of the actors* who played those part — actors famous at the Théâtre du Marais. Indeed, the reason that the Marais had closed down for a while, so leading to its re-opening in April 1655, was the departure of Noel Hauteroche, leader of the Marais troupe, for the rival L'Hôtel de Bourgogne. Thus, well-known actors were taking parts in their own names, so breaking the dramatic illusion very deliberately, as in Gougenot's *La comédie des comédiens* of 1632.

Although *The Play-house to be Let* is a precursor of burlesque drama, burlesque is by no means its only constituent, nor was it the only source of 'the conscious stage' in Restoration and eighteenth-century theatre. Indeed, as *The Play-house to be Let* is so very different from Davenant's earlier plays, especially those written before the theatres closed in 1642, it might well be asked whether there was any other source which gave him the idea for his novelty of 1663, besides *Four Plays in One* and the very doubtful suggestion of Quinault's *La comédie sans comédie*.

The dramatist whom one would expect to be particularly influential in establishing the satirical and rehearsal forms is Jonson. There is no doubt that Jonson's *general* influence was immense and his characterisation by types lasted in comedy, and later in melodrama, well into the nineteenth century, but when one looks at details of performances of his plays, the picture is less clear.

Allardyce Nicoll describes Jonson's influence as being 'cast over the whole period' 1700–50, his work being amongst that of the early seventeenth-century writers which was 'eagerly ransacked'.[16] Although *Volpone*, *The Alchemist*, *Epicoene* and *Bartholomew Fair* were very frequently performed during the Restoration, and *Catiline* had a few performances in 1668–9 and 1675, Robert Gale Noyes lists only a single performance of any other play by Jonson before 1725: *Every Man Out of His Humour* in 1675. In 1725, *Every Man In His Humour* was revived and it became popular in Garrick's version from 1751.[17] John Downes, however, does state in *Roscius Anglicanus*, 1708, that *The Devil is an Ass*, both *Everyman* plays and *Sejanus* were acted if 'but now and then'.[18] Although *The Poetaster* was available (and listed), Gunnar Sorelius says it was 'evidently never performed'.[19] The only plays by Jonson to be published in editions of their own in the Restoration were *The Alchemist* (1680) and *Catiline* (1669 and 1674), and although in the eighteenth century there were many editions of the four more popular plays, from the closing of the theatres until this century, none of the seven 'induction plays' was in sufficient demand to require an edition in its own right.[20]

Needless to say, this does not mean that there could be no influence from performances of Jonson's induction plays after the re-opening of the theatres in 1660, and editions of the *Works* were available. Downes was writing long after the events he describes from memory and there may have been a few performances of these plays which have left no record. But, were the influence of these induction plays of any great extent, we should expect to hear more about them, and to have records of more performances, than we do. The position is well summarised by Emmett L. Avery and Arthur Scouten in *The London Stage 1660-1700*:

> Surprise may be registered, however, at the place of Ben Jonson in the repertory. From the universal chorus of adulation for the work of this Elizabethan dramatist that extends throughout the period and from the repeated references to scenes in his plays, one would certainly have expected to see his plays carried in stock. And they may have been, as fifteen titles were distributed between the King's Company and The Duke's Company. Nevertheless, our Calendar of Performances shows no increase in the known productions of Jonson's plays. Performances are recorded for only seven of his dramas (*Bartholomew Fair*, *Catiline*, *Every Man In His Humour*, *Every Man Out of His Humour*, *The Alchemist*, *The Silent Woman*, and *Volpone*) and only the last three of these appeared with any frequency. Further research, hopefully, may disclose additional productions.[21]

Although the general influence of Jonson is not to be denied, and Davenant and later dramatists could not but know of his induction plays, it may well be that it is to two of the 'Sons of Ben' that we must look for direct inspiration for Davenant and, perhaps, for dramatists of the eighteenth century. Two plays by two different dramatists associated with Jonson stand out: Thomas Randolph's *The Muse's Looking-Glass* (1629 or 1630) and Richard Brome's *The Antipodes* (1637). These plays are described by Joe Lee Davis as 'unique in the drama of the period'; they have, he says, 'the unique distinction of being thought-provoking comedies about the art of comedy'.[22] 'Unique' may be over-used here. There is nothing unique about the representation of several scenes or plays within a play, and although Brome and Randolph pay particular attention to the value and effect of comedy, Massinger had not only presented three plays beautifully integrated within a fourth in his tragedy, *The Roman Actor* (1626), but had made in that play a lively defence of the stage and the profession of acting, and suggested that the drama had curative powers.[23] That said, however, it is apparent that Davenant had, in *The Muse's Looking-Glass* and *The Antipodes*, excellent precedents for *The Playhouse to be Let*. Indeed, it might even be argued that rather than Quinault's play being a source for Davenant's, that Quinault had Randolph's play in mind. The plays not only have a similar structure and tone, but both have a conversion element and both were probably plays used to mark the opening (the re-opening in the case of the Théâtre du Marais) of theatres.[24] If, as is suggested, *The Muse's Looking-Glass* was the play that opened the Salisbury Court Theatre, it could hardly have escaped Davenant's notice at the time — and Davenant was, of course, himself one of the Tribe of Ben.

Although there are similarities in the structures of *The Muse's Looking-Glass* and *The Antipodes*, it is the former which was probably more influential on Davenant and on Restoration and eighteenth-century dramatists. Although Randolph is an even more obscure figure than is Brome today, his work was not only popular before the theatres were closed in 1642, but remained so for 150 years. The style of Randolph's play seems to have been better suited to the Restoration and eighteenth-century temperaments.

Whereas Joe Lee Davis sees 'the end of comedy' for Randolph as being 'primarily moral education ... a form of delightful teaching' which 'strives towards the correction of typical vices and follies through laughter' (p. 74), to Brome 'the end of comedy is primarily psychological therapy' (p. 75). It is from such an approach as Randolph's that burlesques and rehearsal plays in which social and political satire was predominant might readily spring. Brome is so much more concerned with the curative powers of drama. He is, indeed, three centuries ahead of those who would nowadays use drama for therapeutic purposes. Joyless's jealousy of his wife, Diana, is cured; Martha's 'love melancholy' is cured; most strikingly of all, Peregrine's sexual impotence is cured — through drama. This is not to suggest that an audience of *The Antipodes* would not be made conscious of the stage at various points in the play. Letoy gives advice to the players after the manner of Hamlet:

> Let me not see you act now
> In your scholastic way you brought to town wi' ye
> With see-saw sack-a-down, like a sawyer;

Nor in a comic scene play Hercules Furens,
Tearing your throat to split the audients' ears.
And you, sir, you had got a trick of late
Of holding out your bum in a set speech,
Your fingers fibulating on your breast,
As if your buttons or your band-strings were
Helps to your memory. ...

(II.i, p.278)[25]

More intriguing are his comments on Byplay's extemporal acting, some
of which stems from his not knowing his lines properly:

Well, sir, my actors
Are all in readiness, and I think all perfect
But one, that never will be perfect in a thing
He studies; yet he makes such shifts extempore,
(Knowing the purpose what he is to speak to)
That he moves mirth in me 'bove all the rest.
For I am none of those poetic furies,
That threats the actor's life in a whole play
That adds a syllable or takes away.
If he can fribble through, and move delight
In others, I am pleas'd.

(II.i, p.276)

Two-and-a-half centuries later, Olive Logan was to describe this
'winging a part' on the modern stage.[26] Brome actually writes-in such
'winging' for Byplay:

Byplay: Oh, are you here? My lady and myself
Have sought you sweetly —
Letoy: You and your lady, you
Should ha' said, puppy.

(II.ii, p.284)

Perhaps most intriguing of all is the anticipation of the arrangement of
performers and stage audiences which anticipates *The Real Inspector Hound*
by over three centuries. As the play-within-the-play is about to start, the
Doctor takes Peregrine to one side, music sounds for Quailpipe to enter
to speak the Prologue, but he is preceded by another stage audience which
enters, masked, so as not to be seen by Peregrine:

>   *Hautboys. Enter Letoy, Joyless, Diana, Martha, Barbara in masks.*
>   *They sit at the other end of the stage.*
> Letoy: Here we may sit, and he not see us.

(II.ii, p.282)

In fact, they can be seen, but not recognised. A little later on Peregrine will see Letoy and his guests and ask, 'What are those?' and the Doctor will tell him 'All Antipodeans' (p. 286).

Nevertheless, I am inclined to the view that it is not *The Antipodes* but *The Muse's Looking-Glass* which was to prove so influential. *The Antipodes* does not appear to have had a very active dramatic life after the theatres re-opened,[27] and after the edition of 1640 it was not reprinted during the Restoration and eighteenth century. The matter is quite otherwise with *The Muse's Looking-Glass*.

Randolph is now virtually forgotten,[28] yet his short dramatic career (much of it at the University of Cambridge) was attended by condiderable success. It is probable that in 1630 he became playwright to the new Salisbury Court Theatre, perhaps, as G. E. Bentley suggests, 'under contract, as Richard Brome was to the theatre 1635–8'.[29] Not only was *The Muse's Looking-Glass* frequently reprinted, but the popularity of Randolph's *Aristippus* was considerable — Joe Lee Davis describes its popularity as 'immense' (p. 105) — for it was issued nine times between 1630 and 1640. Randolph, very clearly, was a very popular dramatist in this decade — the decade in which Davenant wrote five masques, *The Witts* (1634) and *Love and Honour* (1634).

The Muse's Looking-Glass was printed with Randolph's poems in 1638 (*RSTC* 20894); 1640 (two issues, *RSTC* 20895 and 20895.5); 1643, 1652, 1664 and 1668. It was also popular in its own right being printed in 1643 and then in 1706 (with a Preface by Jeremy Collier). Thereafter it was included by Dodsley (who adapted Randolph's *The Conceited Pedlar* as *The Toy-Shop*, 1735) in his *Select Collection of Old Plays*, appearing in volume 6 in 1744; and in volume 9 in 1780 and 1825. It was also included in volume 2 of *The British Drama* (1810). This is a quite remarkable popularity, especially as compared with printings of Jonson's plays with inductions. Furthermore, as late as 14 March 1748, the play was revived at Covent Garden, and again on 9 March 1749. According to Carew Hazlitt it appeared 'in an altered version ... under the title of the "Mirrour" in 1758' (p. 174), but Reginald Clarence states that it was not acted, giving the author's name as H. Dell. The British Library has copies of editions of 1756 and 1757.[30] But possibly nothing will better suggest the long-lasting life of *The Muse's Looking-Glass* than the fact that

Tate Wilkinson thought it worth adapting for presentation in York as late as 1782. What is more, he reproduces part of what he has 'adapted to the present age' in *The Wandering Patentee* in 1795 (II, 127–31). The scene he prints includes Mediocrity's speech in Act V, Scene i of Randolph's play in which the Masque of the Virtues is introduced. Wilkinson, in fact, has not adapted this speech at all. When it is concluded he has a stage direction 'Here all the characters are discovered' and then he completes the rest of Mediocrity's speech, as in Randolph. The only difference, indeed, is that we do not have in Wilkinson an indication that the Virtues dance together. His adaptation was, presumably, a reduction from five acts to two.

Randolph, is fond of using Jonson's device of induction and intermean. *Amyntas, or The Impossible Dowry* (1630) begins with a Nymph and Shepherd arguing as to who will speak the Prologue:

> *Nymph*: I'll speak the prologue.
> *Shepherd*:   Then you do me wrong.
> *Nymph*: Why, dare your sex compete with ours for tongue?
> *Shepherd*: A female prologue!
> *Nymph*:   Yes, as well as male!
> *Shepherd*: That's a new trick.
> *Nymph*:   And t'other is as stale.

They agree that the Nymph will speak to the women (who included the Queen) and the Shepherd to the men (who included Charles I). They do not appear in the play nor is the Epilogue assigned to either of them. This, of course, is precisely how *Cynthia's Revels* and Jonson's masque, *A Challenge at Tilt* begin. *Amyntas* 'provided material for the anonymous *The Fickle Shepherdess*' (1703), according to Nicoll (p. 141).

Randolph's *Hey for Honesty!* (1627) is an adaptation of the *Plutus* of Aristophanes and opens with an 'Introduction' between Aristophanes, the Translator (i.e. Randolph), and the Ghost of Cleon. There are several references in the play to Elizabethan drama — thus:

> *Chremylus*
> *(to Plutus)*: Did not Will Summers break his wind for thee?
>   And Shakespeare therefor write his comedy?
> (p. 397)

'Jeronymo' is mentioned twice (pp. 414 and 469) and on p. 434 there is a comparison, 'Like Falstaff's regiment, you have one shirt among you'.

The play was certainly modified after Randolph's death in 1635 because there are references in the printed version to Prince Rupert at Marston Moor (p. 478). It is evident that Randolph is here again making his audience aware that they are in the theatre, so breaking the continuity.

Randolph's *Aristippus, or The Jovial Philosopher* begins with a Praeludium in which Show enters 'whipt by two Furies'. It was printed in 1630 and is said by Harbage and Schoenbaum to have been performed in 1626 at Trinity College, Cambridge. In 1627 they record the performance of a monologue, *The Conceited Pedlar*, by Randolph. *The Conceited Pedlar* is quite short and it is possible it was used as an afterpiece, perhaps to a repeat of *Aristippus*. The afterpiece is not otherwise recorded before mid-winter 1676–7 in England, according to R. W. Bevis. In a companion piece to his translation of Racine's *Bérénice*, the tragedian Thomas Otway brought out Molière's *Les Fourberies de Scapin* as *The Cheats of Scapin*. The experiment was not repeated, however, until November 1696 (by Betterton's company at Lincoln's Inn Fields). In a footnote, Bevis states that the 'afterpiece was established on the French stage by 1650, and the satyr-play provides a classical precedent'.[31] Randolph could possibly have anticipated Otway, following classical practice.

The Conceited Pedlar is a tour-de-force requiring a single able actor to deliver a long monologue (with songs) in which he describes, to satirical effect, what he has to sell. Thus, he brings forth a looking-glass and remarks,

> it hath strange operations, viz., if a cracked chambermaid dress herself by this looking-glass, she shall dream the next night of kissing her lord, or making her mistress a she-cuckold, and shall marry a chaplain, the next living that falls. ... An usurer cannot see his conscience in it nor a scrivener his ears. ... Corrupt takers of bribes[32] may read the price of their consciences in it.   (p. 43)

Whether *The Conceited Pedlar* was an afterpiece or not, it was as an afterpiece that Dodsley's *Toy-Shop* was performed at Covent Garden on 3 February 1735.[33] Instead of being a tour-de-force by one actor, there are four ladies, four gentlemen, a beau and two old men who visit the Master of the Toyshop and to whom he explains his wares. The intention is certainly satirical, although in a somewhat moralistic vein. In the Introduction, the Master is called 'a very impertinent silly fellow' because, as the First Gentleman says, he sometimes tells people of their faults. The equivalent passage to that quoted from Randolph's original includes this:

a coquette may see her vanity, and a prude her hypocrisy. Some ladies may see more beauty than modesty, more airs than graces, and more wit than good-nature. ... If a beau was to buy this glass, and look earnestly into it, he might see his folly almost as soon as his finery.

The Muse's Looking-Glass makes the most extended use of induction and intermean in Randolph's work. Two puritans affect to condemn the theatre though content to earn their livings by it. Roscius asks them whether, in selling the players their goods, they do not as much live by sin as these actors whom they condemn:

Roscius: O dull ignorance!
          How ill 'tis understood what we do mean
          For good and honest! They abuse our scene,
          And say we live by vice. Indeed, 'tis true,
          As the physicians by diseases do,
          Only to cure them.
                                        (I.ii, p.183)

In Act I, Scene iv there is a debate between Comedy, Tragedy, Mime and Satire which is concluded by Tragedy proposing that 'On this stage / We'll plead a trial; and in one year content / Which shall do best'. A masque is presented (which Mistress Flowerdew mishears to her horror as 'a mass' — the Vice at his old trick of mistaking the word yet again, just as in the play on 'troupe' in *The Play-house to be Let*, p. 113 above), and then Roscius tells the audience:

          And here — unless your favourite mildness
          With hope of mercy do encourage us,
          Our author bids us end.

Just like *Too True to Be Good* (1932), Shaw's 'Political Extravaganza', *The Muse's Looking-Glass* ends at the close of Act I — unless we wish to stay:

          All he can plead
      Is a desire for pardon; for he brings you
      No plot at all, but a mere Olla Podrida,
      A medley of ill-plac'd and worse-penn'd humours.

Roscius proposes to expose the vices in single scenes (much as Jonson has done in effect) and,

> ... if you can endure to hear the rest,
> You're welcome; if you cannot, do but tell
> Your meaning by some sign, and all farewell.
>
> (pp. 193–4)

As Shaw's Monster put it, 'The play is now virtually over; but the characters will discuss it at great length for two acts more. The exit doors are all in order. Goodnight. [*It draws up the bedclothes round its neck and goes to sleep*]'.

The two puritans of *The Muse's Looking-Glass* then sit and watch the thirteen scenes and the Masque of Virtues, presented by Mediocrity, who says she is 'that even course, that must be kept / To shun two dangerous gulfs' (v.i,p. 261). Most of the vices are presented in symbolic form with Greek names, the noteworthy exception being in IV.iii when the extremes of Justice are presented by Justice Nimis and Justice Nihil and their Clerks, Plus and Parum. Perhaps the most interesting character to be introduced is Bomolochos in IV.v, described as 'a conceited fellow of his own wit', who is straight out of Aristophanes via Jonson.[34] His part is somewhat limited. He has eight speeches in all. Seven of these are 'O, O, O!' and the eighth and last is 'O, O, O, O, O, O, O,!'.[35] The upshot of the whole play is that, as one of the puritans Mistress Flowerdew puts it,

> I have pick'd
> Out of the garden of this play a good
> And wholesome salad of instruction!
>
> (p. 259)

This is very much in accord with Jonson's didactic aims and there is also a close similarity between the 'revue' techniques of Randolph and Davenant, both showing what the theatre can do by presenting a demonstration before 'on-stage critics'.

Might it not be that it was Randolph's, not Jonson's or Beaumont's, work that so greatly influenced that post-1660 drama which made conscious use of reference to the theatre and dramatic art? This is not to say that 'Randolph is better than Jonson', but simply that Randolph proved the more accessible to later dramatists in this particular mode. There is a telling difference between Jonson and Randolph that may well confirm the significance of the latter's influence. Randolph, though his classical background and his didacticism are akin to Jonson's, is much more playful than Jonson. There is a great deal of fun in his approach and it is this element that is so evident in *The Play-house to be Let* and the two burlesques of the early 1670s, to which attention can now be turned.

The subject of this study is not, of course, burlesque as such; burlesque itself is of no special concern here: What is relevant is drama, which, via the Jacobean induction, can be traced back to the technique of direct address. Villiers's *The Rehearsal* (1671) and Duffett's *The Mock Tempest* (1674) satirise serious and great drama respectively. There is a certain irony in the fact that the object of Villiers's attack is the extravagant heights of heroic drama scaled by Davenant himself and this aspect of *The Rehearsal*, and the theatre war of which *The Mock Tempest* is part, are well enough known. It is not what is burlesqued that matters here (and particular lines of some twenty plays by at least seven dramatists are glanced at),[36] but the innovation of using the rehearal technique for a whole play. The purpose, as in Jonson, is didactic as the Prologue maintains:

> *We might well call this short Mock-play of ours*
> *A Posie made of Weeds instead of Flowers;*
> *Yet such have been presented to your noses,*
> *And there are such, I fear, who thought 'em Roses.*
> *Would some of 'em were here, to see, this night.*
> *What stuff it is in which they took delight.*
> *Here brisk insipid Rogues, for wit, let fall*
> *Sometimes dull sence; but oft'ner none at all:*
> *There, strutting Heroes, with a grim-fac'd train,*
> *Shall brave the Gods, in King Cambyses vein.*
> *For (changing Rules, of late, as if man writ*
> *In spite of Reason, Nature, Art and Wit)*
> *Our Poets make us laugh at Tragoedy,*
> *And with their Comoedies they make us cry.*[37]

The constant allusions to specific plays — allusions nowadays completely lost in production — could not but recall the theatre of the time, but it is much more the minutiae of theatrical production that serves to make us aware that we are in a theatre. *The Mock Tempest* does not use the rehearsal format and though at first it strikes an audience as breaking the dramatic illusion because of the burlesque of Shakespeare's play, soon creates a world of its own. The introduction is all that involves direct acknowledgement of the audience. Joseph Haines, the comedian (1638–1701), enters alone and addresses the audience:

> You are of late become so mutinous,
> Y'ave forc'd a reverend Bard to quit our House.

Since y'are so soon misled to ruin us,
I'le call a Spirit forth that shall declare,
What all your tricks and secret Virtues are.
What? ho *Ariel*!
     Enter Betty Mackarel.
Here's *Betty* — Now rail if you dare:
Speak to 'em *Betty* — ha! asham'd, alass poor Girl,
Whisper me! — Oh I'le tell 'em — Gentlemen! she says,
Y'are grown so wild she could not stay among ye,
And yet her tender heart is loath to wrong ye.
Spare 'em not,
Whom kindness cannot stir, but stripes may move.

He offers an interesting comment on Betty Mackarel's origin:

Think of thy high calling *Betty*, now th' art here,
They gaze and wish, but cannot reach thy Sphere,
Though ev'ry one could squeeze thy Orange there.

And he concludes, coincidentally, in the manner of Barnabas in *Nice Wanton*:

... — make thy Cursy *Betty*.
Now go in Child, I have something to say to these
Gentlemen in private.   [*Exit Betty*]

Betty leaves the stage and he then speaks the Prologue in which he assures the audience:

Let Language, Wit and Plot, this Night be safe,
For all our business is to make you laugh.[38]

Rather surprisingly, the rehearsal form (and even burlesque) enjoyed little further success at the time. Estcourt's *Prunella* was introduced as an interlude in a revival of Villiers's *The Rehearsal* at Drury Lane on 12 February 1708; and, as previously noted, Settle adapted Beaumont's play in 1711 as *The City Ramble*.[39] However, Simon Trussler explains in his introduction to Gay's *The What d'ye Call It* (1715):

The What d'ye Call It has its descent not so much from *The Rehearsal* as from a little-known play by Thomas Duffett dubbed *The Mock-*

Tempest. Duffett's bawdy-house version of Shakespeare's romance was written in 1674, and virtually marked the eclipse of that false dawn of burlesque which brightened the early Restoration theatre. Forty years were to elapse before Gay's *What d'ye Call It* revived the tradition — a tradition, in this case, of travesty rather than of close textual parody.[40]

As Trussler points out, *The What d'ye Call It* is concerned with 'emotional falsity' in drama. It presents a play within a frame, but does not use the rehearsal technique. Nevertheless, *The What d'ye Call It* does have one or two matters of direct interest here. In his mock-serious Preface, Gay inaccurately claims that he is the first to offer 'this kind of Dramatick entertainment' (p. 59). Apart from Duffett, mentioned by Trussler, the obvious 'first example' must be Beaumont's *Knight of the Burning Pestle*. It is inconceivable that Gay was unaware of this, so, presumably, this claim is there to be resisted. More interesting is Gay's claim that in order to

> avoid the cavils and misinterpretations of severe Criticks, I have not call'd it a Tragedy, Comedy, Pastoral, or Farce, but left the name entirely undetermin'd in the doubtful appellation of *The What d'ye Call It*, which name I thought unexceptionable; but I added to it a *Tragi-Comi-Pastoral Farce*, as it comprized all those several kinds of the Drama.　(p. 62)

The broken logic here is a pleasant joke — I have not allocated it to *a genre* so have given it a 'doubtful appellation' *as title* but have called it 'a mixture of genres' — but the ingenuousness of that doubtful appellation has taken in at least one critic. Trussler, for example, in a footnote says 'the phrase was already familiar as a substitute for a forgotten name or place. "His Father was Squire what d'you call him, of what d'you call 'em Shire"' (Dryden, *The Kind Keeper*, 1678). However, Gay is surely using the name Touchstone gives Jaques (III.iii.79), the reference being to a jakes, or privy. As with Jaques, the inevitable reference to 'the real world' is insisted upon.

The What d'ye Call It includes, in the form of a ghost of a child unborn, one of the spectres that will comically haunt burlesques throughout the century. Fielding, for example, not only used the killing of the ghost as a source of comedy in *Tom Thumb*, but extracted further comedy from his defence of this incident in his Preface and, at the same time, showed how he was ridiculing empty language. Critics, he says, have objected to the killing of a ghost:

This (say they) far exceeds the Rules of Probability; perhaps it may; but I would desire these Gentlemen seriously to recollect, whether they have not seen in several celebrated Plays, such Expressions as these, *Kill my Soul, Stab my very Soul, Bleeding Soul, Dying Soul, cum multis aliis*, all which visibly confess that for a Soul or Ghost to be killed is no Impossibility.[41]

Perhaps the most interesting aspect of *The What d'ye Call It* in this context is the way that the 'real life' story of the frame and the 'stage-story' of the play-within-the-frame are interrelated. Sir Roger's Steward, by the device of having his daughter marry Sir Roger's son in their roles in the inset play, ensures that she actually does marry him in the 'real' world of the frame by having a 'genuine' priest, not an actor, marry them. In this way, as the Steward explains in an aside to the audience near the start of the play 'the conduct of this play may retrieve her folly' in permitting herself to be 'debauched! and by that booby Squire!', and thus 'preserve her reputation' (p. 66). Of course, 'real' and 'genuine' have to be marked off by quotation marks because these words are being used anomalously. The priest is only 'genuine' in so far as the frame world is 'real' and thus is only 'real' with respect to the play-world it encloses. There are two contrasting worlds of illusion here but they are contained within a total stage-world; the audience simply 'overhears', apart from the occasional direct address of an aside. Direct attention is not drawn to being in a theatre, as in the Jonsonian inductions and the rehearsal plays.[42]

Two years later Colley Cibber was to play a self-caricature in *Three Hours After Marriage* (1717) for seven consecutive nights without realising it, and when he belatedly withdrew, the play came off.[43] In 1721 D'Urfey's sequel to *The Rehearsal* was produced: *The Two Queens of Brentford; or, Bayes No Poetaster*, and in this recall of its origins in Villiers and Jonson there is a sense of a new dawn for the rehearsal play.

In 1724 and 1727 two satires which purported to dramatise the health of the English stage were performed and printed: *The British Stage; or, The Exploits of Harlequin*, purporting to show the bad effect of French pantomime on British drama; and *The English Stage Italianized* which, as Nicoll puts it, while 'directed mainly against the continental type of pantomime, it may be taken here as showing the general trend of satirical opinion against the *commedia dell' arte*'.[44] The awareness of the theatre within the theatre is clearly becoming noticeable in this decade and Nicoll illustrates this amusingly by an extract he quotes from *The British Stage*:

Enter the Dragon, *spitting Fire* ... [*The whole Audience hollow with*

Applause, and shake the very Theatre]. [*An ass*] *endeavours to mount the*
Dragon, *falls down, the* Dragon *is drawn up in the Air by Wires.*
[*The Audience ring with Applause*]
Enter Windmill.
Harl[equin]. Advance, Mr *Windmill*, and give some Entertainment to
    this great Assembly.
[*The Audience hollow and huzza, and are ready to break down the House*
    with Applause]
They dance with the Ghosts, Devils, and Harlequin.
[*The Audience clap prodigiously*]

(p. 257)

As Jean Kern notes, absurd stage directions 'illustrate the extravagance of
the stage business of pantomime performance' and she specifically
mentions the splendid direction 'Enter Windmill'.[45]

The turning point came in 1728 when not ony were *Peri Bathous* and
the first, three-book, version of *The Dunciad* published, but Gay was
triumphantly successful with *The Beggar's Opera*. This ushered in a decade
of intense political satire in drama for which the rehearsal formula proved
most adaptable. It provided, as Jean Kern says, 'a built-in commentator
on the play-within-the-play', plus spectators and critics, who could all
direct the audience's attention to the satire. There was little necessity for
plot, and thus the rehearsal format could easily become a hodgepodge, 'a
miscellany of satire with too many objects of attack'. Most of these
rehearsal-type plays were 'literary satires on bad dramatists, poor acting,
terrible poetry, pedantic critics or the low state of theatrical taste' (pp.
146–7).

The Beggar's Opera is first and foremost a satire. Its chief objects are
Italian opera (and it does not hesitate to borrow one of Handel's best
tunes, the march from *Rinaldo* for 'Let us take the road'), Walpole's
administration, and social corruption. It is set in a very slight theatrical
frame, opening with a short dialogue between an actor and a beggar, and
concludes with the Player expostulating on the evident intention of
hanging the hero, at which point a reprieve is called for. As the Player
explains, 'All this we must do, to comply with the taste of the town'
(III.xvi.17–18).[46] From *The Beggar's Opera*, attended as it was with such
success, it was but a short step to rehearsal drama that, in effect,
constantly broke the dramatic illusion by ever insisting upon the nature of
the theatrical event. Odingsells in 1729 combined the rehearsal formula
and the opera-within-a-frame of Gay for his *Bayes' Opera*, the name Bayes
again referring back to Villiers's *The Rehearsal.* Jean Kern summarises its

plot as 'an allegory of Pantomime capturing the throne of Wit' and the blame for the success of pantomime is placed squarely 'on the shoulders of all Englishmen who are corrupt enough in taste to become the followers of this new foreign form of entertainment'.[47] The attack on the audience is significant.

It was Fielding who capitalised most effectively upon the work of Gay and Odingsells. It is as a novelist that Fielding has earned his reputation of course and it is ironic that it should have been the restrictions of Parliament through the Licensing Act of 1737 that should have actually benefited English literature. Needless to stress, it was wholly unintentional. Although Fielding is often a lively dramatist, that was only so in his irregular drama,[48] and it is not likely that upon that basis that he would have been able to develop a drama of the quality of his novels. His work in regular drama is worth a moment's attention in order that his burlesque of stage conventions can be seen in proper perspective.

The Universal Gallant is a comedy in five acts, performed at Drury Lane without success in 1734. Aaron Hill wrote disparagingly of it in *The Prompter* on 18 February 1735:

> The last Piece brought on the Stage, this Season, was the *Universal Gallant*; or, *Different Husbands*, wrote by the prolifick Mr *Fielding*. — And, as in the *Toy-shop*, I had the Pleasure of remarking, that the good Taste of the Town wanted only to be *awakened* to become as *strong* as ever, so here I had an Opportunity of making an Observation very much in Favour of the Town, *viz.* That the Accusation of BAD TASTE is very *falsly* and *unjustly* brought against them, since if the *Town* had really the bad Taste, they are represented to have, this Play would have run the remaining Part of the Season, in an *uninterrupted* Course of *Applause*. I had likewise an Opportunity of observing much more *Impartiality* than I had expected, in the Behaviour of the *Audience*, for till almost the third Act was over, they sat very quiet, in hopes it would mend, till finding it grew still *worse* and *worse*, they at length lost all Patience, and not an *Expression* or *Sentiment* afterwards passed its *deserved Censure*.[49]

The play is a comedy firmly in the tradition of Shirley's *The Lady of Pleasure* (1635) of a century earlier and still holding the stage in Sheridan's *School for Scandal* (1777) forty years after the production of Fielding's play. It is, in the main, a fourth-wall-removed drama in which the audience 'overhears' what is said on-stage, but it makes great use of monologues and asides. The monologues may be slightly disguised, as is the very first by Mr Mondish in which he reads out a letter he has received (x, 39–40).[50] Captain Spark does the same in Act IV (x, 96), making comments *en passant*. Several monologues provide story links or add a little to character delineation, such as Mr Gaylove's (x, 86) or Mr Mondish's (x, 97 and 100):

> *Mondish*:　A letter dropt! To Captain Spark — the rogue counterfeits a woman's hand exceeding well. But he could not counterfeit her hand so exactly without having seen letters from her — Why then may not this be from her? Is she not a woman, a prude? — the devil can say no more.
>
> 　　　　　　　　　　　　　　　　　　　　　　　　　(x, 97)

In quite crude dramatisation, Sir Simon Raffler has a whole series of monologues in Acts IV and V explaining how he will use a counterfeit letter, purportedly from his wife, to discover who is supposedly cuckolding him. The monologues show him carrying out his plot, dressed as a woman and attempting to imitate her voice:

> [*Enter Sir Simon Raffler, in Women's Clothes*]
> *Sir Simon Raffler*:　My evidence is posted, the colonel is in the closet, and can overhear all — The time of appointment draws near. I am strangely pleased with my stratagem. If I can but counterfeit my wife's voice as well as I have her hand, I may defy him to discover me; for there is not a glimpse of light — I am as much delighted as any young whore-master can be in expectation of meeting another man's wife. And yet I am afraid I shall not discover myself to be what I fear, neither; and if I should not I will hang myself incontinently. Oh! thou damned couch! thou art not ten years old, and yet what cuckoldom hast thou been witness of — I will be revenged on thee; for I will burn thee this evening in triumph, please Heaven! — Hush, hush, here he comes.
> [*Lies on a couch*]
> 　　　　　　　　　　　　　　　　　　　　　　　　　(x, 107–8)

Sir Simon's villainy is deliberately undercut — 'placed' — not only by the absurdity of his behaviour, but by his expostulation to the couch. The absurdity is made the more ridiculous when the presumed lover, stumbling about in the dark, unable to find the couch, provokes Sir Simon into making an aside addressed to the couch: 'Oh! thou damned villain! I wish thou couldst feel torments, that I might be an age in burning thee' (X, 108). We are not far removed from Coomes in *The Two Angry Women of Abingdon* kissing the stage post (see p. 89 above). In tone, the comedy differs little from comedies of manners of the period. It is witty and ever concerned with deception and the uncertain relationships of men and women. This is Sir Simon's jaundiced view of matrimony:

> *Sir Simon Raffler*: Is not this intolerable? is not this insufferable? this is the comfortable state that a man is wished joy of by his friends; and yet no man wishes a man joy of being condemned, or of getting the plague. But when a man is married, 'Give you joy, sir,' cries one fool; 'I wish you joy,' says another; and thus the wretch is ushered into the galleys with the same triumph as he could be exalted with to the empire of the Great Mogul.
>
> (X, 57)

The response of the independently-minded woman is given later in the play by Mrs Raffler:

> *Mrs Raffler*: A woman never acts as she should, but when she acts against her husband. He is a prince who is ever endeavouring to grow absolute, and it should be our constant endeavour to restrain him. You are a member of the commonwealth of women, and when you give way to your husband, you betray the liberty of your sex.
>
> (X, 104)

Fielding is obviously at ease with the most stereotyped of theatrical conventions. He is, as his advertisement puts it, simply 'getting a livelihood in an honest and inoffensive way' by providing the theatre with standard fare. Possibly the most interesting characteristic of the play is the manner in which Fielding has Mr Gaylove unwittingly pick up the way that Captain Spark has read Colonel Raffler's counterfeit letter.

Captain Spark: 'Sir, — as Sir Simon will be abroad this evening, I
shall have an opportunity of seeing you alone.' —
hum — 'if you please, therefore, it shall be in the
dining room at nine — there is a couch will hold us
both.' — The devil there is — 'The company will be
all assembled in the parlour, and you will be very safe
with your humble servant, Mary Raffler.' Pooh! Pox,
what shall I do? I would not give a farthing for her —
Ha! can't I contrive to be surprised together? That
ridiculous dog, Mondish, sups here — If I could but
convince him of this amour, he will believe all I ever
told him — now if he could but see this letter some
way without my showing it him — Egad, I'll find
him out, and drop it before him. By good luck here
he is.

(x, 96)

When Mondish picks up the letter, after Colonel Spark has conveniently
dropped it, he shows it to Gaylove, who reads it in this manner:

Gaylove: To Captain Spark — Sir Simon — abroad this evening — In
the dining-room — couch will hold us both — Ha, ha! The
captain improves — Safe with your humble servant — Mary
Raffler — Well said, my little Spark — Now, from this
moment shall I have a great opinion of thee — thou art a
genius — a hero — to forge a letter from a woman, and
drop it in her own house — there is more impudence
thrown away on this fellow than would have made six court
pages and as many attorneys — he is an errant walking
contagion on women's reputations, and was sent into the
world as a judgment on the sex.

(x, 98)

This anticipates the style of speech used by Dr Pother in Charles Dibden
Jnr's *The Farmer's Wife* (1814):

Doctor: I'll follow, the moment I have digested all this. Make a capital
story. Farmer and wife — Rural affection — husband abroad
— wife at home — intriguing baronet — elopement —
pursuit — red-hot poker — old Nick in the chimney — down
he comes — fat in the fire — and the devil hauled over the

coals. [*Looks out of window*]. There they go! Now, Peter —
now, Robin. Peter puffs — Robin at his heels — Peter at the
pond — can't cross in time to go round — Robin seizes him
— struggle — pull-haul — wrestle — and there they go
plump into the pond together. Huzza! it will make as good a
story as my history of the debating-society. I wish there were
anybody here to tell it to.[51]

And this elliptical style has, of course, been made familiar to us through
Dickens's Mr Jingle who appeared in *The Pickwick Papers* in 1836, four
years after Dickens became an actor.

The very conventional nature of *The Universal Gallant*, especially its use
of monologues and asides, is also to be found in the short, related, musical
farces, *An Old Man Taught Wisdom, or, The Virgin Unmasked* (1735) and
its sequel, *Miss Lucy in Town* (1742). *An Old Man Taught Wisdom* opens
with the aged father outlining the action to the audience and a little later
his fifteen-year old daughter, Lucy, has a monologue which includes a
debate within the monologue of the kind that has a long theatrical
tradition:

Let me see, I'll practise a little.
Suppose that chair was my husband; and ecod! by all I can find, a chair
is as proper for a husband as anything else; now says my husband to
me, 'How do you do, my dear?' Lard! my dear, I don't know how I
do! not the better for you. 'Pray, my dear, let us dine early to-day?'
Indeed, my dear, I can't. 'Do you intend to go abroad to-day?' No,
my dear! 'Shall we ride out?' No, my dear. 'Shall we go a visiting?'
No, my dear. — I will never do any thing I am bid, that I am resolved.
(x, 12–13)

These afterpieces include songs in the manner of Gay's ballad opera and
both would repay revival in the right context.

Thus, in his 'regular' drama although he uses monologues and asides,
Fielding is clearly working within the conventions of his time and the
audience is not asked to examine or laugh at those conventions and nor is
the theatre as theatre drawn to the audience's attention. Not so,
however, with his irregular drama.

With one remote exception, Fielding's regular drama has survived
neither on the stage nor in the study. The exception is a modern

adaptation of *Rape upon Rape* (1730) a five-act comedy, which was adapted by Bernard Miles for his Mermaid Theatre in 1957 as a musical romp called *Lock Up Your Daughters*;[52] the adaptation was revived in 1978.

Although there can be little doubt that plays critical of aspects of the drama produced during the 1720s, coupled with the great success of *The Beggar's Opera*, and perhaps Odingsell's example of 1729, must have prompted Fielding to adopt the rehearsal form, there can also be no doubt that he was influenced by Jonson. Thus, Arthur Scouten, in his study of the London Stage between 1729 and 1747, remarks that Fielding 'revived induction scenes' in his period as manager of the New Haymarket.[53] Fielding admired Jonson's plays and refers to them in his own work. In his Preface to *Plutus, the God of Riches* (1742), he remarks that 'Genteel comedy' has banished Shakespeare, Fletcher and Jonson from the stage, and there are references to *The Alchemist* in *Tom Jones*, for example, and *Bartholomew Fair* in *The Champion*.[54] He had the work of many dramatists in his library, according to the auction catalogue of his books. He owned the 1716 six-volume edition of Jonson's works, and among other play-wrights were Aristophanes, Euripides, Plautus, Seneca, Shakespeare (in eight and nine-volume editions), Beaumont and Fletcher, Shirley, and at least ten of the Restoration dramatists, as well as a set of the 1744 edition of Dodsley's Old Plays. Randolph's works are not mentioned and *The Muse's Looking-Glass* appeared in Dodsley only after Fielding had given up writing plays. It is possible the play was known to Fielding, however. The catalogue of his books at auction does not show all his reading matter, especially in literature, and the play was doubtless available having been reprinted in 1706.[55]

Fielding first revives the induction in *The Welsh Opera* (1731) and its two revisions *The Genuine Grub Street Opera* (1731) and *The Grub Street Opera* (1731). It is also used in *Don Quixote in England* (1734), *Pasquin* (1736), *Tumble-Down Dick* (1736), *Eurydice* (1737), *The Historical Register* (1737) and *Eurydice Hissed* (1737). All these plays were produced at his own Haymarket Theatre, with the exceptions of *Eurydice* (Drury Lane), *The Grub Street Opera*, which seems to have been suppressed, and *The Genuine Grub Street Opera*, which was printed but not performed.[56] However, he not only revived the induction but the use of critical comment throughout the play, as in *Pasquin*, *Tumble-Down Dick*, both *Eurydice* plays, and *The Historical Register*. In *The Author's Farce* (1730) there is a puppet Show, as in Jonson's *Bartholomew Fair*, and an Epilogue featuring four poets, assembled to write the epilogue between them, Luckless (the author), a Player and a cat.

4 Poet:	Well, let us now begin.
3 Poet:	But we omit
	An epilogue's chief decoration, wit.
1 Poet:	It hath been so, but that stale custom's broken;
	Though dull to read, 'twill please you when 'tis spoken.
	[*Enter Luckless*]
Luckless:	Fie, gentlemen, the audience now hath stayed
	This half hour for the epilogue.
All Poets:	'Tis not made.
Luckless:	How! Then I value not your aid of that,
	I'll have the epilogue spoken by a cat.
	Puss, puss, puss, puss, puss, puss, puss,
	[*Enter Cat*]
1 Poet:	I'm in a rage.
	When cats come on, poets should leave the stage.
	[*Exeunt Poets*]
Cat:	Mew, mew.
Luckless:	Poor puss, come hither pretty rogue.
	Who knows but you may come to be in vogue?
	Some ladies like a cat, and some a dog.
	[*Enter a Player*]
Player:	Cass, cass, cass, cass! Fie, Mr Luckless, what
	Can you be doing with that filthy cat?
	[*Exit Cat*]
Luckless:	Oh, curst misfortune! What can I be doing?
	This devil's coming in has proved my ruin.
	She's driven the cat and the epilogue away.

(p. 79)

Fortunately for Luckless, the cat returns — as a woman — and reads the Epilogue.[57]

Fielding's interest in the induction is nowhere more apparent than in the three versions written for the various manifestations of *The Grub Street Opera*. Apart from the first fifteen lines of the two 'Grub Street' versions, the three inductions are quite different in content, though their form is the same — a dialogue between Scriblerus (the supposed author) and either a Player or the Master of the Playhouse.[58] Fielding's satirical attitude to the drama of the time (despite his own writing within the existing conventions, as in *The Universal Gallant*) is quite clear from the opening of the first induction (or 'The Introduction' as he calls it). After the Player has expostulated on the speed with which Scriblerus writes plays — 'or something like plays' — faster than they can be acted or danced, he asks whether Scriblerus thinks the town will expect Welsh in his play (perhaps with a glance at what Jonson did in *For the Honour of Wales*). 'No, sir,' replies Scriblerus:

> ... the town is too well acquainted with modern authors to expect anything from a title. A tragedy often proves a comedy, a comedy a tragedy, and an opera nothing at all. I have seen a tragedy without any distress, a comedy without a jest, and an opera without music.
>
> *Player:* I wish, sir, you had kept within the rules of probability in your plot, if I may call it so.
>
> *Scriblerus:* It is the business of a poet to surprise his audience, especially a writer of operas. The discovery, sir, should be as no one could understand how it could be brought about, before it is made.
>
> (pp. 76–7)

It would seem from the first of these three inductions that Fielding had thought of intermean-like comments:

> *Player:* Sir, I wish you would be so kind to stay here to comment upon your opera as it goes on.
>
> *Scriblerus:* Hey, to be a sort of walking notes!
>
> (p. 78)

It is not, however, until *Pasquin*, five years later, that he adopts this Jonsonian technique, and thereafter uses it in all his plays with inductions. This first induction concludes with the entry of a second player bearing news of a series of those little local disasters that strike dramatic productions, and to which the audience's attention is drawn on a number of occasions by Fielding:

> *Second Player:* Sir, Mr Davenport will not go on without a pair of white gloves, and Mrs Jones, who played Huncamunca, insists on a dram before she goes on for Madame Apshinken. As for Mrs Clark, the king has fall'd so heavy upon her that he has almost squeezed her guts out, and it's a question whether she will be able to sing or no.
>
> (p. 78)

The induction to *Don Quixote in England* (1734) consists chiefly of a dialogue between the author and the theatre manager — one and the same at the Haymarket: Fielding himself. This induction is concerned with the matter of prologues (there is none for this play, though the author claims to have three in his pocket, each of which he describes), and the manipulation of the audience's response:

> [*Enter a Player*]
> *Player*: Sir, the audience make such a noise with their canes, that if we don't begin immediately, they will beat the house down before the play begins; and it is not advisable to put them out of humour: for there are two or three of the loudest catcalls in the gallery that ever were heard.
> *Author*: Be not frightened at that: those are only some particular friends of mine, who are to put on the face of enemies at first, and be converted at the end of the first act.
>
> (IX, 440–1)

The Author having himself arranged for these signs of protest at the delay in starting can show greater equanimity than does Cordatus in the induction to *Every Man Out of His Humour*, who maintains that such 'protraction is able to sowre the best-settled patience in the Theatre' (ll. 287–8).

In being so open about audience manipulation, Fielding not only criticises this habit, but ensures a special relationship with *his* Haymarket audience, as author and manager. Following the ill-reception of his *Eurydice* at Drury Lane, in Stephen's edition described as 'A Farce: as it was d-amned at the Theatre Royal, in Drury Lane' (vol.x, p.233), Fielding returned to his own audience with *Eurydice Hissed*. This has the revealing sub-title 'A Word to the Wise'. The author Spatter describes the play as being 'of a most instructive kind' that 'conveys to us a beautiful image of the instability of human greatness, and the uncertainty of friends'. The curtain is drawn to reveal Pillage, the author of a farce. Thus Fielding, dramatist and manager, presents Spatter, who presents Pillage, who presents a farce, upon which Spatter comments to Sourwit. Pillage bribes out-of-work actors to applaud his farce. All agree, except Honestas who hopes for the time 'when none / Shall come to censure and applaud, / But merit always bear away the prize' (vol.x, p.264). Alas, despite Pillage's precautions, 'Eurydice is damned'. Only Honestas does not desert Pillage:

Pillage: Honestus here! will he not shun me too?
Honestus: When Pasquin ran, and the town liked you most,
             And every scribbler loaded you with praise,
             I did not court you, nor will shun you now.

(x, 270)

If it were not that Fielding is so much involved in the damning of *Eurydice*, this would smack of playfulness to an almost absurd degree, but to dramatise the rejection of his farce and recall the success of *Pasquin* at two removes as it were, suggests that this technique may involve more personal feeling than one sometimes supposes. The satire directed at politics and society is clearly felt,[59] but there is so much that is jokey about the theatrical satire, despite the animosity apparent, say, in the address to John Lun (that is, John Rich, manager of Drury Lane), 'Vulgarly called Esquire', which precedes *Tumble-Down Dick*, that the depth of Fielding's own feelings is in danger of being overlooked.

Tumble-Down Dick satirises the vogue for pantomime and Italianate entertainments. It has some splendid moments, from the title-page, the list of dramatis personae (with its final all-inclusive 'Constables, Watch, Fiddlers, Lanthorns, Suns, Moons, Whores, &c, &c, &c'), its Harlequinade, complete with *lazzi*, to the induction and intermeans. Two quotations will suffice to show Fielding's contempt for the kind of entertainment that was said to be driving serious drama from the stage. Machine, the author of the entertainment, complains early on:

> ... But Mr Prompter, I must insist that you cut out a great
> deal of *Othello*, if my pantomime is performed with it, or the
> audience will be palled before the entertainment begins.
>
> *Prompter:* We'll cut out the fifth act, sir, if you please.
> *Machine:* Sir, that's not enough, I'll have the first cut out too.
> *Fustian:* Death and the devil! Can I bear this? Shall Shakespeare be
> mangled to introduce this trumpery?
> *Prompter:* Sir, this gentleman brings more money to the house than all
> the poets put together.
> *Machine:* Pugh, pugh, Shakespeare! — Come, let down the curtain,
> and play away the overture. — Prompter, to your post.

(x, 280)

A little later, Machine explains to Fustian, the author of the tragedy:

> ... Mr Fustian, in tragedies and comedies, and such sort of

> things, the audiences will make great allowances; but they
> expect more from an entertainment; here, if the least thing
> be out of order, they never pass it by.
>
> (x, 284)

It is easier to understand Fielding's satirisation of pantomime at the expense of Shakespeare, than his attacks on drama not dissimilar from his own *The Universal Gallant*. It might be advanced that were better plays than *The Universal Gallant* being written at the time, pantomime might not have swept all before it. The pantomime evidently had a life and variety not strongly evident in Fielding's Drury Lane drama.

It is in *Pasquin*, however, that Fielding dramatises most extensively every aspect of dramatic composition and production. It is seen, correctly, as its sub-title puts it, as 'A Dramatic Satire on the Times', and the political and social satire are, of course, much to the fore. But the satire on drama is so pervasive, and the destruction of the world of dramatic illusion so complete, that one cannot but wonder that *Pasquin* could appear only a little over a year after *The Universal Gallant* had been put on at Drury Lane. One wonders whether the Licensing Act did not, in fact, come just in time for Fielding the creative artist!

Pasquin involves the rehearsal of two plays, Trapwit's comedy, *The Election*, and Fustian's tragedy, *The Life and Death of Common-sense*. The plays themselves provide many opportunities for satire on the drama of the time. Thus, Trapwit assures Fustian that he understands 'the laws of comedy better than to write without marrying somebody' (vol.x, p. 139), and that he inculcates 'a particular moral at the end of every act' (x, 145). The principles underlying plotting are expounded by Trapwit. He has just explained to Fustian that with the fourth act the plot will begin to open.

> *Fustian*: Is not the fourth act a little too late to open the plot, Mr
> Trapwit?
> *Trapwit*: Sir, 'tis an error on the right side; I have known a plot open
> in the first act, and the audience, and the poet too, forget it
> before the third was over; now, sir, I am not willing to
> burden either the audience's memory, or my own; for they
> may forget all that is hitherto past, and know full as much of
> the plot as if they remembered it.
>
> (x, 150)

The two dramatists also discuss dialogue and its relationship to character:[60]

Trapwit: Sir, in this play, I keep exactly up to nature; nor is there anything said in this scene that I have not heard come out of the mouths of the finest people of the age. Sir, this scene has cost me ten shillings in chair-hire, to keep the best company, as it is called.

Mrs Mayoress: Indeed, my lord, I cannot guess it at less than ten pounds a yard.

Lord Place: Pray, madam, was you at the last ridotto?

Fustian: Ridotto! the devil! a country mayoress at a ridotto! Sure, that is out of character, Mr Trapwit?

Trapwit: Sir, a conversation of this nature cannot be carried on without these helps; besides, sir, this country mayoress, as you call her, may be allowed to know something of the town; for you must know, sir, that she has been a woman to a woman of quality.

Fustian: I am glad to hear that.

(x, 141)

But a little later Fustian remonstrates again with Trapwit that the Mayoress is not truly in character:

Fustian: How comes this lady, Mr Trapwit, considering her education, to be so ignorant of all these things?

Trapwit: 'Gad that's true; I had forgotten her education, faith, when I writ that speech; it's a fault I sometimes fall into — a man ought to have the memory of a devil to remember every little thing; but come, go on, go on, go on — I'll alter it by and by.

(x, 142)

Fustian explains the rules of dramatic writing to the critic, Sneerwell, in the course of the rehearsal of his tragedy:

. . . you do not understand the practical rules of writing as well as I do: the first and greatest of which is protraction, or the art of spinning, without which the matter of a play would lose the chief property of all other matter, namely, extension; and no play, sir, could possibly last longer than half an hour. I perceive, Mr Sneerwell, you are one of those who would have no character brought on, but what is necessary to the business of the play. — Nor I neither — But the business of the play, as I take it, is to divert, and therefore every character that diverts is necessary to the business of the play.

(x, 174)

There are the almost inevitable jokes about ghosts. Fustian has no less than three successively rising and descending, complete with crowing cock, and he is astonished that Sneerwell does not immediately recognise the first of them, for is he not the ghost of Tragedy who 'has walked all the stages of London for several years'? Unfortunately he has not come to rehearsal 'floured', because the theatre barber has gone to Drury Lane 'to shave the Sultan in the new entertainment' (vol.x, p.174) — another hit at the 'taste of the town'. In fact, Trapwit's comedy is rehearsed first because Fustian's 'ghost being ill' he 'cannot get up without danger' and he would not risk the life of a ghost on any account. And quite right, too, agrees Trapwit, 'for a ghost is the soul of tragedy' (x, 131).

There are comments on actors and critics; on dedications and prologues; on dancing and opera and epic; there is even a scene to be played in silence:

> *Trapwit*: Now, Mr Fustian, the plot which has hitherto been only carried on by hints, and opened itself like the infant spring by small and imperceptible degrees to the audience, will display itself, like a ripe matron, in its full summer's bloom; and cannot, I think, fail with its attractive charms, like a loadstone, to catch the admiration of every one like a trap, and raise an applause like thunder, till it makes the whole house like a hurricane. I must desire a strict silence through this whole scene. Colonel, stand you still on this side of the stage; and, miss, do you stand on the opposite. — There, now look at each other.
>
> [*A long silence here*]
>
> *Fustian*: Pray, Mr Trapwit, is nobody ever to speak again?
>
> *Trapwit*: Oh! the devil! You have interrupted the scene; after all my precautions the scene's destroyed; the best scene of silence that ever was penned by a man. Come, come, you may speak now; you may speak as fast as you please.
>
> (x, 158–9)

Only the epilogue itself, spoken by a ghost, is directly serious in its appeal to the theatre and its audiences. 'Our Author then in jest throughout the play, / Now begs a serious word or two to say'. It is here that Fielding reveals not only his intent, but the impasse in which he finds himself in the theatre of his time:

> Can the whole world in science match our soil?
> Have they a Locke, a Newton, or a Boyle?

Or dare the greatest genius of their stage,
With Shakespeare, or immortal Ben engage?
Content with nature's bounty, do not crave
The little which to other lands she gave;
Nor like the cock a barley-corn prefer
To all the jewels which you owe to her.

(x, 190)

There was no way in which Fielding could move forward as a dramatist.
He wished to write conventional drama, such as *The Universal Gallant*,
but his best work was in dramatic satire which exposed not only the
corruption of politicians, but, through the medium he used, the very kind
of theatre in which he hoped for success. His dramatic talents would find
their outlet in his novels — in, for example, the excellent 'scenes' of
Joseph Andrews. Paradoxically, though the drama of the eighteenth
century was never more than modestly regarded as literature, and at its
best when seemingly undermining the very art it proclaimed, *the theatre*,
as some of these extracts may have suggested, was extremely lively.
Pantomimes and harlequinades, dragons spitting fire, and interminable
petty quarrels may have been predominant, but there can be no doubt
that the theatre had life. What the Licensing Act may have done that it
did not intend (besides ensuring that Fielding became a novelist[61]) was to
preserve something of the wonder of the theatre. That a ghost is merely
a man be-floured is true enough, but if the illusion of drama is to work,
then we cannot have its mechanics too insistently drawn to our attention
(as nowadays in programmes of rejected film and television 'takes'). The
trappings of the theatre are essentially artificial — a deceit. The irony is
that, given a Shakespeare or an 'immortal Ben', it is through that illusion
that audiences can glimpse truth. In the absence of such dramatists — and
he must include himself — Fielding was in danger of throwing out baby
and bathwater. Aaron Hill spoke truer than perhaps he knew when he
wrote of *Pasquin* in *The Prompter* on 2 April 1736, a little after the first
performance on 5 March:

The very great run *Pasquin* has already had, and is still like to have, is
the severest Blow, that cou'd be given to our Theatres, and the
strongest Confirmation of an Opinion, I have ventured, *singly*, to
advance, *viz. That the Stage may*, (and as it may, ought to) *be supported
without* PANTOMIME. While our Theatrick Sovereigns, with the best
Actors the Age can afford, are forced to call in the Assistance of
wonderful Scenary, surprising Transformations, beautiful Landscapes, Dancers

(the very best, both in the graceful and humourous Manner) and in short, all the attendant Powers of *inexplicable Dumb Shew*, at a very great Expence; a Gentleman, under the Disadvantage of a very bad House, with scarce an Actor, and at very little Expence, by the single Power of *Satire, Wit*, and *Common Sense*, has been able to run a Play on for 24 Nights, which is now, *but* begining to *rise* in the Opinion of the Town.[62]

Fielding had shown that the soul of drama lay in language, not in painting and carpentry — as Jonson had expostulated with Inigo Jones — but he was not capable of providing such language himself in the drama, and he was in danger of giving not merely a severe but a mortal blow to the theatre.

The Licensing Act put paid to Fielding's dramatic career, and, pretty well, to political satire in the theatre for a considerable time, but it by no means put an end to self-awareness in the theatre. Samuel Foote found a variety of means whereby he might circumvent the Licensing Act. By ostensibly inviting his friends to a dish of chocolate or a cup of tea, he presented *The Diversions of the Morning* for thirty-six days from 25 April 1747, later changing the time to 6.30 in the evenings for the greater convenience of his friends.[63] The *Diversions* purported to be training sessions for those aspiring to become actors. What was offered was evidently a frequently varied 'revue' within a rehearsal framework. Some of the most substantial changes were included by Tate Wilkinson in *The Wandering Patentee* (1795),[64] the original second act of 1747 appearing in volume IV, pp. 237–50, and the version acted from 1758 in volume I, pp. 285–99 (p. 299 being misnumbered p. 290). There are a number of interesting aspects to these productions, slight as 'plays' though they were.

First of all, like so much of Foote's work, there is direct and indirect awareness of the theatre; the audience was forever being reminded in one way or another that it was in a theatre. When Foote lost a leg in 1766, following a fall from a horse, he proceeded to write plays for one-legged men, in which, of course, he acted. In *The Devil upon Two Sticks* (1768), Foote played the Devil, materialising from a bottle in a chemist's shop to the sound of thunder (I.iii).[65] Harriet, before whom he appeared, naturally registered surprise, and Foote then gave himself lines which commented upon the strange figure that he cut:

I am not surprised, miss, that you are a little shocked at my figure: I could have assumed a much more agreeable form; but as we are to be a little better acquainted, I thought it best to quit all disguise and pretence; therefore, madam, you see me just as I am.   (p. 380)

And not only Harriet but the audience saw Foote, without disguise, just as he was, *in propria persona*. A little later in the scene he describes how he 'got lame on this leg, and obtained the nickname of the Devil Upon Two Sticks' (p. 381). As if that were not enough, after a graduation ceremony in a university college, the play concludes with the Devil recommending Harriet to offer herself as a singer to either Drury Lane or Covent Garden. Alas, he says, he can be of no service to her at those theatres as instead of being under his direction as formerly, 'they are now directed by the Genius of Insipidity' (p. 392). Invoice says he has heard of a new playhouse in the Haymarket, licensed for the summer season only, but Foote — its real-life manager — dismisses this at first: 'What, Foote's? Oh, that's an eccentric, narrow establishment; a mere summer fly! He!' However, he agrees it might do for a '*coup d'essai*, and prove no bad foundation for a future engagement'. Foote then concludes the play by making his last speech (in the role of the Devil) a kind of epilogue. Invoice and Harriet propose to try the Haymarket and the Devil replies:

> By all means: And you may do it this instant; he opens tonight, and will be glad of your assistance. I'll drop you down at the door; and must then take my leave for some time. *Allons*! but don't tremble; you have nothing to fear: the public will treat you with kindness; at least, if they shew but half the indulgence to you, that they have, upon all occasions, shewn to that manager. [*Exeunt omnes*]   (p. 393)

The dramatic illusion is not so insistently broken in *The Lame Lover* (1770) but Foote assumed a name, Sir Luke Limp, which drew attention to the amputation, and his loss of a leg was referred to directly:

Charlotte:	And though the loss of a leg can't be imputed to Sir Luke Limp as a fault –
Serjeant Circuit:	How!
Charlotte:	I hope, sir, at least, you will allow it a misfortune?
Serjeant Circuit:	Indeed!
Charlotte:	A pretty thing truly, for a girl, at my time of life, to be tied to a man with one foot in the grave.
Serjeant Circuit:	One foot in the grave! the rest of his body is not a whit nearer for that. There has been only an execution issued against part of his personals; his real estate is unencumbered and free –

(p. 395)

Although Foote did not act under his own name, the stress placed on his physical loss has much the same effect as that of La Fleur, Hauteroche, Chevalier and La Roque acting in their real-life names in Quinault's *La comédie sans comédie*.

According to Wilkinson, audiences soon became unconscious of the fact that Foote lacked a leg. He makes a very interesting distinction between the way he imitated Foote's acting and the way others, such as Bannister or Carey, did. Wilkinson never imitated Foote by pretending to be lame, whereas others 'one and all do the likeness as lame, and as only with one leg'.[66]

This leads directly to the second characteristic of Foote's work relevant here: he incorporated a great deal of imitation of others in his performances so that there was frequently direct reference to a world outside that performance. This might take the form of ridiculing the very successful lectures being given at the time by Thomas Sheridan (1719–88, father of Richard Brinsley Sheridan), as in *The Orators* (1762), especially those on different kinds of oratory. Within the *Diversions* Wilkinson would imitate Foote, and Foote would imitate Macklin training actors. The complexity of illusion-breaking and creating must have taxed the resourcefulness of the audiences' response, but the oft-repeated performances over a period of thirty years indicate how successful was this kind of act with the public, if not with Dr Johnson. When Boswell remarked that Foote had 'a singular talent for exhibiting character', Johnson replied: 'Sir, it is not a talent; it is a vice; it is what others abstain from. It is not comedy, which exhibits the character of a species, as that of a miser gathered from many misers, it is a farce which exhibits individuals.' Boswell then asked if it were not correct that Foote had considered exhibiting Johnson, to which he replied — harping inevitably on Foote's amputation: 'Sir, fear restrained him; he knew I would have broken his bones. I would have saved him the trouble of cutting off a leg; I would not have left him a leg to cut off'.[67]

Although by no stretch of imagination can the *Diversions* be regarded as drama of any depth, Foote's entertainment is of particular interest for what it suggests of the way that good performers can manipulate an audience's suspension of disbelief, and it provides some evidence for how a text, however trivial, can be used as a basis for good theatre.

The original second act was first presented with pasteboard figures instead of by live actors, apart from Foote as Fustian (a name obviously carried over from Fielding). The following note appears below the Dramatis Personae:

N.B. When this piece was first acted by Mr Foote, with PASTEBOARD FIGURES, it entirely failed in the effect; but with PERFORMERS, *accoutred ridiculously pompous*, and in *fierce whiskered high tragedy*, the effect those dumb actors had assisted my Imitations, and received unbounded applause. (I.286)

Among the actors playing in the revised version was Tate Wilkinson.

In the replacement second act, first given in 1758, Fustian has disappeared. Wilkinson plays Puzzle, evidently imitating Foote, who, during the course of the act has to imitate Macklin. However, when Foote acted Puzzle, an additional character, Bounce, was included and he was played by Wilkinson. The scene between Puzzle and Bounce 'was meant in mimicry of Macklin's teaching Barry Othello' (IV, 244). The way in which characters can be included or dropped to suit convenience of performance will be noted. A modern parallel might be actors in an Ayckbourne play deciding by the toss of a coin before the play begins what the outcome will be on a particular night. This extract is from the imitation of Macklin's lesson in acting:

Puzzle: ... Begin at 'Othello's occupation's gone'. Now catch at me, as if you would tear the very strings and all. Keep your voice low – loudness is no mark of passion. – Mind your attitude.
Bounce: Villain –
Puzzle: Very well!
Bounce: Be sure you prove my love a whore –
Puzzle: Admirable!
Bounce: Be sure on't –
Puzzle: Bravo!
Bounce: Give me the occular proof –
Puzzle: Lay your emphasis a little stronger upon occ-occ-occ-
Bounce: Occ-occ-occular proof –
Puzzle: That's right!
Bounce: Or by the worth of my eternal soul, thou had'st better be born a dog –
Puzzle: Grind dog – a d-o-o-g, Iag –
Bounce: A do-og, Iago, than answer my wak'd wrath.
Puzzle: Charming! – Now quick – [*Speaking all the time*]
Bounce: Make me to see it, or at least so prove it,
That the probation bears no hinge or loop,
To hang a doubt on; – or wo –

Puzzle: A little more terror upon woe — wo-o-e, like a
            mastiff in a tanner's yard — wo-o-o-e-
            [*They answer each other* — wo-o-o-e, &c.]

                                                              (IV, 245)

As if this were not enough, a footnote on p. 249 gives a clear indication of
authorised *ad libbing* (though it is somewhat elliptically expressed): 'Here
Mr Wilkinson in the character of Mr Foote, as Puzzle, gave an imitation
of Mr Foote and Mrs Clive, in Mr and Mrs Cadwallader, and other
characters, which filled up more than a quarter of an hour' (IV, 249).
The Cadwalladers appeared in Foote's play *The Author* (1757), an
afterpiece on the trials of authorship doubtless suggested by Fielding's
The Author's Farce.

It should not be assumed from this that Wilkinson, who ran a very
successful provincial company in Yorkshire for twenty-five years,
approved of the total freedom of the actor to do with his part what he
would. He tells an interesting anecdote which demonstrates that his
attitude to *ad libbing* was akin to Shakespeare's. One of his actors,
Fawcett, was playing Jemmy Jumps in O'Keeffe's *The Farmer* (1787)
with Darcy as Captain Valentine:

> The night before *The Farmer* was acted, Mrs Fawcett (to the pride and
> joy of her *young* husband) was brought to bed. In the Park scene,
> Valentine, who had not seen Jemmy Jumps till then, and did not even
> know who he was, inquired warmly after the health of Jemmy Jumps's
> wife, which Jemmy answered with great pleasure, by assuring him,
> that she had the night preceding 'produced a chopping boy, and was as
> well as could be expected, considering her condition'. Yet, notwith-
> standing the absurdity and glaring impropriety, instead of being
> properly reprobated, the audience actually applauded, though so coarse
> and out of all character; and while any audience will permit a favourite
> actor to so o'erstep the modesty of Nature, there never can be any
> wonder that comedians will take advantage, though so greatly to their
> own discredit and judgment, with every auditor who will not be at the
> trouble of one minute to think for himself, and properly resent such an
> affront offered to his understanding. What a pity for the actor's real
> reputation such liberties are not reprobated as soon as heard; for were
> that the case, the best comedians would be more guarded. I do not
> wish to be too rigid, for I have known many an impromptu be of
> infinite service to the piece, and the actor of course to the audience; but
> the actor should have such a curb on his wit, as to be careful that what

he lets off from the fire of whim and his genius, is strictly in time, place, and character, and then let him be as witty as he pleases; but beware in any play of Shakespear's, for the true value is as different as a French Assignat to a Bank Note of Old England; the intrinsic worth of which, I truly hope, will never be diminished or held in distrust or disesteem either at home or abroad.　(III, 29–30)

Alas, Wilkinson's hopes for the Bank Note of Old England have been disappointed, his *Wandering Patentee* being published in 1795!

Wilkinson's imitating of other actors, his ability to extemporise for a quarter of an hour, and yet his very clear conception of the proper place for *ad libbing*, together with Foote's manipulation of the planes of theatrical illusion, give considerable insight into the relationship of stage illusion to audience. Continuity can be completely broken and, *in certain circumstances*, restored, but to understand and work this requires great theatrical skill and experience. It is not surprising that Wilkinson not only put on Randolph's *The Muse's Looking-Glass* in 1782, but regularly performed Villiers's *The Rehearsal* between 1777 and 1783, Sheridan's *The Critic* between 1781 and 1790, and *The Beggar's Opera* for a longer period than any of these works — 1772–92.

Foote and Wilkinson were not alone in capitalising upon the audience's capacity to apprehend a performance on-stage and be aware of the theatre as theatre at the same time. The most famous play of the period which did this was Sheridan's *The Critic* (1779), still capable of successful production today and well-enough known to not demand comment. But there were a number of other plays which, if they did not go to the lengths that Foote, Wilkinson and Sheridan did, successfully played upon double theatrical illusion. Of these, Arthur Murphy's *The Apprentice* (1756), David Garrick's *A Peep Behind the Curtain* (1767), Isaac Jackman's *All the World's a Stage* (1777) and Frederick Reynolds's *The Dramatist, or Stop Him Who Can!* (1789) are worth at least brief mention. The first three were given their initial productions at Drury Lane and *The Dramatist* at Covent Garden. *The Apprentice* (in two acts) was also performed at Edinburgh and was in Tate Wilkinson's repertoire. It was described recently by Robertson Davies as 'an undistinguished farce',[68] but a preliminary note to the play in one of the early nineteenth-century collections, when the play was still in the repertoire, takes a different view.

It is an ingenious satire on young people who without the requisite talent, lose their time and reputations in attempts on the works of authors who would be unable, in such hands, to recognise their own offspring. After its first performance it induced a great reform; though many stage-struck heroes still 'leave their calling for the idle trade'.[69]

Murphy's biographer, Jesse Foot, says that the sole intention of *The Apprentice* was,

> ... to expose the absurd passion, at that time so prevalent among apprentices and other young people, who, with no talent or education, assembled themselves in bodies, under the title of Spouting Clubs; and all this to the loss and destruction, not only of their time but their reputation. Of these curious meetings he had been a frequent spectator.[70]

It is not a great play and it is to be doubted whether it really effected so sweeping a reform — if it did, it must be one of the few plays directly to change society.[71] It did not prevent Ned Corvan (1830–65), an apprentice sailmaker from Newcastle upon Tyne running off to join the theatre and later writing a music-hall song called 'The Stage-Struck Keelman',[72] nor the ineffable McGonagall attempting to earn his living as tragedian and poet instead of in a Dundee jute mill.[73] Nevertheless, *The Apprentice* is rather better than 'undistinguished' and it dealt with a real enough issue, and one involving not only apprentices:

> All through the eighteenth century, and increasingly in the early nineteenth century, amateur performers had been admitted, not only in provincial companies, but even at Drury Lane and Covent Garden. Early nineteenth-century records of the two great theatres reveal amateur Iagos, Macbeths, Hamlets, Richards. It suited the management for one reason or another — either because the amateurs paid for the privilege, or because they were likely to draw a good house through their honourable connections. The result was often deplorable, as a review by Hazlitt shows in *The Examiner* of October 1st, 1815.[74]

Tate Wilkinson records how, in December 1785, a considerable stir was caused in Hull when 'a gentleman tonsor' called Dixon wished to act with a professional company but was refused permission by the actors. Wilkinson gives as a precedent for Dixon's acting, a London hairdresser who had acted with professionals in October 1756 (the year *The Apprentice* was printed).[75] Inevitably, in a production of this kind, especially if a large number of the amateur's friends were present, the interaction of the theatrical and outside worlds could not but be apparent. Furthermore, in *The Apprentice* there are over seventy patently obvious quotations from a score of plays (six of which are by Shakespeare) as the stage-struck apothecary's apprentice, Dick, prepares himself for the time when the world shall see, posted up in capitals, 'The part of Romeo by a young gentleman, who never appeared on the stage before!'. When Dick is found reading Shakespeare in the dispensary, Wingate, his master, says to his friend Gargle:

> Ay, that damned Shakespeare! I hear the fellow was nothing but a deer-stalker in Warwickshire: Lookers! if they had hanged him out of the way, he would not now be the ruin of honest men's children. But what right had he to read Shakespeare! Wounds! I caught the rascal, myself, reading that nonsensical play of *Hamlet*, where the prince is keeping company with strollers and vagabonds: a fine example, Mr. Gargle![76]

Although failure is not the common meat of farce, Dick has to give up all hope of a stage career and resign himself to becoming an apothecary, for, as he says to his intended, 'we are brought to the last distress'. He reconciles himself to his ordained way of life with the thought that he and his wife will see plays 'and since we don't go on the stage, 'tis some comfort that the world's a stage, and all the men and women merely players'. The thought is hardly surprising, but in its context it does effectively juxtapose real and stage worlds. There is also implicit in the play the suggestion that the realities of the stage life are very different from the world of theatrical make-believe.

Garrick's *A Peep Behind the Curtain, or The New Rehearsal* (one act with an inset burlesque) is slight enough. A fashionable couple arrange to elope under cover of attendance at a rehearsal at Drury Lane. Its interest here is in its carrying on, but in a very mildly satirical manner, the rehearsal formula of the preceding hundred years. Two women are discovered sweeping the stage and then the Prompter and Master Carpenter discuss their problems, drawing the audience's attention to the artifice of theatrical entertainments:

> *Hopkins:* Hark'ye, Saunders? the managers have ordered me to discharge the man at the lightning; he was so drunk the last time he flashed, that he has singed all the clouds on that side the stage. [*Pointing to the clouds*]
>
> *Saunders:* Yes, yes, I see it; and, hark ye? he has burnt a hole in the

new cascade, and set fire to the shower of rain–but mum––
Hopkins: The deuce! he must be discharged directly.[77]

The current vogue for showing clips of rejected film and teleplay-takes
continues this tradition. The Manager, Mr Patent, discusses the idio-
syncracies of actresses and actors and their quarrels about their parts, and
Glib, the author, talks in an excitable, disjointed fashion (a topical parody
presumably) about his play and the fashionable visitors who are coming to
see the rehearsal.

> Patent: ... Will Sir Macaroni be here?
> Glib: Why, he promised, but he's too polite to be punctual — You
>   understand me? ha, ha, ha! — however, I am pretty sure we
>   shall see him — I have a secret for you — not a soul must
>   know it — he has composed two of the songs in my bur-
>   letta — An admirable musician, but particular — He has no
>   great opinion of me, nor indeed of anybody else; a very tolerable
>   one of himself — and so I believe he'll come — You under-
>   stand me — ha, ha, ha!
> Patent: I do, sir — But, pray, Mr. Glib, why did not you complete
>   your burletta — 'tis very new with us to rehearse but one act
>   only?
> Glib: By a sample, Mr. Patent, you may know the piece: if you
>   approve, you shall never want novelty; I am a very spider at
>   spinning my own brains, ha, ha, ha! always at it, spin, spin,
>   spin — you understand me?
>
> (v, 182)

When the 'burletto' is rehearsed (as an inset play), Garrick provides Glib
with no lines but instructs that he *ad lib*:

> *During the burletto, Glib, the author, goes out and comes in several times
> upon the stage, and speaks occasionally to the performers, as his fancy prompts
> him, in order to enliven the action, and give proper comic spirit to the perfor-
> mance* (v, 186)

The play concludes with Glib more concerned that his rehearsal is spoilt
than that a social *blague* has occurred:

> Patent: 'Tis true, Mr. Glib, the young lady is gone off, but with
>   nobody that belongs to us — 'tis a dreadful affair!

Glib: So it is, faith! to spoil my rehearsal — I think it was very ungenteel of her, to choose this morning for her pranks. Though she might make free with her father and mother, she should have more manners than to treat me so; I'll tell her as much when I see her. The second act shall be ready for you next week — I depend upon you for a prologue — your genius —

Patent: You are too polite, Mr. Glib — have you an epilogue?

Glib: I have a kind of address here, by way of epilogue, to the town — I suppose it to be spoken by myself, as author — who have you can represent me? — no easy task, let me tell you — he must be a little smart, dégagée, and not want assurance.

(V, 189)

Jackman's *All the World's a Stage* (a two-act farce), was revived over a period of at least fifty years, being performed at Drury Lane in 1777, 1819 and 1824 and in Edinburgh in 1782. It is concerned with the performance in a private house of *The Beggar's Opera*. There is a rehearsal scene but no performance and perhaps the best moment of the play comes when the stage-struck Steward of the household, instead of attending to the needs of Sir Gilbert and his guests, is found 'kneeling at the foot of the sideboard as if lamenting the death of Statira'. When asked to explain himself he explains as he rises 'I was only striving to cry over Statira!'. The dangers of performing plays in country houses, which were later so to exercise Fanny at Mansfield Park, are only too well demonstrated, for Sir Gilbert's ward marries 'Macheath', though when begging forgiveness for the deception, she promises never to do it again! There is again a warning of the danger of drama, Sir Gilbert telling Charles: 'let her never read a play, or go within the doors of a theatre; if you do, I would not underwrite her'.[78]

The final play of the group was easily the most successful. Reynolds's *The Dramatist*, a five-act comedy, was presented by Tate Wilkinson in 1790, the year after its first production at Covent Garden, and by him at Bath and Wakefield in 1791. It was produced in the early nineteenth century at the Haymarket, Drury Lane, and the Lyceum in 1806, 1818 and 1822 respectively; and in this century at the Bijou in 1903 and the Haymarket in 1927. The play shows a certain Jonsonian influence in its use of type-characters with descriptive names — Ennui, 'whose only business in life is to murder the hour',[79] Lady Waitfor't and Lord Scratch. The love intrigue, which is of no great distinction, is, however, related to a theatrical theme and again might have attracted Jane Austen's attention.

Ennui has found in 'private acting' — private theatricals — a way of killing time. The dramatic theme is centred on Lord Scratch, who cannot bear drama — 'Acting! — never talk to me about the stage — I detest the theatre, and everything that belongs to it' (p. 12) — and Vapid, the dramatist who believes that 'to give a true picture of life, a man should enter all its scenes' (p. 15). The satire of bad drama, false sentiment, and trivial entertainment, which so exercised Jonson and Fielding, has gone and there is now no more than amused affection at the foibles of theatricals. Reynolds does offer some excellent comedy in lines and situations, which doubtless explains the play's long life. Much of this centres on the single-minded dramatist, Vapid. When he is introduced to Lord Scratch, his greeting is the slightly unconventional: 'Very warm tragedy weather, sir!' (p. 23). He has a catch-phrase of the kind popular with the lesser Elizabethan dramatists (such as Master Flower's 'it is a good conceit', reiterated endlessly in *The Fair Maid of the Exchange*, 1602): 'Here's incident', a result of his search for the true picture of life for his dramatic writing. When Marianne asks him: 'Do you really love me, Mr. Vapid?', he replies: 'Hey day! recovered! — here's incident' (p. 62). It is the sort of material a good comedian can use to very great effect for the farcical comedy comes across even on the page. Just as Lord Scratch is about to sign a marriage contract with Lady Waitfor't, and simultaneously to arrange that Louisa shall marry Willoughby against her will — clearly a tense moment of the intrigue — Vapid bursts out of a closet in which he has been communing with his muse, smashing china in all directions, clutching his epilogue and exclaiming excitedly that he's got the last half-line that has so far stumped him:

Vapid:	'Die all! die nobly! die like demi-gods-Huzza, Huzza! 'tis done! 'tis past! 'tis perfect!
Floriville:	Huzza! — the poet at last! 'Stop him who can!'
Lady Waitfor't:	Confusion! .

Of course, Lady Waitfor't's 'Confusion' is the most obvious of clichés, but the structuring of the dramatic moment is perfect, from the reversal of fortune, via the use of the play's sub-title at a crucial moment (something not spurned by Mozart and da Ponte in *Cosi fan Tutte*, 1790), and Lady Waitfor't's cliché, to the farcical outcome. This is the staple of the regular drama and its interest here is that the world of the theatre is presented in the theatre, even if the illusion at this late date is broken only very gently. This is well illustrated by Vapid's response to Marianne's telling him she is to be sent to a convent:

Marianne: Indeed, I can't bear the thoughts of it, — Oh do speak to
            her Mr. Vapid — tell her about the nasty monks, now do, a
            convent! Mercy! What a check to the passions? Oh! I can't
            bear it. [*Weeping*]
Vapid: Gad, here's a sudden touch of tragedy — pray, Lady
            Waitfor't, reflect — you can't send a lady to a convent
            when the theatres are open.

                                                              (p. 61)

There is just a little more here than the theatre's image being kept before
the audience. Although the satirical edge has been blunted, it is noticeable
in this comedy, and in Garrick's farce, that part of the comic effect stems
from such single-minded devotion by Vapid and Glib to the drama that
they have no time for the normal human relationships and emotions of
everyday life.[80] It may be unintentional, and it does not go very deep in
either play, but Garrick and Reynolds do expose something of that
narrowing of emotions which, in the theatre, can go with their too-ready
professional expression.

After Fielding, the Jonsonian inductions and intermeans have been
assimilated and their critical edge dulled. The rehearsal formula is no
longer a vehicle for a sharp political and social satire, but a means of entertaining an audience by offering a sort of insight into an intriguing world
of make-believe, peopled by men and women seemingly larger than life.
At the end of the nineteenth century, Pinero was to offer one worthwhile
drama of the theatre that still holds the stage (*Trelawney of 'The Wells'*,
1898), but in this century, it has been left to the film industry to provide,
usually affectionate, and not always too accurate, representations of the
world of 'show biz'. But these are only remote descendants of a tradition
that started with direct address and the critical induction.

There are, however, three kinds of theatrical entertainment that still
require brief mention: the Shakespearean burlesque, melodrama and
Planché's revues.

The nineteenth century saw a great many burlesques of Shakespeare's
plays, starting with John Poole's *Hamlet Travestie* in 1810 and reaching a
climax and an end, as Stanley Wells puts it, with Gilbert's *Rosencrantz and
Guildenstern* (performed 1891), 'significantly co-incident with the beginnings of musical comedy'.[81] Poole, in fact, was anticipated in a very
interesting way by Arthur Murphy and although his burlesque was never
performed,[82] the reason for its being written, and its content, throw
considerable light on attitudes to theatrical tradition, especially as it
affects Shakespeare. It is also better burlesque than any of the nineteenth
century.

Murphy was much angered by Garrick's adaptation of *Hamlet*, performed at Drury Lane in 1772 (and holding the stage there until 1779). Foot describes how Murphy's veneration for Shakespeare, and his 'close connexion with Dr Johnson', whom he constantly met at Streatham, led to his being 'provoked ... to write a *Parody*, which he called *Hamlet with Alterations*, in three acts' (p. 254). Foot obviously shares Murphy's and Dr Johnson's attitude for he says such 'altered scraps' are predestined to no better purpose than 'as Milton has expressed it ... "to make winding sheets in Lent for pilchards"' (p. 255).

The cast is composed of David Garrick; his brother George, the Assistant Manager; Becket, Garrick's bookseller; Hopkins, the Prompter; and Johnson, the propertyman. Originally Colman was included but Murphy excised his part in revision. Act I is closely modelled on the opening of *Hamlet*. Johnson and Hopkins are sentinels on watch over Drury Lane Theatre, which David Garrick rules as King. The obvious implication is that there is something rotten in the state of Garrick's kingdom. The ghost of Shakespeare enters twice in Act I, but, as in *Hamlet*, does not speak to the sentinels.

In Act II, Garrick has a soliloquy in which he justifies his need to murder Shakespeare's plays and in which he complains of the competition he faces from Samuel Foote's Haymarket Theatre:

> Yet so far hath discretion fought with nature,
> That we think now to alter all his plays.
> O, that that too, too solid house, which Foote
> Has in the Haymarket, would melt at once,
> Thaw, and resolve itself into a dew!
> Or that the Royal Pleasure had not fix'd
> A patent for the summer in his hands!
> Fie on't! O fie! — Foote's an unweeded garden,
> That grows to seed; things rank, and gross in nature,
> Possess him merely ...
>
> (p. 263)

George and Becket tell David Garrick that his favourite, Shakespeare, has appeared and in the final soliloquy to Act II, Garrick reflects:

> The Ghost of Shakespear seen! all is not well.
> There's something rotten in the state o' th' stage:
> Something offends him. Would the time were come!
> Till then sit still, my soul. His Plays will rise,

Though ev'n my pen o'erwhelm them, to men's eyes.
(p. 267)

When Shakespeare's ghost appears to Garrick in Act III, Garrick inevitably cries out 'Ye ministers of Drury Lane defend us!' (p. 268). As in *Hamlet*, the ghost beckons and Garrick follows him as he leaves the stage. When they are alone the ghost addresses Garrick:

> I am Shakespear's Ghost.
> For my foul sins, done in my days of nature
> Doom'd for a certain time to leave my works
> Obscure and uncorrected; to endure
> The ignorance of players; the barbarous hand
> Of Gothic editors; the ponderous weight
> Of leaden commentator; fast confin'd
> In critic fires, till errors, not my own,
> Are done away, and sorely I the while
> Wish'd I had blotted for myself before . . .
>   (p. 270)

He asks Garrick to revenge the 'Murder most foul' of his works (p. 271) and, in a long speech, Shakespeare's ghost complains of what has been done to his plays, especially by Garrick:

> Thus was I, ev'n by thy unhallowed hand,
> Of both my *grave-diggers* at once dispatch'd.
>   (p. 272)

This refers to Garrick's omission of the grave-diggers and what he regarded as coarse humour, probably under the influence of Voltaire's strictures against the 'barbarity' of *Hamlet*: 'Attempt no more, nor let your soul conceive / Aught 'gainst my other plays . . .' (p. 273).

The ghost departs with the coming of morning and Garrick determines he will 'wipe away all trivial modern bards' and ensure that Shakespeare's plays shall be 'Unmix'd with other matter than my own' (p. 273). When his brother and Becket enter, Garrick tells them to advertise in the *St. James's Chronicle*:

> This Ghost is pleas'd with this my alteration,
> And now he bids me alter all his Plays.
> His plays are out of joint; — *O cursed spite!*

That ever I was born to set them right.

(p. 274)

Murphy's burlesque is lively, well written and has real critical bite. It could stand performance today, requiring only the change of Garrick's name and the up-dating of the specific changes that Garrick made. Murphy would doubtless not haunt a modern adapter of his burlesque provided he shared his concern for the integrity of Shakespeare's drama!

An audience at Murphy's burlesque would be conscious not only of Shakespeare's original, but of the particular production to which exception had been taken. Thus there would be three planes of theatrical illusion: Garrick's confrontation with the ghost of Shakespeare; Shakespeare's original; and Garrick's adaptation. In contrast, the Victorian burlesques might be said *just* to break dramatic illusion but they lack critical purpose.[83] Their chief significance in the context of this study is that they were performed in theatres presenting 'straight' drama and also in those offering illegitimate drama (for example, as part of minstrel shows). In this way the Victorian burlesques of Shakespeare provided a slight link between the two traditions at a time when they were becoming increasingly separated.

Melodrama would seem a natural subject for burlesque but there would appear to have been relatively few attempts to guy this genre, bearing in mind its enormous popularity. V. C. Clinton-Baddeley suggests that possibly the 'melodrama was too popular, at that time, to be held up to full-length ridicule' although certain aspects of melodrama — the ghost, for example — 'were evidently burlesqued at a very early date'.[84] It could be argued that burlesques of *Richard III* filled the gap, but there is probably more to be investigated here.

The characteristic of melodrama that requires mention is the element of audience participation which was often a part of performances and which can still be experienced, if somewhat falsely stimulated. The hisses and boos directed at the villain, often encouraged by the villain himself through his asides to the audience, break the dramatic illusion. However, the performer's engaging directly with the audience may well have provoked deeper involvement in the production as a whole, as in the music-hall tradition.

Finally, Planché — a most interesting man of the theatre. Ernest Reynolds, writing nearly fifty years ago, remarked

> Planché is clearly a figure of some importance, and deserves to be better known. He is important because he set himself out to improve the wretched state of 'illegitimate' comedy in the middle of the century.[85]

Planché, who was of Huguenot descent, was a prolific writer for the stage and also something of a scholar. He wrote on the history of costume and was, from June 1866, Somerset Herald. Among his works are five volumes of extravaganzas, two of which repay attention here.[86] The term 'extravaganza' belies their name, as Ernest Reynolds noted: 'Their whole purpose was to tone down the extravagance of the contemporary burlesque.' Planché wrote frequently for Madame Vestris and she, with Charles Mathews, 'set a new standard of refinement and moderation in staging and acting', which played a part in preparing the way for the revolutionary work of Tom Robertson (whom Pinero celebrates in *Trelawney of 'The Wells'*), in his 'Caste' plays, for example, *Society* (1865), *Ours* (1866), *Caste* itself (1867), *Play* (1868), *Home* (1869), *Birth* (1870) and *War* (1871).[87]

Both extravaganzas present 'the theatre in review — or revue'. Planché had been writing revues, as he called them, since 1825, the first being given at the Adelphi. He was required to produce not only a special Christmas show, but also one for Easter. *The Drama's Levée; or, A Peep at the Past* was presented at the Royal Olympic Theatre on Easter Monday, 16 April 1838, and *The Drama at Home; or, An Evening with Puff* at the Theatre Royal, Haymarket, on Easter Monday, 8 April 1844, following the passing of the act ending the theatre monopoly. *The Drama's Levée* has this opening stage direction: *The stage represents the British stage in a deplorable condition. The Drama is discovered in a languishing state upon it, surrounded by the different Theatres* (vol.II, p.11). The 'characters' include the Drama, described as being 'in a critical state of health'; Legitimate Drama and Illegitimate Drama, her sons, 'on the worst possible terms with each other'; Praise and Censure, 'Old friends of the Drama, but rather differing in opinion'; Fancy, 'a well-intentioned busybody'; and the Green Coat Man. There is a noise off-stage:

Drama:	Hark! Them, again! — that worse than O. P. riot;[88]
	Why don't they let the Drama die in quiet?
	So, part those children; bid them both appear!
	Enter Legitimate Drama in a Roman Toga
Leg. Drama:	He whom they own Legitimate is here!
Drama:	You naughty boy! When I'm so poorly;
	You have been fighting with your brother, surely.[89]

Of course, the rhymes are too pat, but the idea of an audience being shown in a play the wretched state of the drama in this manner continues Fielding's technique, but now applied solely to the stage. In Planché there is no social or political satire (but that will return over a hundred years later with Osborne in *The Entertainer*). Illegitimate Drama enters 'in a dress half harlequin and half melo-dramatic', and the ensuing dialogue and song take place:

> *Ill. Drama*:   Behold! (*striking an attitude*)
> *Drama*:   Unnatural son!
> *Ill. Drama*:   Is't thus I'm styled?
>   I always thought I was your *natural* child.
> *Leg. Drama*:   He puns! He'll pick a pocket the next minute![90]
> *Ill. Drama*:   I shan't pick yours because there's nothing in it!
> *Leg. Drama*:   That's because you robb'd me long ago!

After a few more interchanges of this kind, they sing a short duet:

> *Leg. Drama*:   You mimicking fool, do you hope with the town
>   Your trumpery shows will go longer down?
> *Ill. Drama*:   D'ye think they ever would come you to see,
>   If it wasn't for show that you take from me?
> *Leg. Drama*:   Tawdry elf!
> *Ill. Drama*:   Go look to yourself!
>   You've laid till you're mouldy on the shelf.
> *Leg. Drama*:   You lay out in gingerbread all your pelf.
>   (*They attack each other — THEATRES take different sides*)
> *Drama*:   Hence both and each who either cause expouse!
>   You'll drive me mad! A plague on *all* your houses!
>   (*drives them all out*)
>   Unless between themselves they soon agree,
>   These boys, I feel, will be the death of me!
>
>   (II, 12–13)

Legitimate Drama and Illegitimate Drama do not appear again, but the Drama is conducted round the theatres by Censure and Praise 'to see a novelty or two'. There then follows a series of excerpts in which the Theatres present what they are doing. These include Moncrieff's adaptation of *The Pickwick Papers* at the Strand Theatre (*Sam Weller; or, The Pickwickians*, June 1837); *The Magic Flute*, first performed in England at Drury Lane, 10 March 1838; Serle's *Joan of Arc* (1837), a two-act play given at Covent Garden; Balfe's opera, *Joan of Arc*, first presented at Drury Lane, 30 November 1837; and Scribe and Auber's comic opera, *Le Domino Noir*, first performed in Paris in 1837 and in Drury Lane some years after *The Drama's Levée* (in 1846). The Drama also visits a theatre presenting illegitimate drama in Wych Street. The following dialogue ensues:

> *Drama*: What do they play there? Farces, I suppose.
> *Praise*: Burlettas only.
> *Drama*: What on earth are those?
> *Censure*: Nobody ever knew that I could find.
> *Praise*: I wish you'd just look in.
> *Drama*: I've half a mind.
>   Will you go with us?   [*to Censure*]
> *Censure*: To be sure I will.
>
> (II, 23)

Planché adds a footnote to Censure's inability to define burletta: 'I have already commented upon the absurd regulations respecting the performances at the minor theatres'. In fact, as he himself explained, after much controversy, 'burletta' was defined as a drama containing not less than five pieces of music in each act.[91]

In his memoirs, Planché recalls that *The Drama at Home* was written as a result of the ending in 1843 of 'The monopoly of the legitimate drama by the great houses, and the limitation of the season of the minors ... free trade in theatricals was established by law.' Thus, he says, the Drama (again a character in the revue) did not need to emigrate.[92] The Puff of the subtitle also appears in the revue and there is a direct allusion to Sheridan's Mr Puff of *The Critic*, in which Charles Mathews had had a great success (p. 270). The Drama is again depicted *in extremis*: 'The Drama, like a dog, has had her day' she says, and she concludes her first speech with:

> Othello's occupation's gone indeed!
> Oh, Fate! I'll lay me down at once and die!
> (II, 276)

Puff enters, cries 'Die? — nonsense!' and there is a series of tableaux of current productions with interspersed comments by Puff and the Drama. Thus Puff:

> ... who cares for acting now-a-days! The public want startling effects, madam, not fine language or natural acting; 'good worts, good cabbage', as Falstaff says.[93] Get your effects, madam, no matter how, but get them, and the faster the better. (II, 283)

Puff's philistinism is also shown in his response to Shakespeare. After a statue of Shakespeare has cried out, with reference to Worrell's Richard III at Drury Lane, 'Awake! Beware of fibbers! That Richard's none of mine — 'Tis Colley Cibber's!!' (i.e. the 1700 adaptation), Puff responds to The Drama's reaction with:

> Rot that Shakespeare, he always speaks the truth!
> I wonder what the devil they stuck him up there for.
>
> (II, 280)

He maintains that *William Tell* draws more than William Shakespeare and a tableau from the former is presented, with music. The Drama is forced to murmur 'Well, that is very sweet, I must admit' (p. 280). Spectacle, Shakespeare, opera and ballet are reviewed. After a ballet-leap in imitation of one by Carlotta Grisi (from *The Peri*, 1843), Puff calls out:

> Brava, Bravissima. Dancing has charms to soothe the savage breast!
>
> *Drama*: 'Music' in the original text.
>
> *Puff*:   Congreve's — but he knew nothing of dancing. Had he lived in these days he would have changed his tune, or written, 'Ballet-music hath charms'. Music is making great strides I allow, but dancing jumps over everything — clears a fortune at a bound — *exempli gratia*.
>
> (II, 281)

Delight in presenting the theatre in the theatre never quite died out. After the success of his sweetened version of *The Beggar's Opera* (1920), Nigel Playfair produced in 1927 a version of George Lillo's *The London Merchant* (1730), set in a frame provided by a dramatisation of extracts from *Nicholas Nickleby*. The play was advertised as 'acted by Mr Vincent Crummles's company'. The prologue, 'arranged from Dickens', included, for example, 'Miss Ninetta Crummles — Hermione Baddeley' and 'Master Crummles — Ernest Thesiger'. The cast list for *The London Merchant* then showed 'George Barnwell — Master Crummles' and 'Maria — Miss Ninetta Crummles'. The play was followed by 'The Harlequinade' (and Columbine was Miss Ninetta Crummles) and 'The Epilogue', spoken by Miriam Lewes, Nadine March and Ernest Thesiger '*in propriâ personâ*'.[94]

In 1948, Terence Rattigan's farce *Harlequinade* was produced with a distinguished cast (including Eric Portman, Mary Ellis and Marie Löhr).

This shows how the past catches up with an ageing theatrical family touring *Romeo and Juliet* round the less well-favoured provincial towns. The play makes pleasant fun of theatricals (and it is still a favourite with amateur companies) and ends with much the same device as Davenant's *The Play-house to be Let*. Arthur Gosport, the leader of the company, has been trying to get the lighting right and is also anxiously attempting to place a pot in just the right place. The rehearsal has almost run into the time when the evening performance is due to begin:

Jack: ... take it down more, Will. And try those thunder and lightning cues 2, 3, and 4.
           [*The lights suddenly go out*]
           My God! They've fused.
           [*Summer lightning is now playing fitfully on the scene*]
Arthur: [*calling*] House lights. House lights.
           [*The house lights go up. Mr Burton rushes on*]
Burton: [*in a frantic voice*] Take those lights out! It's seven thirty. There's an audience in front. Look!
           [*He points. A row of startled faces gaze at the now visible audience, and then they scatter in panic to the wings. The house lights go out. There's a moment's black-out, disturbed by summer lightning and a roll of thunder. Then the stage lights come on again, revealing an empty stage. Arthur comes on slowly, carrying his pot*]
Jack: [*off, whispering frantically*] Mr Gosport! Mr Gosport! The audience is in front.
           [*He beckons him to the wings. Other faces and other beckoning figures appear, but Arthur is oblivious. He walks slowly round the pot, then dissatisfied with its appearance, picks it up once more and walks slowly out to the strains of the overture*]
           THE CURTAIN FALLS[95]

Planché's *The Drama at Home* is not *The Critic* or *The Rehearsal*, and he is not a Fielding or a Jonson, but he does have a strong sense of purpose and the belief in the value of a worthwhile theatre.[96] There is a critical sense in these two revues and the audience of each had theatre as theatre brought before them. Ironically, the ending of the legal distinction between legitimate and illegitimate, though it allowed a 'free trade in theatricals', could not ensure good drama, and it hardened as never before the distinction between these two forms. Although it was early days, Planché's The Drama in *The Drama at Home* expresses disappointment after the wonders that Puff has displayed: 'I see no rising drama worth the name, / And now the law is scarcely to blame'. But public taste could not be raised by Act of Parliament, even though Parliament must share the blame for lowering it. Just as Richard II could shorten Gaunt's days but not a minute give, Parliament could destroy but not create drama. Then, a series of events coincidentally occurring — the establishment of music halls, the new consciousness of realism in the theatre, the darkened auditorium, and the new seriousness of the drama with their middle-class audiences — conspired together, unwittingly, to ensure that hardly had the theatres been freed but, in a sense, the drama shackled itself for the better part of a century. In one kind of theatre there would be direct address to the audience (music hall); in another very formal overheard drama, so that even Shakespeare became fashioned, so far as it was practicable, as overheard drama. The same theatre buildings could, from 1843 onwards, house either form, and audiences were able to respond to each form, but the forms themselves were separated to a degree that not even the closing of the theatres in 1642, or the Licensing Act of 1737, had been able to achieve.[97] Planché's *The Drama at Home*, therefore, comes at the tail-end of a tradition in which complex theatrical illusion was *de règle*, or at least, a commonplace.[98]

It might well have been that, with the coming of realism, and the attempt by the theatre to rival the photograph and the film in the simulation of actuality, that the capacity of the English audience for multiconscious apprehension would have been lost. The increasing separation of the legitimate and illegitimate dramas, despite what Planché called the 'free trade in theatricals', could well have led to a permanent loss to theatre far greater than the manifold gains brought by realism. That the theatre has not lost its capacity to arouse wonder, its power of sheer theatricality, nor its audiences their ability to respond to direct address and to 'overhear' in the same act, is largely due to music hall.[99] When serious English drama once again made its appeal direct to the audience, adopting the techniques of Pirandello and Brecht, the two traditions of direct address, native and Continental, came into conflict. It is these developments and their effects on contemporary drama that form the subject of *Contemporary Drama and the Popular Dramatic Tradition in England*.

Appendix I: A Chronological List of Plays and Acts Discussed

As some of the plays and acts discussed are not well known, a chronological list might prove a useful reference guide. It should be noted that not every play can be precisely dated and acts, though recorded at a specific time, were repeated over many years. They have therefore been related to decades rather than years.

c. 1300	*Dux Moraud*
1435–50	*Shepherds' Plays*
	Mactatio Abel
1450	*Play of the Sacrament*
1490–1520	*The Three Kings of Cologne* (Welsh)
1497	Medwall: *Fulgens and Lucres*
1538	Bale: *King John*
1539	Redford: *The Marriage of Wit and Science*
1550	*A Nice Wanton*
1552	Udall: *Ralph Roister Doister*
1553	*Respublica*
1554	Udall or Hunnis(?): *Jacob and Esau*
1559	Wager: *The Longer Thou Livest*
1561	Preston: *Cambises*
1587	Marlowe: *Tamburlaine*, Part 1
1588	Porter: *The Two Angry Women of Abingdon*
1590	Kyd: *The Spanish Tragedy*
1591	Shakespeare: *Richard III*
1592	Marlowe: *Dr Faustus*
	A Knack to Know a Knave
1593	Shakespeare: *The Two Gentlemen of Verona*
1594	*Titus Andronicus*
1595	*Love's Labours Lost*
	Richard II
1596	*The Merchant of Venice*
1597	*1 Henry IV*

1598	*Much Ado About Nothing*
1599	*Henry V*
	As You Like It
	Jonson: *Every Man Out of His Humour*
1601	Shakespeare: *Hamlet*
	Jonson: *Cynthia's Revels*
1602	Shakespeare: *Troilus and Cressida*
	The Fair Maid of the Exchange
	Chapman: *The Gentleman Usher*
1603	Jonson: *The Satyr*
1604	Shakespeare: *Othello*
	Chapman: *All Fools*
	Marston: *The Malcontent*
1606	Jonson: *Hymenaei*
	The Barriers
1607	Shakespeare: *Antony and Cleopatra*
	Beaumont: *The Knight of the Burning Pestle*
1608	Jonson: *The Hue and Cry after Cupid*
	Armin: *The Two Maids of Moreclack*
1609	Shakespeare: *Cymbeline*
1611	Jonson: *The Masque of Oberon*
1612	*Love Restored*
1613	Shakespeare: *Henry VIII*
	Jonson: *The Irish Masque*
	A Challenge at Tilt
1614	*Bartholomew Fair*
1616	*The Masque of Christmas*
1618	*Pleasure Reconciled to Virtue*
	For the Honour of Wales
1621	*The Masque of Augurs*
1622	Middleton and Rowley: *The Changeling*
1623	Jonson: *Time Vindicated*
1624	*Neptune's Triumph*
1626	Randolph: *Aristippus*
	Massinger: *The Roman Actor*
1627	Randolph: *Hey for Honesty!*
	The Conceited Pedlar
1629/30	*The Muse's Looking-Glass* (printed: 1638, 1640, 1643, 1652, 1664, 1668, 1706, Dodsley — 1744)
1630	*Amyntas*

1632	Jonson: *The Magnetic Lady*
1633	Ford: *'Tis Pity She's a Whore*
	Marmion: *A Fine Companion*
1634	Shirley: *The Triumph of Peace*
1635	Ford: *The Fancies Chaste and Noble*
1637	Jonson: *The Sad Shepherd*
	Brome: *The Antipodes*
1642	THEATRES CLOSED
1655	Quinault: *La comédie sans comédie* (in Paris)
1658	Davenant: *The Cruelty of the Spaniards in Peru*
1659	Davenant: *The History of Sir Francis Drake*
1660	THEATRES RE-OPENED. Davenant and Killigrew form the two Patent Companies, the King's and Duke of York's.
(1662	Butler: *Hudibras*, part 1)
1663	Davenant: *The Play-House to be Let*
(1664–5	Cotton: *Scarronides*)
1671	Villiers: *The Rehearsal*
1674	Duffett: *The Mock Tempest*
1676	Wycherley: *The Plain Dealer*
1700	Congreve: *The Way of the World*
1708	Estcourt: *Prunella* (interlude in *The Rehearsal*)
1711	Settle: *The City Ramble* (adaption of *Knight of the Burning Pestle*)
(1712–14	Pope: *The Rape of the Lock*)
1715	Gay: *The What d'ye Call It*
1721	D'Urfey: *The Two Queens of Brentford*
1724	*The British Stage*
1727	*The English Stage Italianized*
1728	Gay: *The Beggar's Opera*
	(Pope: *The Dunciad*, Books 1–3)
1729	Odingsells: *Bayes' Opera*
1730	Fielding: *The Author's Farce*
	Tom Thumb
1731	Fielding: *The Welsh Opera* (*The Grub Street Opera*)
1732	*The Covent Garden Tragedy*
1734	*Don Quixote in England*
	The Universal Gallant
1735	*An Old Man Taught Wisdom*
	Dodsley: *The Toy Shop* (adapted from *The Conceited Pedlar*)
1736	Fielding: *Pasquin*
	Tumble-Down Dick

1737	*The Historical Register*
	Eurydice
	Eurydice Hissed
	THE STAGE LICENSING ACT
1747	Foote: *Diversions of the Morning*
1747 and	
1748	Randolph's *The Muse's Looking Glass* revived
1756	Murphy: *The Apprentice*
1757	Foote: *The Author*
1758	*Diversions of the Morning* revised
1759	Garrick: *The Guardian*
1760	Colman: *Polly Honeycombe*
1764	Foote: *The Orators*
1767	Garrick: *A Peep Behind the Curtain*
1768	Foote: *The Devil upon Two Sticks*
1770	*The Lame Lover*
1772	Murphy: *Hamlet with Alterations*
1777	Jackman: *All the World's a Stage*
1779	Sheridan: *The Critic*
1787	O'Keeffe: *The Farmer*
1789	Reynolds: *The Dramatist*
1810	Poole: *Hamlet Travestie*
1814	Dibdin Jnr: *The Farmer's Wife*
1834	Planché: *The Red Mask*
1838	*The Drama's Levée*
1843	THEATRE REGULATION ACT ending the Patent Theatre Monopoly
1844	Planché: *The Drama at Home*
(1859	Darwin: *On the Origin of Species*)
Mid-late nineteenth-century	Minstrel shows
1863	*A Thin Slice of Ham let* [*sic*]
1866	*Hamlet! The Ravin' Prince of Denmark!!*
1882	A. C. Hilton: *Hamlet, or, Not Such a Fool as He Looks*
1932	Shaw: *Too True to be Good*
1930s and 1940s: Flanagan and Allen	
	Murgatroyd and Winterbottom
c. 1940	'The Proposal' (Askey and Murdoch)
1940s	*ITMA*
1948	Rattigan: *Harlequinade*

Appendix II: Recordings of Music-Hall Performances Quoted

A detailed consideration of the part played by music hall in the development of contemporary drama is given in *Contemporary Drama and the Popular Dramatic Tradition*. A much fuller discography is therefore given in that volume as Appendix II. The short list printed here gives details of acts to which reference is made in this volume.

Arthur Askey and Richard Murdoch: 'The Proposal' — recorded before an audience of soldiers about 1940; HMV C3173 (78 rpm); re-recorded by the BBC, 138M, *50 Years of Radio Comedy*, 1972.

Murgatroyd and Winterbottom: (Tommy Handley and Gilbert Frankau): 'About Cruises'; Parlophone A6585 (78 rpm).

Flanagan and Allen: 'Digging H"OI"les'; Columbia DO1479 (78 rpm).

Notes

Journal titles have been abbreviated as follows throughout the notes:

ELH	*Journal of English Literary History*
JEGP	*Journal of English and Germanic Philology*
MLN	*Modern Language Notes*
MLQ	*Modern Language Quarterly*
MP	*Modern Philology*
PMLA	*Publications of the Modern Language Association*
PQ	*Philological Quarterly*
SB	*Studies in Bibliography*
SP	*Studies in Philology*
SQ	*Shakespeare Quarterly*

NOTES TO THE PREFACE

1. *Songs of the British Music Hall . . . a Critical History of the Songs and their Times*, written in 1965 and published in 1971. The references to the problems of producing Brecht's work in England are on pp. 234-5.
2. 'The Theme and Structure of *The Roman Actor*', Aumla, 19 (1962) 39–56. I disagree, therefore, with Anne Righter that in *The Roman Actor* Massinger takes 'delight in playing with illusion for its own sake, confusing art with life' (*Shakespeare and the Idea of the Play*, p. 205).
3. Compare Anne Righter: 'Harried by Parliament, urged by her counsellors to execute Mary of Scotland without further delay, Queen Elizabeth tartly reminded her advisors that princes, like actors, stand upon a stage in the sight of all the world' (*Shakespeare and the Idea of the Play*, p. 113; no reference is given).
4. See, for example, Una Ellis-Fermor, *The Jacobean Drama*, ch. XI, p. 202 and *passim*; quoted in P. H. Davison, 'The Serious Concerns of *Philaster*', *ELH*, 30 (1963) 1–15.
5. *George a Greene, The Pinner of Wakefield*, possibly by Robert Greene, *c*. 1592, scene vii. See also P. H. Davison, 'La Dramaturgie en Angleterre à la veille de la Guerre Civile: John Ford et la comédie', *Dramaturgie et Société*, ed. Jean Jacquot, vol.II, p.806.

Mais Beaumont et Fletcher eux-mêmes, dans l'intervention du villageois dans *Philaster* par example, peuvent faire un usage sérieux de cet héritage dramatique.

Il me semble que c'est ce moyen d'expression dramatique que Ford développe dans *The Fancies Chaste and Noble*. Cependent il ne se contente pas de juxtaposer le comique et le non-comique, il essaie de faire quelque chose de plus subtil: il cherche à produire une interaction entre diverses sortes de comique.

6. See particularly, Olive Mary Busby, *Studies in the Development of the Fool in the Elizabethan Drama*; Leonard Dean, '*Richard II*: the State and the Image of the Theater', *PMLA*, 67 (1952) 211–18; Doris Fenton, *The Extra-Dramatic Moment in Elizabethan Plays before 1616*; Robert J. Nelson, *Play within Play: the Dramatist's Conception of his Art: Shakespeare to Anouilh*; Anne Righter, *Shakespeare and the Idea of the Play*; Thelma N. Greenfield, *The Induction in Elizabethan Drama*; J. A. B. Somerset, 'The Comic Turn in English Drama to 1616', unpublished Ph. D. thesis (University of Birmingham, 1966), part of which is distilled in '"Fair is foul and foul is fair"': Vice-Comedy's Development and Theatrical Effects', *The Elizabethan Theatre*, vol. v, ed. G. Hibbard (Waterloo, 1975) pp. 54–75; and Robert Weimann's splendid study, *Shakespeare and the Popular Tradition in the Theater: Studies in the Social Dimension of Dramatic Form and Function*, ed. Robert Schwartz (1978; originally published in German in a somewhat different version in 1967). The most important influence on this book has been S.L. Bethell's *Shakespeare and the Popular Dramatic Tradition*. Bethell's principle of multiconscious response — the ability of an audience in Elizabethan times and in popular drama (e.g. music hall) 'to respond spontaneously and unconsciously on more than one plane of attention at the same time' (p. 29) — has proved particularly stimulating. I have referred to it in earlier work and it underlies much that is said in this book and in *Contemporary Drama and the Popular Dramatic Tradition in England*. It has recently been reprinted in vol. 8 of *Literary Taste, Culture, and Mass Communication: Theater and Song*, ed. Peter Davison, Rolf Meyersohn and Edward Shils (Cambridge, 1978).

NOTES TO CHAPTER ONE: INTRODUCTION

1. For a brief discussion, see P. H. Davison, 'Popular Literature', *Encyclopaedia Britannica*, 15th edn vol. xx, pp. 804–7.

2. 'Epilogue to the Actor' (1913); reprinted in *An Anthology of German Expressionist Drama*, ed. Walter H. Sokel, pp. 6-8. Kornfeld advises the actor 'not to be ashamed of the fact that he is acting' (p. 7).

3. See Bertolt Brecht, 'Alienation Effects in Chinese Acting', in *Brecht on Theatre*, trans. by John Willett, pp. 91-9.

4. Bram Stoker, *Personal Reminiscences of Henry Irving*, p. 180.

5. See his *Shakespeare and the Popular Dramatic Tradition*, esp. p. 28. See also my 'Contemporary Drama and Popular Dramatic Forms', pp. 157-8, and certain reservations suggested to me discussed in *Contemporary Drama and the Popular Dramatic Tradition*. Louis James has pointed out to me James Grant's *Sketches in London* (1838), in a shortened version in *Theatre Quarterly*, no. 4 (1971) p. 17:

> The dramatis personae of the Penny Theatres keep up, in most cases, a very close intimacy with the audience. In many instances they carry on a sort of conversation with them during the representations of the different pieces. It is no uncommon thing to see an actor stop in the middle of some very interesting scene to answer some question asked by one of the audience, or to parry any attempted witticism at his expense. This done, the actor resumes his part of the performance as if nothing had happened; but possibly before he has delivered half a dozen sentences more, some other question is asked, or some other sarcastic observation made by one of the auditory, in which case the performer again stops to answer or retort, as if by way of parenthesis. A cross fire is thus sometimes kept up between audience and actors for several minutes at a time.

Guido Almansi amusingly discusses the way a television actor can make a 'non-linguistic commentary upon the linguistic message' by appealing directly to the audience 'through the camera' (as did Daneman in Richard III in the BBC series *The Age of Kings*), in his inaugural lecture 'The Mysterious Case of the Abominable Tongue-in-Cheek', University of East Anglia, 28 October 1976 (unpaginated).

6. The picture, one half of a diptych dated 1498, is to be seen in Bruges Museum. It is illustrated and briefly described in *Flemish Painting from the Van Eycks to Metsys*, by Leo van Puyvelde (1968; English trans., 1970) plate xxxiv and p. 209. Although Sisamnes' 'skin' looks very like a cloak, it is worth mentioning that the first part of the diptych, showing Sisamnes' arrest, also uses *décor simultané*. In the background

we can see Sisamnes accepting the bribe that led to his arrest.

7. Peter Burke, for example, gives as an instance of cultural flow the withdrawal of the upper classes from the theatres in early seventeenth-century England and the establishment of private theatres with higher prices. The public theatres, he says, 'where Shakespeare had been played to noblemen and apprentices alike, were no longer good enough for the upper classes' (*Popular Culture in Early Modern Europe*, p. 277). Though there is something in this, the distinction is exaggerated by the modern interpretation of 'public' and 'private' which seems sometimes to be implied. According to seventeenth-century usage, the nationally-financed theatres of London would be 'private' whereas Regent's Park Open Air Theatre might be said to be 'public' — at least, when rain has not driven the audience into the marquee. Robert Weimann is surely right in suggesting that although Alfred Harbage (in *Shakespeare and the Rival Traditions*) draws a useful 'general border between public and private theater' it results in a 'somewhat uncritical approach to the poetic and dramatic achievements of both'. Their co-existence, he argues, 'fostered that extremely effective balance between dramatic enchantment and disenchantment ... in the varying forms of the popular theater'. Weimann suggests that a much more fruitful approach to the relationship of 'ritual' and 'realism' 'would emphasize the continuing interplay between embodiment and representation rather than the replacement of one at the expense of the other' (*Shakespeare and the Popular Tradition*, pp. 247–9). Ann Jennalie Cook has recently argued that English Renaissance drama was performed primarily before privileged people rather than plebeians (see *The Privileged Playgoers: Shakespearean Theater Audiences* [Princeton, N. J., 1981]).

8. According to Andrew Sarris in *Interviews with Film Directors*, *Sullivan's Travels* is a 'Swiftian glimpse at Hollywood' with 'occasional flirtations with social consciousness' (p. 513). For further examples of 'The Idea of the Film' see *Contemporary Drama and the Popular Dramatic Tradition*.

9. Published in a slightly shortened form in *Times Literary Supplement*, 21 January 1977, pp. 77–81.

10. The separation of the classes has not always been dictated by the more affluent. Peter Burke records that in 'sixteenth-century Sienna, plays were written by members of a club called the "Rustics" (*Rozzi*), from which people of high status were formally excluded' (*Popular Culture in Early Modern Europe*, p. 102).

11. Quoted in *An Actor's Handbook*, ed. E. R. Hopgood, p. 40.

NOTES TO CHAPTER TWO: THE MEDIEVAL TRADITION

1. *Popular Culture in Early Modern Europe*, pp. 22–3, referring to Robert Redfield, *Peasant Society and Culture*, pp. 41–2. Burke's modification is on p. 28.
2. See Burke, pp. 29 and 58. He gives interesting examples of direction of cultural flow on pp. 59–62 (but see p. 173, note 7). His reference to the mediating effect of the chapbook is on p. 63. The reference to midcult is from *Against the American Grain* (New York, 1972) pp. 34 ff. Compare also Keith Thomas on laughter, p. 10 above.
3. *English Mystery Plays*, p. 245.
4. *Transactions of the Connecticut Academy of Arts and Sciences*, vol. 14 (March 1910) 291–414; see especially pp. 305–12.
5. Jacques de Vitry, *Exampla, or Illustrative Stories from the Sermones Vulgares*, ed. T. F. Crane (1890) pp. lxviii–lxix. The quotation from *The Divine Comedy* is from 'Paradise' (29, 115–17.)
6. G. K. Hunter, *John Lyly: the Humanist as Courtier*, p. 138. What I am stressing should not be misinterpreted as a denial of those other influential sources of medieval drama, from *Quem Quaeritis* to the tournament; see especially Glynne Wickham, *Early English Stages 1300–1660*, vol.i,pp. 13–50. Olive Mary Busby argues in *Studies in the Development of the Fool in the Elizabethan Drama* that although there are very few traces of Fool Societies in England (about the only exception being the prohibition in 1348 of 'a certain disreputable society known as the "Order of Brothelyngham"'), 'it seems possible that the influence of the Feast of Fools upon the English clown operated largely through the "sociétés joyeuses" of France' (p. 16). A feature of the mock services of the Feast of Fools in France, which 'later played a prominent part in the performances of Fool Societies' was the 'sermons joyeux' which parodied the religious sermon and the rhetorical disquisition of the schools. She describes the sermons as 'ridiculous medleys of mock-pious exhortations, learned allusions and scurrility, full of dog-Latin and religious tags' and points to 'but two examples in the English [*sic*] drama': Folly's description of various classes of fools at the end of Lindsay's *A Satire of the Three Estaits* (1540), and the discourse of Herod's fool in Nicholas Grimald's *Archipropheta*, a Latin play of 1547. This is 'based nominally on the opening verses of Genesis, but in reality [consists] of a disquisition on folly and satire of society, particularly women' (p. 15). She stresses that 'foreign influence must not be exaggerated . . . there was a purely native influence at work in the development of

the stage fool' (p. 18). It may be, therefore, that such mock sermons had some slight influence in the development of comic 'dialogue' within the monologue.

7. *A Study of Three Welsh Religious Plays*, p. 67.
8. Jones, p. 147, ll.215–26. The scene shifts back immediately to Herod and his Queen.
9. Norman Davis, *Non-Cycle Plays and Fragments*; see also Richard Axton, 'Popular Modes in the Earliest Plays', *Medieval Drama* (1973) esp. pp. 32–5.
10. J. M. Manly, *Specimens of the Pre-Shakespearean Drama*, vol.I,p. 243.
11. *English Moral Interludes*, p. 108. David L. Jeffrey likens this Prologue to Gower's in *Pericles* (1608). He suggests that the frame served to answer those critical of the use of the Bible for dramatic purposes, hence the author's care to point out that his play is 'as the bybull sayeth' ('English Saints' Plays', *Medieval Drama* (1973) pp. 73–4).
12. W. A. Armstrong (ed.), *Elizabethan History Plays*, p. 37.
13. Quoted by Anne Righter, *Shakespeare and the Idea of the Play*, p. 209, fn 27; David Bevington (ed.), *The Macro Plays*, l. 551. Bevington suggests the more precise date of 1460–3 (p. vii).
14. Manly, vol.I, p.37, l.183.
15. *The Tudor Interlude: Stage, Costume, and Acting*, pp. 24–5.
16. Richard Axton argues persuasively that a solo performer could hardly bring off *Dame Sirith*. He would in any case need a dog. The entertainment (as he calls it) opens with a first person narrator, though he, unlike the Dux Moraud, disappears, leaving the characters to speak for themselves ('Popular Modes in the Earliest Plays', *Medieval Drama* (1973) pp. 16–19). See also p. 180, n. 19.
17. Steven C. Young suggests that 'the most important influence in the structure and setting of the frame in all European drama may be found in the Bible. The *Book of Job* displays a frame-like structure in its prologue in heaven between God and Satan, and in God's speech to Job at the end of the book' (*The Frame Structure in Tudor and Stuart Drama*, p. 9).
18. pp. xix–xx. Edmund Creeth agrees in his edition, *Tudor Plays: an Anthology of Tudor Drama*, p. xvi, as does Glynne Wickham in his *English Moral Interludes*, p. 37. Creeth points out that 'A glimpse into Morton's household about the time of these festivities may be had in the opening pages of More's *Utopia*' (p. xvi, fn 9). I have quoted from Wickham's modernised text though with an eye on Creeth's old-spelling edition.
19. J. M. McDowell, 'Tudor Court Staging: a Study in Perspective',

JEGP, 44 (1945) 199. He deduces from *Gorboduc* (1562) 'the probability that the raised stage was established early in Elizabeth's reign' (p. 200). He does not refer to *Fulgens and Lucres*.

20. pp. xvi–xvii, particularly the reference to the lawsuit brought against him after Morton's death.

21. Boas and Reed, p. xxii; Thelma N. Greenfield, *The Induction in Elizabethan Drama*, pp. 3–4; Wickham's comment, in *English Moral Interludes*, p. 39. Wickham's students performed *Fulgens and Lucres* in Bristol University's Reception Room in 1964 in conditions which simulated those of 1497, so that he judges with the knowledge of practical experience.

22. 'The Tudor Interlude and Later Elizabethan Drama', *Elizabethan Theatre*, p. 37.

23. 'Popular and Courtly Traditions on the Early Tudor Stage', *Medieval Drama*, p. 100.

24. *Shakespeare and the Idea of the Play*, p. 38.

25. David Bevington remarks 'Medwall was, after all, in touch with the popular forms of drama, as were the humanist writers generally' ('Popular and Courtly Traditions', *Medieval Drama*, p. 99).

26. As Glynne Wickham puts it, II.665–70 disposes of 'the claims of birth and inherited wealth at a stroke, substituting natural ability and personal achievement as the only criteria for respect and promotion' (*English Moral Interludes*, p. 38).

27. Creeth, p. 538, n 4.

28. Creeth, pp. xii–xiii. On p. xiv Creeth reports Reed's suggestion that the Senate is omitted because of the difficulty of presenting it in session with only a few actors. There is no basis for this suggestion. The decision could easily have been reported.

29. Wickham suggests that they use broom and mop as spears and that Joan, when she helps them arm, dresses them up with 'saucepans as helmets, the lids as shields and dish-cloths as slings or harnesses for the lances' (*English Moral Interludes*, 1165 fn). This is in the manner of Ambidexter's armour in *Cambises* (1561), where the stage direction reads: 'Enter [Ambidexter] *the Vice*, with an olde capcase on his hed, an olde pail about his hips for harnes, a scummer and a potlid by his side, and a rake on his shoulder' (Creeth, *Tudor Plays*, pp. 455–6). In *Early English Stages 1300-1660*, Wickham describes the origin and practice of Running at Quintain and he calls it a popular imitation of the knightly tournament (vol.I,pp. 38–41). However, in *Fulgens and Lucres* something more fundamental is indicated by the expression, jousting 'at fart-prick-in-cule'. No shield seems to be called for

because as the joust is described in the play, one contestant charges his doubled-over opponent with a staff gripped between the upper arm and body, the hands being tied behind the back.

The joke of kitchen-utensil armour lasted well. Thomas Nashe in *The Unfortunate Traveller* (1594) has the Anabaptists following John of Leiden armed in chamber-pots and dripping-pans [*The Works of Thomas Nashe*, ed. R. B. McKerrow (1904–10; Oxford, 1958) vol.II,pp. 232–3].

NOTES TO CHAPTER THREE: SHAKESPEARE AND THE COMICS

1. The phrase is taken from Arthur Brown's 'The Play within a Play: an Elizabethan Dramatic Device', *Essays and Studies*, n.s. 13 (1960) 37. Brown is discussing the paradox of removing 'the main action one stage further from actuality in order to stress a deeper reality, a purpose which often seems to lie behind the introduction of a play within a play'. Compare also, Norman Sanders's account of Greene's *James the Fourth* in which the audience is 'simultaneously distanced from and brought closer to the world of the play' ('The Comedy of Greene and Shakespeare', *Early Shakespeare* (1961) p. 51).

2. Compare the dispute in *Fulgens and Lucres* as to who failed to keep time (see p. 31 above).

3. Dover Wilson in the New Cambridge edition (1926) argues that 'Touchstone is not criticising the setting but the rendering'. Agnes Latham in the New Arden edition (1975) glosses 'the note was very untuneable' as 'I think it sounded very disagreeable', with no implication that the boys sang out of tune. The music is by Thomas Morley and exists in manuscript and in his *First Book of Ayres* (1600). A comparison of the versions in William Chappell, *Popular Music of the Olden Time* (1859) vol.I,p. 205, and *Classical Songs for Children*, ed. Countess of Harewood and Ronald Duncan (London, 1964) pp. 16–18, is instructive.

4. For a discussion of Ford's experiment, see P. H. Davison, 'La Dramaturgie en Angleterre à la veille de la Guerre Civile: John Ford et la comédie', *Dramaturgie et Société*, vol.II,pp. 805–14.

5. These could take the form of 'etc.', and she lists 26 plays with this indication (p. 19, fn 28), or such charming directions as '*Enter Forester, missing the other taken away, speak anything, and exit*' (*The Trial of Chivalry*), or '*Iockie is led to whipping ouer the stage, speaking some wordes, but of no importance*' (Heywood's *Edward IV*), quoted on p. 17. Sir Walter Greg considered that about a quarter of some two

or three thousand plays produced between 1558 and 1642 had survived (his edition of *Henslowe's Diary*, vol.II,p. 146). Over two hundred plays with extra-dramatic moments represent, therefore, upwards of 30 per cent of the plays extant.

6. For example, she lists an instance from Marston's *The Dutch Courtesan* in III.i of Halliwell's edition of Marston's *Works* (p. 155), but does not discuss the curious use of empty brackets at IV.i.65 and IV.iv.17; nor the parentheses enclosing only a dash (–) at IV.vii.57 to indicate the omission of an obvious rhyme word. Fredson Bowers, in his edition of *Patient Grissil* (1600; *The Dramatic Works of Thomas Dekker*, vol.I,p. 292), suggests that such brackets indicate stage business — he proposes an indecent movement of the legs — and J. A. B. Somerset has suggested in his Ph. D. thesis that the omitted word at IV.vii.57 is to be called out by the audience. See also note to IV.i.65 in my edition of *The Dutch Courtesan* (Edinburgh, 1968) p. 101.

7. See Introduction to the Johnson Reprint Company facsimile (New York and London, 1972), ed. J. P. Feather. Enid Welsford remarks scathingly of *Tarlton's Jests* that it is 'of the conventional jest-book type, full of unreliable anecdotes, and dull jests, and gives us little idea of the famous clown, in spite of the fact that the author seems to have been acquainted with the leading facts of his hero's life' (*The Fool*, p. 287).

8. It can conveniently be read in the New Penguin edition of *2 Henry IV*, ed. P. H. Davison (Harmondsworth, 1977) p. 20. Jonson suggests a similar breaking of the illusion, probably with Armin, when Drugger asks 'did you neuer see me play the foole?' in *The Alchemist* (IV.vii.69).

9. The Queen's Players were Queen Elizabeth's Men. Richard Tarlton is included amongst twelve named actors recorded in the city records. For a suggestion as to how Armin developed Tarlton's theming in the form of his *Quips upon Questions* (1600), and his use of Tarlton's 'jest of a Gridiron', see my 'Henry V in the Context of the Popular Dramatic Tradition', *Contexts and Connexions* (Winchester, 1981). The motto of Metro–Goldwyn–Mayer was *Ars gratia artis*.

10. I am indebted to Malcolm Evans who drew this to my attention and kindly obtained a photocopy of the original for me. Notice the reference to the Vice as late as the 1630s. The reading 'newe' is doubtful but may refer to Richard Kendall, wardrobe keeper at Salisbury Court Theatre, taking on a role at short notice. An account of this Kendall is given by G. E. Bentley in *Jacobean and Caroline Stage*,

vol.II, p.491. He toured in 1634–5, visiting Oxford and Norwich, and 'no doubt he was drafted for minor roles'.

11. I am indebted to Dr James Binns for this information.

12. *Hamlet, The First Quarto*, ed. Albert B. Weiner (Great Neck, 1962) pp. 121–2, ll.21–36. The passage is erroneously set as verse in Q1, F2$^{r/v}$. If Q2 is based on Shakespeare's foul papers — his final draft before the fair copy was produced — and F reflects the finished version and an authorised performance, and as neither contains this passage, it is unlikely that it was written by Shakespeare. The manuscript underlying Q2 antecedes Q1, and the manuscript underlying F was written later than Q1, so far as we can ascertain. As recently as 1978, however, Maurice Charney in *Comedy High and Low*, warned 'we shouldn't automatically equate [Hamlet's] special views about clowns with Shakespeare' (p. 46). On p. 19 he does equate Jaques with a jakes, incidentally. See also K. M. Lea, *Italian Popular Comedy*, vol.II,pp. 385–7. Roy W. Battenhouse presents a strong case that Hamlet's advice is not Shakespeare's, but he is not specifically concerned with the advice to the clowns ('The Significance of Hamlet's Advice to the Players', *The Drama of the Renaissance*, ed. E. M. Blistein (Providence, 1970) pp. 3–26.

13. *The Shakespeare Apocrypha*, ed. C. F. Tucker Brooke, I,72–90.

14. There is no evidence that Armin played Lear's Fool, but apart from the fact that the role seems to have been peculiarly suited to him, there is a puzzling line in Armin's *Nest of Ninnies* that has not been satisfactorily explained but which might suggest his relationship with that part. *A Nest of Ninnies* is an modified version of *Fool upon Fool* (1600 and 1605). The printing history and the relationship of the editions is well described by H. F. Lippincott in his *A Shakespeare Jestbook: Robert Armin's 'Foole upon Foole' (1600)*, pp. 33–9. In the 1608 edition, beginning after the verse on G3^v, there appears the sentence 'Ther are as Hamlet sayes thinges cald whips in store'. Lippincott's note reads:

> As Collier comments, there is no such line in *Ham*. Perhaps Armin is recalling 'Use every man after his desert, and who shall 'scape whipping?' (2.2.534) and conflating it (as he does with fused proverbs) with 'For who would bear the whips and scorns of time?' (3.1.70). Tilney-Bassett (p. 52) sees the passage 'as a reference to not a quotation from the play'. (p. 147)

It is, one supposes, unlikely that if Armin played Lear's Fool he would confuse *Hamlet* and *King Lear*, though even someone with as proverbially good a memory as an Elizabethan (and an actor to boot) could presumably be confused. However, did he, one wonders, have in mind the line addressed to him in *King Lear* at I.iv.123: 'Take heed, sirrah; the whip'? Or is Armin recalling a line *ad libbed* in *Hamlet*? So much were his clowns in his mind when he wrote for them that Shakespeare sometimes used their own names, instead of those of the characters they were to play, in his drafts. Thus Kempe and Cowley stand for Dogberry and Verges in *Much Ado About Nothing* (Q1) derived from Shakespeare's foul papers.

15. See Sir Walter Greg, *Marlowe's 'Doctor Faustus': 1604-1616*, and Fredson Bowers, 'Marlowe's *Doctor Faustus*: the 1602 Additions', *SB*, 26 (1973) 1–18. Bowers is concerned with additions to the B Text. The passages discussed here are added to the A Text. Although A is a much abridged text, the 'farcical scenes that are preserved tend to be expanded' in what Greg describes as 'vulgar elaboration' (pp. 35–6). Leo Kirschbaum drew the parallel between the *ad libbing* and Hamlet's advice to the players and in particular to the extended version in *Hamlet*, Q1 ('The Good and Bad Quartos of *Doctor Faustus*', *The Library*, IV, 26 (1946) 272–94).

16. *The Adventures of Arthur Roberts by Rail, Road and River* told by himself and chronicled by Richard Morton (Bristol, 1895) pp. 72–5.

17. The joke may depend upon a topical allusion to a particular person's barren inheritance or there might be a relationship, now lost to us, between 'stavesacre' (delphinium seeds used to kill personal vermin) and 'knavesacre', where the plant knavery might grow. Knavery is Bog Asphodel; it grew on marshy ground and as it was considered harmful to sheep, it made the ground on which it grew valueless.

18. The words 'leave your jesting' in B are erroneously placed earlier in A (at line 385). This is a clue to how A originated but it does not affect the matter of *ad libbing*.

19. 'Performing dogs scarcely figure in a modern notion of legitimate drama, but they were a standard feature of medieval entertainments and the "gleeman's bitch" was a proverbial phrase to Langland. An improvised diversion caused by a weeping dog is described in the eleventh-century romance *Ruodlieb*, a work liberally sprinkled with set-pieces, culled from the repertoire of the Spielleute or play-folk. ... (That the tradition survived into Shakespeare's time is suggested by the character of Launce in *The Two Gentlemen of Verona*, with a name that suggests something of his bawdy humour as go-between as he woos for his master Proteus, equipped with an "understanding staff" and a dog that will not weep)' — quoted from 'Popular Modes

in the Earliest Plays', *Medieval Drama*, p. 18.) Nevertheless, there have been some remarkable performing dogs in productions of Shakespeare at Stratford-upon-Avon and Birmingham in recent years. Most remarkable in my experience was the dog who participated ('performed' might be misconstrued) in a full version of Mendelssohn's music to *A Midsummer Night's Dream*, with actors speaking the lines. This took place in Birmingham Town Hall as part of the celebrations which marked Britain's entry into the Common Market and that dog is my liveliest memory of that occasion. Robert Weimann discusses the popular tradition and *The Two Gentlemen of Verona*, in *Shakespeare and the Popular Tradition*, pp. 253–60.

20. The minstrel examples come from *The Witmark Amateur Minstrel Guide* (1899) by Frank Dumont of Dumont's Minstrels, which performed for many seasons at Eleventh Street Opera House, Philadelphia, from about 1888. Dumont was the author of successful burlesques presented in New York and San Francisco as well as Philadelphia. He was also a member of the first minstrel troupe to cross America to play in San Francisco. On the way the company was attacked by Indians and its comedian, Hughey Dougherty, was 'reported killed and scalped' (pp. 3–5).

21. See for a play upon 'hair/air' in a particularly absurdist context, their act 'Digging H"OI"les', Columbia record DO1479 (78 rpm), part of which is reproduced in P. H. Davison, 'Contemporary Drama and Popular Dramatic Forms', *Aspects of Drama and the Theatre*, p. 171.

22. See *The Wakefield Mystery Plays*, ed. A. C. Cawley (Manchester, 1958) for the full text.

23. See especially v.iii.90–111.

24. Revised edition (1962) pp. 35–6.

25. *Jacob and Esau*, ed. John Crow and F. P. Wilson (Oxford, 1956) ll. 644–55. The pattern continues for a further eight lines.

26. *The ITMA Years* (London, 1974) pp. 93–4; script by Ted Kavanagh.

27. K. M. Lea, *Italian Popular Comedy*, vol.I, pp. 108–9.

28. Adapted slightly from *Wit and Science*. A complete text will be found in J. M. Manly, *Specimens of the Pre-Shakespearean Drama*, vol.I, pp. 436–9 (ll.452–94). Idleness maintains he is 'playing the schoolmistress' (l.450) so this is probably what would now be termed a drag part. The act can easily be further adapted, with actions, for a contemporary pantomime audience.

29. Harry Tate's car has broken down; the wheels won't go round; the diameter of a wheel depends upon π; π is 22 over 7; 7 won't go into 22; therefore the wheels won't go and neither will the car . . . and so

on. This act can also still be made to — 'go'. It is one of many which delight in number play and similar routines are to be found in legitimate drama in Strindberg's *Dream Play* and Ionesco's *The Lesson*. Some of Tate's act is printed in P. H. Davison, *Contemporary Drama and the Popular Dramatic Tradition*.

30. Recorded about 1940 on HMV C3173; recently re-issued as part of *50 Years of Radio Comedy*, BBC, rec. 138M (1972). Hugh Lloyd and Terry Scott rehearsed an act to defeat a proposal of marriage (by John Laurie to Scott's 'mother') in their television show, *Hugh and I*, 3 January 1965.

31. See the Regents edition (with *The Longer Thou Livest*), ed. R. Mark Benbow (London, 1968) ll.305–53. *The Longer Thou Livest* is of course, much taken up with 'teaching the fool'.

32. Reprinted in *Shakespeare Criticism, 1935-1960*, ed. Anne Ridler, p. 100. For the use of the 'con-' prefix in *Henny V*, see Adrian Colman, *The Dramatic Use of Bawdy in Shakespeare*, pp. 105-6.

33. Anne Righter, *Shakespeare and the Idea of the Play*, p. 21.

34. See, for example, suggestions for the use of steps at the side of the stage in J. W. Saunders, 'Staging at the Globe 1599–1613', *SQ*, 11 (1960) 401–25.

35. Simon Forman (1552–1611) gives accounts of his attendance at three of Shakespeare's plays: *Macbeth*, *The Winter's Tale* (15 May 1611) and *Cymbeline*, in a manuscript entitled, 'The Bocke of plaies and Notes herof . . .'.

36. After Q1 of *Mucedorus* appeared in 1598, there were at least sixteen further editions of the play in the seventeenth century, fourteen being published before the theatres were closed in 1642. There are a number of references to its performance and there can be little doubt that it was a 'popular' success. Shakespeare's using a similar incident cannot have escaped notice. The play was, on occasion, attributed to him and it is included in *The Shakespeare Apocrypha*, ed. C. F. Tucker Brooke. In his introduction, Brooke mentions performances of *Mucedorus* given by strolling players after the theatres had been officially closed in London as late as 1652 (p. xxv). *Mucedorus* was revived by Shakespeare's company at Court and the Globe just prior to the production of *The Winter's Tale*. Jonson's *Oberon*, which just precedes *The Winter's Tale*, also features bears — see the reference to its 'fighting beare' (p. 105).

37. It is with this quotation that James Brown begins his essay 'Eight Types of Puns', *PMLA*, 71 (1956) 14–26. The quotation comes from the *Spectator*, 61.

38. 'Eight Types of Puns', p. 16. fn 4.
39. These and other burlesques are reprinted in *Nineteenth-Century Shakespeare Burlesques*, ed. Stanley Wells, with M. E. Kimberley, vol.IV.
40. *The Sad Shepherd* (1637) I.vi.9–13. Some editions (e.g. the Everyman) italicise *One* and *want-*ed in the manner used in printing nineteenth-century burlesques. In their Commentary, the editors quote Dyce's comparison with Lodge's *Rosalynde* (1590), B2: 'Women are *wantons*, and yet men cannot *want one*' (X, 372; italicisation as in Lodge).
41. Bede, *Historical Works*, Loeb Classical Library, trans. J. E. King (London and Cambridge, Mass., 1930) vol.I,pp. 201 and 203. The pun on Deira reads in Latin 'Deiri, de ira eruti, et ad misericordiam Christi vocati' (vol.I,pp. 200 and 202).
42. 'Chaucer's Pun', *PMLA*, 71 (1956) 225–46. Vinsauf is quoted on p. 225. See also a further article by Baum on the same subject, *PMLA*, 73 (1958).
43. See also Brown, 'Eight Types of Puns', pp. 16–17, and Edward Le Comte, *A Dictionary of Puns in Milton's English Poetry* (London, 1981).
44. *The Yale Edition of the Works of Samuel Johnson*, vol.VII: *Johnson on Shakespeare*, ed. Arthur Sherbo, p. 74. Maurice Morgann splendidly demonstrates how Shakespeare converts 'base things into excellence' through the 'miserable pun' in 'For if the Jew do but cut deep enough, / I'll pay the forfeiture with all my heart', in *Merchant of Venice*, IV.i.278–9 (*Shakespearian Criticism*, ed. D. A. Fineman, p. 185).
45. 'Popular Fallacies, ix: That the Worst Puns are the Best', *New Monthly Magazine*, January 1826 (reprinted in *The Works of Charles and Mary Lamb*, ed. E. V. Lucas, vol.II,p. 258).
46. 'A Proposal for Correcting the English Tongue', *Polite Conversation, Etc.*, ed. Herbert Davis with Louis Landa, pp. 263–4. The 'coffin' joke is still a commonplace: 'It's not the cough that carries you off but the coffin they carries you off in'.
47. J. Brown, 'Eight Types of Puns', p. 15.
48. *The Dunciad*, B, IV, 247n. Nevertheless, the poem has many brilliant puns.
49. 'Diction of Common Life', p. 101.
50. *Ambiguity in Greek Literature*, p. 35.
51. Ibid, p. 38.
52. *Agamemnon* l.688, ed. A. W. Verrall (1889). Though some authorities amend the manuscript reading to the Attic form, Verrall argues

that 'the exceptional form could hardly be avoided, if the point was to be made at all' (p. 85).

53. In the *Mabinogion*, for example, Lleu Llaw Gyffes gains his name in a very significant manner and his story is told against a strongly onomastic setting which accounts for many of the place names of Wales. His name means 'the fair one with the deft hand' — he was fair-haired and could break the leg of a wren by hurling a stone at it. The greatest living Welsh-language dramatist, Saunders Lewis, deliberately changes 'Lleu' to 'Llew' (meaning 'lion') so distorting the myth and its significance [see *Presenting Saunders Lewis*, ed. Alun R. Jones and George Thomas (Cardiff, 1973) p. 201]. With unwitting irony the editors explain: 'Llew is also the Welsh for *lion*' — as well, that is, as being part of Llew Llaw Gyffes's name, as Lewis has it — 'This ambiguity is fairly extensively used in [the Welsh of] the play: all this has been lost in the translation' (p. 200). What has been lost, of course, should never have been there in the first place. Kipling's use of names needs no explanation.

54. The source of this example escapes me, I'm afraid.

55. T. S. Eliot, *The Complete Poems and Plays, 1909-1950*, p. 122.

56. Gwennan Jones, *A Study of Three Welsh Religious Plays*, p. 6.

57. According to Sir John Harington in his *A Supplie or Addicion to the Catalogue of Bishops to the Yeare 1608*, ed. R. H. Miller, Dr Toby Mathew, Archbishop of York, confessed that his predilection for puns was 'a recreation of his wearied spirits, after more painful and serious studies'. Harington compares this punning to the bending of a bow the contrary way so that thereby it might 'cast the better in his right bent' (p. 179). Contrast Benjamin Franklin's resolve to break his habit of punning in a programme of *moral* improvement (*Autobiography*, ch. 6).

NOTES TO CHAPTER FOUR: JONSON AND HIS CONTEMPORARIES

1. '*Cambises*', ed. Edmund Creeth, *Tudor Plays*, ll.142–57. See also Ambidexter's own account of the wicked judge, Sisamnes, in which he is said to have 'plaid with bothe hands, but he sped il favouredly' (l.606). Sisamnes' death by flaying (see above, p. 7) is described by Ambidexter with malicious humour:

> *Executioner*: Come, M[aster] Sisamnes, come on your way, my office I must pay.
> Forgive therfore my deed.
> *Sisamnes*: I doo forgive it thee, my freend. Dispatch therefore

	with speed.
	Smite him in the neck with a swoord to signify his death.
Praxaspes:	Beholde (O king) how he dooth bleed, being of life bereft.
Cambises:	In this wise he shall not yet be left.
	Pul his skin over his eares to make his death more vile.
	A wretch he was, a cruel theef, my Commons to begile.
	Flea him with a false skin.
Otian:	What childe is he of natures mould could bide the same to see,
	His father fleaed in this wise? Oh, how it greeveth me!
Cambises:	Otian, thou seest thy father dead, and thou art in his roume.
	If thou beest proud, as he hath been, even therto shalt thou come.
Otian:	O king, to me this is a glasse, with greefe in it I view
	Example that unto your Grace I doo not prove untrue.

(ll.458–70)

Unlike David's picture, Sisamnes is skinned when dead but in both works the lesson of his wickedness is brought home to the son, Otian.

2. '"Fair is foul and foul is fair": Vice-Comedy's Development and Theatrical Effects', pp. 64–5 and 67.

3. See *1 Henry IV*, II.iv.460–6 and introduction to New Penguin edition (1969), ed. P. H. Davison, pp. 33–4.

4. The prayer rhymes 'quenes' with 'things' so there is no doubt that the original rhyme-word was 'kings'. The play was printed in 1560, in Elizabeth's reign, but must have been written in the reign of Edward VI, who died in 1553.

5. The tradition has not wholly died out. A similar pattern is adapted for the end of a London Living Newspaper production, *Busmen* (1938). This was presented at the Unity Theatre so naturally there is no prayer for the monarch! Instead, at the end of a direct exhortation to the audience, they join in singing 'Daisy'.

6. See John Feather's introduction to the play in his edition of Armin's *Collected Works*, vol. 2.

7. Christ's Hospital, or the Blue Coat School, hence the reference to 'a

blew-coat boy with him', C3^r. On the title-page a figure, presumably Armin as John, can be seen wearing the School's long blue coat, still worn, with yellow wool stockings, on occasion to this day.

8. *The Complete Works of Christopher Marlowe*, ed. Fredson Bowers (Cambridge, 1973) vol.I,p. 77.

9. Ed. Matthew W. Black (Philadelphia, 1966) II.i.52–62.

10. *The Changeling* is one of a number of plays which show, if slightly, knowledge of *commedia dell'arte*. As Miss Lea has pointed out, Lollio likens the crazy Antonio to a Magnifico. Of plays mentioned here, *As You Like It, Volpone, The Dutch Courtesan, Othello, The Taming of the Shrew*, and *Every Man Out of His Humour* are but a few of the plays that refer to *commedia* characters. For the relationship of *commedia* to the English stage, see K. M. Lea, *Italian Popular Comedy*, especially vol.2, pp. 350 ff. The technique of continuous asides was used for many years in comedy of intrigue. This example succinctly shows its use by David Garrick in *The Guardian* (1759):

> [*Enter a servant*]
>
> Mr Heartly: Carry this letter —
> [*An action escapes from Harriet, as if to hinder the sending of the letter.*]
> Is it not for Mr Clackit?
>
> Harriet: [*peevishly*] Who can it be for?
>
> Mr Heartly: [*to the servant*] Here, take this letter to Mr Clackit [*Gives a letter*]   [*Exit servant*]
>
> Harriet: [*aside*] What a terrible situation!
>
> Mr Heartly: [*aside*] I am thunderstruck!
>
> Harriet: [*aside*] I cannot speak another word!
>
> Mr Heartly: [*aside*] My prudence fails me!
>
> Harriet: [*aside*] He disapproves my passion, and I shall die with confusion!
> [*Enter Lucy*]
>
> Lucy: [*aside*] The conversation is over, and I may appear. Sir Charles is without, sir, and is impatient to know your determination. May he be permitted to see you?
>
> Mr Heartly: [*aside*] I must retire to conceal my weakness   [*Exit*]
>
> Lucy: Upon my word, this is very whimsical! — What is the reason, miss, that your guardian is gone away without giving me an answer?
>
> Harriet: What a contempt he must have for me, to behave in this manner!   [*Exit*]

> *Lucy:*   Extremely well this, and equally foolish on both sides!
> But what can be the meaning of it?

Just as it is uncertain whether a soliloquy is being directly addressed to the audience (see p. 3 above), it may also not be clear whether an aside to an audience is intended — Harriet's last speech is an example. In *Titus Andronicus*, when Demetrius and Chiron quarrel (II.i), Aaron has a line, 'Clubs! clubs! these lovers will not keep the peace' (1.37). Most editors do not mark this as an aside (though the 1895 Temple edition does, for example). 'Clubs! clubs!' is a conventional rallying cry for London apprentices (and this effectively places Demetrius and Chiron), but if 'these lovers will not keep the peace' is directly addressed to the audience, as I believe, it modifies the scene, still further stressing the absurdity of these two men 'braving' one another. Robert Weimann comments interestingly on the aside in *Shakespeare and the Popular Tradition*, pp. 224 ff.

11. See the Regents edition edited R. Mark Benbow.
12. *'Tis Pity She's a Whore* (1633), ed. N. W. Bawcutt (London, 1966) III.vii.8–13, 18–20 and 30–4.
13. *Henslowe's Diary*, ed. R. A. Foakes and R. T. Rickert (Cambridge, 1961). On 22 December 1598, £5.00 was paid by Henslowe for the second part of the play and a further £2.00 on 12 February following. On 31 January £9.00 was put on taffeta for two women's gowns for the play and on 12 February £2.00 for 'divers thinges' for the play (pp. 102, 104–5). The edition of the *Two Angry Women of Abingdon* referred to is that in Havelock Ellis (ed.), *Nero and Other Plays* (London, 1888).
14. The induction to *The Malcontent*, written by Webster, is not included in Marston's four. The summary appears as Appendix 2, pp. 161–6.
15. Quotations are from *The Dramatic Works in the Beaumont and Fletcher Canon*, ed. Fredson Bowers (Cambridge, 1966) vol.I. This play was edited by Cyrus Hoy.
16. The lines are based on Hotspur's in *1 Henry IV*, I.iii.201–5.
17. The direct influence of performances of Beaumont's and Randolph's plays in the Restoration period is mentioned below, pp. 89–90, 110–11, 120–4.
18. See her *The Induction in Elizabethan Drama*, esp. pp. 67–9 and 79. She suggests, for example, that the induction to *Cynthia's Revels* was 'doubtless modeled on the Prologue's speech in *Poenulus* by Plautus' (p. 69).

19. There is more in common between the inductions of Marston and Jonson than is, perhaps, implied here, and one can see that Webster, when he writes an induction for Marston's *The Malcontent*, picking up Jonson's request that he be censured 'Where I want arte' as Asper puts it in *Every Man Out of His Humour* (Grex, 60–1), and relating it to the price paid for admission. Thus Webster, in 1604, has Sly say 'any man that hath wit, may Censure (if he sit in the twelve-penny room)'. Ten years later, Jonson, in the contract with the audience that precedes *Bartholomew Fair*, agrees that 'It shall bee lawfull for any man to iudge his six pen'orth, his twelue pen'orth, so to his eighteene pence, 2. shillings, halfe a crowne, to the value of his place' (*Ind.*, ll.87–90). In 1632, in *The Magnetic Lady*, he is still harping on the same idea. Damplay says, 'I see no reason, if I come here, and give my eighteene pence, or two shillings for my Seat, but I should take it out in censure, on the Stage', with which the Boy agrees, but points out: 'but you will take your ten shilling worth, your twenty shilling worth, and more: And teach others (about you) to doe the like ...' (*Chorus* after Act II,ll.59–65). Within *The Magnetic Lady* itself, incidentally — that is, not in the induction or intermeans — Jonson refers directly to himself: 'No,' says Compass, 'a great Clarke / As any'is of his bulke (*Ben: Jonson*) made it' (I.ii.33–4).

20. *Elizabethan Theatre*, see esp. pp. 229–41.

21. 'Beyond Psychology: the Moral Basis of Jonson's Theory of Humor Characterization', *ELH*, 28 (1961) 316–34. The passage quoted is from p. 330.

22. Thelma Greenfield notes that in the 'much slighter and simpler' induction to Thomas Heywood's *The Four Prentices of London* (1592–*c*. 1600), made up of three prologues, 'The combination of dramatic distance and the obvious direct and immediate application, each one belying the other, add wit and complexity to the statement of the pattern', and she refers to S. L. Bethell's description of a boy actor playing a girl disguised as a boy, as in *As You Like It* (*The Induction in Elizabethan Drama* p. 74).

23. *The Jonsonian Masque*, p. 92.

24. Davenant wrote five masques prior to 1642: *The Temple of Love* (1635), *The Triumphs of the Prince d'Amour* (1636), *Britannia Triumphans*, *Luminalia* (1638), and *Salmacida Spolia* (1640). It is the last of these that is particularly important, in part because it was the last masque to be performed to the Court before the Civil War broke out. It has been badly misinterpreted as being isolated from the troubles brewing, despite H. A. Evans's early comment, 'the

troubles of the times are not obscurely hinted at, and the murmur of the approaching storm is plainly audible in the midst of all the mirth' (*English Masques*, p. 229). For the astonishing significance it had with respect to the political events of the time, and especially the approaching Civil War, see the introduction to this masque in T. J. B. Spencer (ed.), *A Book of Masques*.

25. A useful account of the masque in performance, the significance of the audience, and the role of the author, is given by Stanley Wells in *Literature and Drama with Special Reference to Shakespeare and his Contemporaries*, ch. 3 'The Intent and the Event', pp. 56–84.

26. *Selected Masques of Ben Jonson*, p. 13.

27. *England's Joy* was announced as an historical drama which would be performed on 6 November 1602 by gentlemen and gentlewomen amateurs. Queen Elizabeth was England's Joy. Richard Vennar(d), who promoted the entertainment, disappeared with most of the takings (entry being 1*s*. 6*d*. or 2*s*. 0*d*.). He was arrested but the Justice treated the affair relatively lightly. The hoax is frequently referred to in the literature of the time and Jonson also mentions it in the *Masque of Augurs*: the tavern-keeper and the two barmaids are referred to as 'three of those Gentlewomen that should have acted in that famous matter of *Englands joy* in sixe hundred and three' (*sic*) ll.122–4 (E. K. Chambers, *The Elizabethan Stage*, vol.III,pp. 500–3). An account of this exploit and of Richard Vennar(d) is to be found in 'The Vanishing Act', in *Elizabeth's Misfits* by Arthur Freeman (New York and London, 1978) pp. 145–67.

28. To us, the most famous example of Anglo-Welsh in Elizabethan drama is Fluellen's in *Henry V*. Despite the fun made of his accent, it is worth noting that Shakespeare not only shows him as a worthy gentleman and fine soldier, but putting down the braggart, Pistol. There is much use of comic Welsh in *The Valiant Welshman* (1612), performed by the Prince of Wales's Servants and printed in 1615. According to Clarence's *Cyclopaedia* it was also performed in 1663 and 1727, but 1663 is probably an error for 1613. John Feather attributes the play to Robert Armin and in his introduction points to the way 'many of the elements of Jacobean popular drama' are combined with its classical source, Tacitus (*The Collected Works of Robert Armin*, vol.II). Thus, the setting of popular dialect comedy in the King's Banqueting Hall has a precedent of sorts. *The Valiant Welshman* is, incidentally, one of the plays listed by Thelma Green-field as having an Occasional Induction. The Chorus is presented by a 'Bardh'. Keith Thomas, in his Neale Lecture (1976) says that 'the

comic Welshman reached his peak of popularity about 1620, to be duly superseded as a butt by other denizens of the Celtic fringe' (*Times Literary Supplement*, 21 January 1977, p. 77).

29. *The Jonsonian Masque*, pp. 71–2.

30. John Brand, *Observations on Popular Antiquities*, with additions by Sir Henry Ellis, p. 247. The Bearward's annual payment is said to be twenty shillings (quoting Pennant's *Zoology*, 1776).

31. Brand's *Popular Antiquities*, pp. 245–6. This summarises accounts of disguisings for Prince Richard in 1377 and the plot to kill Henry IV during a disguising recorded in Hall's *Union of the Two Noble Families* (London, 1550) B4ʳ. The device of a murder during a masque was to prove very popular with Jacobean dramatists.

32. *A Challenge at Tilt, The Irish Masque, The Masque of Christmas, For the Honour of Wales, News from the New World in the Moon* (1620), which includes a printer who says he would 'give anything for a good copy now, be it true or false, so it be news', *The Masque of Augurs, Time Vindicated* and *Neptune's Triumph for the Return of Albion*.

33. The masque was 'A magnificent formal gesture' of loyalty to Charles I, according to Clifford Leech (ed.) of *The Triumph of Peace* in Spencer's *A Book of Masques*, p. 277. The gesture followed the imprisonment of Prynne, 'an Vtter Barrester of Lincolnes Inne', for his *Histriomastix* (1632). References are to Leech's edition.

34. The feather-maker's wife is sure her husband sold the masquers most of their feathers. Webster's induction to *The Malcontent* also refers to the trade in feathers in the neighbourhood of Blackfriars and the use of feathers by actors. Harvey Wood's edition notes (p. 238) that the play also refers to feathers in v.ii. Jonson specifically relates the feather-makers to Puritans in *The Alchemist*, Doll saying that 'not a puritane in black–*friers*, will trust [Face] / So much, as for a feather!' (I.i.128–9). One of the two Puritans in Randolph's *The Muse's Looking-Glass* is a featherman, who, though he abhors the stage, makes his money by selling the actors his wares, as Roscius points out:

> . . . you, sweet feather-man, whose ware, though light,
> O'er weighs your conscience, what serves your trade.   (I.ii).

35. Sir Laurence Olivier's 'Trouble with the Scenery' in *The Critic* — or more properly, in Puff's play, *The Spanish Armada* — is illustrated in V. C. Clinton-Baddeley, *The Burlesque Tradition in the English Theatre after 1660*, facing p. 76.

36. See Stephen Orgel's introduction to *The Complete Masques of Ben*

Jonson, and his and Roy Strong's *Inigo Jones: the Theatre of the Stuart Court*.

37. *Jonson: The Complete Poems*, ed. Ian Donaldson, pp. 321–2, ll.25–30, 39–52. Donaldson notes that the partnership between Jonson and Jones was 'more deeply harmonious than Jonson's satire allows' (fn 41).

38. *English Masques*, pp. l-li. The border of the scene — virtually a proscenium arch — is illustrated in Spencer's *A Book of Masques*, plate 15. See also, Glynne Wickham, *Early English Stages, 1300–1660*, vol. 2, pt. I, esp. the frontispiece for the backcloth for *Luminalia* (1638). *A Book of Masques* also illustrates the stage designs for *Salmacida Spolia*; see esp. the ground plan and section of the stage and scenery (plates 20–1), which anticipate the arrangements for the next two centuries.

39. Inigo Jones's designs for the Forum of Peace are illustrated as plates 16 and 17 in *A Book of Masques*. Costumes and head-dresses are illustrated on plates 18 and 19. The design for seating the masquers is reproduced as plate 18b.

NOTES TO CHAPTER FIVE: THE MUSE'S LOOKING-GLASS

1. Introduction to his *Burlesque Plays of the Eighteenth Century*, p. vii.
2. Arthur Colby Sprague, *Beaumont and Fletcher on the Restoration Stage*, p. 21.
3. Ibid, pp. 36–7 and 74.
4. *A History of Early Eighteenth Century Drama, 1700–1750*, p. 266.
5. Ibid., p. 140.
6. Quotations are reproduced from the facsimile of Davenant's *Works*, 1673 (New York, 1968). The Quarto versions of 1658 and 1659 are virtually identical with those printed in the 1673 edition. The order is reversed and the description of the Frontispiece ('An Arch discover'd' — i.e., a proscenium arch) is prefaced only to *The History of Sir Francis Drake*. This means that the purpose of the Frontispiece — the design on the proscenium arch — is omitted, for it was only included in *The Cruelty of the Spaniards*, the first of the plays to be produced and printed. This stated that its design 'is, by way of preparation, to give some notice of that Argument which is pursu'd in the Scene' (A2ʳ). This admirably shows how the proscenium arch was carried over from the pre-1642 masque to the post-1660 public theatre, and how it was linked with the play being presented behind it. The 1673 edition also omits the advertisement that appeared at the end of *The Cruelty of the Spaniards*: 'Notwithstanding the great expence

necessary to Scenes, and other ornaments in this Entertainment, there is a good provision made of places for a shilling. And it shall begin certainly at 3 after noon.' It has been argued that credit for adapting *Sganarelle* should go to Henry Howard (see André de Mandach, 'The First Translator of Molière: Sir William Davenant or Colonel Henry Howard?', *MLN*, 66 (1951) 513–18).

7. *The Restoration Court Stage, 1660-1702*, pp. 115–16.

8. See Felix E. Schelling, *Elizabethan Drama, 1558-1642*, vol.I.pp. 400–1. Both have been attributed to Tarlton as *1* and *2 Seven Deadly Sins*.

9. Howard S. Collins, *The Comedy of Sir William Davenant*, pp. 73–4.

10. Arthur H. Nethercot, *Sir William D'Avenant, Poet Laureate and Playwright-Manager*, p. 381. Footnote 34 gives suggested sources for *The Play-house to be Let*.

11. This effect of a hot summer on the theatre may seem exaggerated today, at least to tourists trying to buy tickets at Stratford-upon-Avon, but hot weather has certainly ended the runs of successful plays. Thus Robertson's *Play* (1868) did well until May,

> when its good fortune received a sudden check, like all things theatrical in that year, which was that of the great drought and most exceptional heat. The big receipts then began to fall of, the sun grew fiercer and fiercer, the theatres more and more deserted, and we felt our play could not last the season out. Its run, which reached a hundred and six nights, was the shortest of all the Robertson comedies.   (The Bancrofts, *Mr and Mrs Bancroft On and Off the Stage*, p. 119).

12. Cyrus Hoy attributes to Field the induction and the Triumphs of Honour and Love, and to Fletcher, the Triumphs of Death and Time ('The Shares of Fletcher and his Collaborators in the Beaumont and Fletcher Canon, iv', *SB*, 12 (1959) 95).

13. William J. Lawrence, *Pre-Restoration Stage Studies*, p. 193.

14. Philippe Quinault, *Théâtre Choisi*, ed. Henri Allouard (Paris, 1882) pp. 60–126. Several of Quinault's plays were adapted for the English stage in the seventeenth century, two by William Lower in 1659 and 1660, one by Dryden in 1667, and others in 1669 and 1698.

15. W. S. Brooks, 'The Théâtre du Marais, Quinault's *Comédie sans comédie* and Thomas Corneille's Illustres ennemis', *French Studies*, XXVII (1973) 271–7, quoted in *La comédie sans comédie*, ed. J. D. Biard (Exeter, 1974) pp. v-vi. Biard accepts Brooks's date. Details of the actors of the Marais are to be found in *La Grande Encyclopédie*.

16. Nicoll, *A History of Eighteenth Century Drama, 1700-1750*, p. 141.

17. Robert Gale Noyes, *Ben Jonson on the English Stage, 1660–1776*, pp. 319–36.
18. *Roscius Anglicanus*, ed. Montague Summers, pp. 8–9. On p. 22 Downes gives a splendid example of an unfortunate *ad lib*, recording also the audience's response. It well illustrates the effect of such an *ad lib* in a straight play (compare pp. 4–5 above). The daughter of John Holden, Davenant's publisher, was appearing in a version of *Romeo and Juliet* on 1 March 1662. She was playing a role called 'Count Paris's Wife', and, as Downes puts it, 'enter'd in a *Hurry*, Crying, O my dear *Count*! She inadvertently left out, O, in the pronuntiation of the Word *Count*! giving it a Vehement Accent, put the House into such a Laughter, that *London* Bridge at low-water was silence to it' (p. 22). Summers explains that Mrs Holden, as he calls her, 'appears only to have played parts that were entirely unimportant' (p. 175).
19. '*The Giant Race before the Flood': Pre-Restoration Drama on the Stage and in the Criticism of the Restoration*, p. 63, n. 3.
20. *Penkethman's Jests . . . extracted from the . . . writings of . . . Ben Jonson* was published in 1721 and a seventh edition was called for in 1761, but that is not quite the same thing. Penkethman played Jonas Dock (alias Timothy Peascod) in *The What d'ye Call It*.
21. p. cxxx. They refer in a footnote to R. G. Noyes, *Ben Jonson on the English Stage, 1660–1776*. This is not to deny the major role Jonson plays as a standard by which what was proper to comedy was judged in the eighteenth century. See, for example, G. Nicholls, 'Aspects of Stage Productions of Ben Jonson, 1660–1776', unpublished Ph. D. thesis, University of Wales (Lampeter), 1972, esp. ch. 2.
22. Joe Lee Davis, *The Sons of Ben: Jonsonian Comedy in Caroline England*, pp. 59 and 208. David Klein called *The Muse's Looking-Glass* 'a piece of propaganda, hardly a play' (*The Elizabethan Dramatists as Critics*, p. 86), but Felix Schelling is nearer the mark when he says 'nothing can detract from the wit, originality, and clever characterisation within the limits of abstractions which mark the personages of this interesting production' (*Elizabethan Drama, 1558–1642*, vol.II,pp. 86–7). Another of the Tribe of Ben, Shackerley Marmion, in the short prologue to *A Fine Companion* (1633), has the Critic impute double standards to 'the tribe':

> yet you may
> Remember, if you please, what entertainment
> Some of your tribe have had that have took pains
> To be contemn'd, and laught at by the vulgar,
> And then ascrib'd it to their ignorance.

James Maidment and W. H. Logan (eds), *The Dramatic Works of Shackerley Marmion*, p. 105. Maidment and Logan say that D'Urfey borrowed from *A Fine Companion* in his *Sir Barnaby Whig, or, No Wit Like a Woman's* (1681) — see p. 101.

23. For an account of *The Roman Actor* from this point of view, see P. H. Davison, 'The Theme and Structure of *The Roman Actor*', *Aumla*, 19 (1962) pp. 39–56.

24. Gerald E. Bentley, 'Randolph's *Praeludium* and the Salisbury Court Theatre', *Joseph Quincy Adams Memorial Studies*, ed. J. G. McManaway, G. E. Dawson and E. E. Willoughby, pp. 775–83, esp. pp. 779–80.

25. Quotations are from the edition in *Six Caroline Plays*, ed. A. S. Knowland (Oxford, 1962).

26. Thornton S. Graves, in 'Some Aspects of Extemporal Acting', *SP*, XIX (1922) 429–56, points out that extemporal acting did not die out as a result of Hamlet's strictures. He gives many examples including a number of instances of *ad libbing* because actors were too lazy, or had insufficient time, to learn their parts. This is described by Olive Logan in *Before the Footlights and Behind the Scenes* as 'winging a part' (pp. 57 ff) and this Graves defines as 'going on the stage to play a part without having studied it' (p. 447).

27. Gunnar Sorelius in '*The Giant Race before the Flood*' records *The Antipodes* only once (p. 43), referring to it as one of the 43 plays performed by the King's Men in 1661. He does not mention *The Muse's Looking-Glass*.

28. The edition used of Randolph's plays is that of W. Carew Hazlitt, *Poetical and Dramatic Works of Thomas Randolph* (London, 1875). It is not certain whether the apostrophe should be before or after the final '*s*' of *Muses*. There is no apostrophe in the original quarto. Hazlitt uses both forms; most modern critics print *Muses'*. I have used the singular form, having Thalia in mind, the Muse of Comedy and Pastoral Poetry. As Comedy, Tragedy, Mime and Satire are all 'characters' in the play, *Muses'* is possible, but *Muse's* better signifies dramatic art as a whole.

29. G. E. Bentley, 'Randolph's *Praeludium* and the Salisbury Court Theatre', p. 777. Bentley suggests that *The Muse's Looking-Glass* may have opened the Salisbury Court Theatre in November 1630, having been 'performed in the summer on the road, when all the London theatres were closed' (*The Jacobean and Caroline Stage*, vol.VI,p. 97).

30. An anonymous play called *The Mirror* was presented from 14 January 1737 by Fielding during his last season as manager of the Haymarket

Theatre. Nicoll gives the subtitle as 'With the Practice of a Dramatick Entertainment called the Defeat of Apollo: or, Harlequin Triumphant, and a farce call'd, The Mob in Despair' (Nicoll, *A History of Eighteenth Century Drama, 1700-1750*, p. 179). It is possible that this was a version of Randolph's play and 'With the Practice of a Dramatick Entertainment' sounds like a rehearsal or revue play. Emmett L. Avery thinks it was 'more likely a satire on pantomime', though *The Daily Advertiser*, in the publicity for the show on 12 January, said it 'proves to be a Satyr on the Rants of Poets, and an Entertainment'. The afterpiece was evidently aimed at Walpole: *The Fall of Bob, alias Gin* (see Emmett L. Avery, 'Fielding's Last Season with the Haymarket Theatre', *MP*, 36 (1939) 284-5).

31. *Eighteenth-Century Drama: Afterpieces*, ed. Richard W. Bevis, pp. vi–vii.

32. Presumably corrupt because they did not fulfil what they were bribed to perform. The *Dictionary of National Biography* says of *The Conceited Pedlar* that 'it would not have discredited Autolycus' (vol. XLVII, p. 281).

33. Leo Hughes describes it as one of Dodsley's 'sentimental or moralizing' afterpieces (*A Century of English Farce*, p. 126).

34. See P. H. Davison, '*Volpone* and the Old Comedy', *MLQ*, 24 (1963) 151-7.

35. The parody is, presumably, of the quadruple 'O' with which Hamlet expires in the Folio version. These have been taken to be actor's interpolations (see Harold Jenkins, 'Playhouse Interpolations: the Folio Text of *Hamlet*', *SB*, 13 (1966) 31-47).

36. These include, in II.i, Davenant's *History of Sir Francis Drake*, and the use of whispers to give orders, as in Mrs Aphra Behn's *The Amorous Prince* (1671). One of the most intriguing plays referred to is Henry Howard's *The United Kingdom* which, as it miscarried on the stage, was not printed. It began, appropriately enough, with a funeral.

37. *Burlesque Plays of the Eighteenth Century*, ed. Simon Trussler, p. 5.

38. '*The Mock Tempest*' in *Shakespeare Adaptations*, ed. Montague Summers, pp. 107-9.

39. Nicoll, *A History of Eighteenth Century Drama, 1700–1750*, pp. 140, 266 and 266, respectively.

40. *Burlesque Plays of the Eighteenth Century*, p. 55. Quotations are taken from this edition.

41. Ibid., p. 148. This incident has the peculiar merit of being one of only two occasions on which Jonathan Swift laughed, if the *Memoirs of Mrs Laetitia Pilkington* (1754) are to be believed. The other was a

trick played by a mountebank's merry-andrew (see Ronald Paulson and Thomas Lockwood (eds), *Henry Fielding: the Critical Heritage*, p. 73).

There has been something of a revival in the killing of ghosts in recent years, especially in the work of Edward Bond. In his *Early Morning* (1968) George dies (p. 51), is alive (p. 60), dies again — presumably as a ghost (p. 66), and steps from a line of ghosts (p. 82), and is next seen in heaven (p. 83). Later in the play the soul is said to die but the body to go on living as a ghost (p. 101). In *Lear* (1972), the ghosts of Bodice and Fontanelle in their youth appear (pp. 38–9) and later a ghost dies (p. 86).

42. Half-a-century later this was still a popular device. Garrick's *A Peep Behind the Curtain* (1767), Jackman's *All the World's a Stage* (1777) and Reynold's *The Dramatist* (1789) all use dramatic rehearsals or the writing of plays as a means whereby marriages, secret or open, may be arranged. See pp. 151–5.

43. Trussler's *Burlesque Plays of the Eighteenth Century*, p. 91.

44. *A History of Eighteenth Century Drama, 1700–1750*, pp. 256–7. Both plays are anonymous, though *The English Stage Italianized* is attributed to D'Urfey — but see Nicoll's footnote. See also Jean B. Kern, *Dramatic Satire in the Age of Walpole, 1720–1750*, pp. 125–6.

45. *Dramatic Satire in the Age of Walpole, 1720–1750*, p. 120. This study provides a good review of the use of satire on the stage and specific attention is given to rehearsal plays (pp. 35, 45–7, 52–3, 94, 121–3, 146–7). Chapter 4, 'Literary Satire', and chapter 5, 'The Form of Dramatic Satire 1720–1750', are particularly worth attention and there is a useful list of plays (pp. 167–79).

46. Ian Donaldson, *The World Turned Upside Down: Comedy from Jonson to Fielding*, shows how Gay burlesqued 'one of the most celebrated tragic moments of the Restoration and eighteenth-century stage', Pierre's heroic ascent of the scaffold, to the toll of a passing bell, in Otway's *Venice Preserved*. Indeed, as if to rub this in, the actor playing Macheath (Walker) had, a few weeks earlier, played Pierre at the same theatre (pp. 161–2). There were in the early performances, therefore, more theatrical allusions that would break the suspension of disbelief than can be evident to a modern audience. It should be noted that, despite his borrowing from *Rinaldo*, Gay and Handel did work together on occasion.

47. Kern, *Dramatic Satire in the Age of Walpole, 1720–1750*, pp. 121–2. A useful account of 'The Infancy of English Pantomime, 1716–1723', by Virginia P. Scott, appeared in *Educational Theatre Journal*, 34

(1970) 125–34. In this she suggests that pantomimes, which 'became enormously popular in England in 1723', began in imitation of the 'Night Scenes' performed in theatres and fairs in London by actors from French fairs between 1702 and 1716, and their popularity was developed by 'French *forain* performances of the Gherardi and Le Sage repertoires in London in 1718–19 and 1719–20' (pp. 125–6). See also Michael R. Booth's introduction to his *English Plays of the Nineteenth Century*, vol.v: *Pantomimes, Extravaganzas, and Burlesques* for a good succinct survey of the field, especially for pantomime, pp. 1–10.

48. Thus, Simon Trussler in *Burlesque Plays of the Eighteenth Century* (p. 143) and Charles B. Woods in his introduction to his edition of *The Author's Farce* (London, 1967) p. xv, argue that it was in the irregular drama that Fielding's excellence as a dramatist lay.

49. Reprinted in Paulson and Lockwood's *Henry Fielding: the Critical Heritage*, pp. 75–6. For Dodsley's *The Toy Shop*, see pp. 122–3 above.

50. References are to *The Works of Henry Fielding, Esq.,* ed. Leslie Stephen, ten vols (unless specific recent editions are noted). *The Universal Gallant* appears in vol.x.

51. *The London Stage* (London,? 1824) vol.iv; Act iii, Sc. iv, p. 14.

52. Some of the songs were recorded on HMV 7EG 8499. The lyrics were written by Lionel Bart.

53. *The London Stage*, pt 3, *1729–1747* (Carbondale, 1961) p. lxxxvi.

54. Quoted in Ioan Williams, *The Criticism of Henry Fielding*, p. 157. See also allusions to Jonson's works in *Tom Jones*, ed. M. C. Battestin and Fredson Bowers (Oxford, 1974) vol.i,p. 493; vol.ii,p. 525. Fielding refers to *Bartholomew Fair* in *The Champion*, no. 53 (Williams, *The Criticism of Henry Fielding*, p. 121).

55. See *Sale Catalogues of Libraries of Eminent Persons*, vol. 7: *Poets and Men of Letters*, ed. Hugh Amory. Jonson's *Works* is listed as item 497, p. 154. Amory says in his introduction that many instances might be cited to show that Fielding possessed books that the auctioneer, Samuel Baker, never saw (p. 131): 'The catalogue gives a rather unreliable account of Fielding's reading, therefore, especially in literature' (p. 132).

56. The circumstances are not wholly clear. The management of the Haymarket advertised that the play would be deferred till further notice. Thereafter, as Edgar V. Roberts notes in his edition (London, 1969), the theatre 'experienced severe governmental repression'. Curiously, Fielding was silent, for, if the play had been suppressed by

Walpole's Ministry, he could have made much capital out of the incident. See Roberts, pp. xv-xvii.

57. *The Author's Farce*, ed. Charles B. Woods.

58. The three versions may be conveniently compared in Edgar Roberts's edition, from which quotations are taken.

59. Jean Kern discusses the objects of Fielding's satire in her *Dramatic Satire in the Age of Walpole, 1720–1750.* See especially political satire, pp. 45–8 and 52–3; social satire, pp. 61–3 and 66–7.

60. Mrs Mayoress and Lord Place are characters in Trapwit's comedy.

61. The Licensing Act of 1737 'limited the number of theatres to those with royal patents and made illegal the performance of any play, prologue or epilogue without the approval of the Licenser from the Lord Chamberlain's office' (Kern, *Dramatic Satire in the Age of Walpole, 1720–1750*, p. 47). For earlier moves to bring in such an act, and the use made of the lost, and possibly spurious play, *The Golden Rump* (with a quotation therefrom), to facilitate passage of the act, see Kern, pp. 47–9. Sterne's use of direct appeal to the reader of *Tristram Shandy* (1759–67) makes an interesting comparison with the use of this tradition in the theatre of his time, especially as a technique for 'undermining' the tradition of the novel.

62. See Paulson and Lockwood's *Henry Fielding: the Critical Heritage*, p. 77. For Pope's objection to the 'Taste of the Rabble' in West End theatres, see *The Dunciad Variorum*, vol.I,2n.

63. See M. M. Belden, *The Dramatic Works of Samuel Foote*, pp. 7–10. Foote, of course, was not the first to exploit such loopholes in the law. Theophilus Cibber used a 'rehearsal' device in 1744 and several ostensible 'concerts' had included dramatic performances: one paid for the music and the drama was thrown in, gratis. For a succinct account of the Licensing Act and these evasions, see Arthur H. Scouten, *The London Stage, 1729–1747: a Critical Introduction* (Carbondale, 1968) pp. xlviii–lx.

64. Scolar facsimile (Menstone, 1973), with index. Quotations are from this text.

65. Quotations from *The Devil Upon Two Sticks* and *The Lame Lover* are from *The Modern British Drama* (1811) vol.v. In *The Maid of Bath*, Foote played Sir Christopher Cripple, hobbling on to take the waters at Bath. Foote endured his misfortune with greater composure than Henry Hughes, who lost a leg in 1756, ten years before Foote. Hughes's colleagues buried his leg at Strata Florida (near Lampeter, Dyfed) with mock ceremony, but Hughes, not appreciating the gesture, emigrated to America. The gravestone to his leg can still be

seen in the cemetery of this ancient monument, adjacent to the yew by which the medieval poet, Dafydd ap Gwilym is reputedly buried.

66. *The Wandering Patentee*, vol.i,pp. 282–3. Apart from the sad irony of an actor called Foote losing a leg (which Wilkinson does not refrain from pointing out, saying that Foote, after his accident, 'was not so good an actor as when cut short', vol.i,p. 282), Wilkinson then broke his leg and though it was not amputated, he became so lame that he went into partial retirement in 1788 (vol.iii,p. 57).

67. James Boswell, *The Life of Samuel Johnson*, p. 205.

68. *Revels History of Drama in English*, vol.vi: *1750–1880*, ed. Clifford Leech and T. W. Craik, p. 156. Murphy prepared an edition of Fielding's plays, incidentally, and this was published in 1762.

69. *The British Drama* (1828), vol.i,p. 69.

70. Jesse Foot, *The Life of Arthur Murphy, Esq.*, p. 103.

71. The obvious, and pretty well solitary, example in English drama is Galsworthy's *Justice* (1910). Winston Churchill, when Home Secretary, was much moved by the dramatisation of the effects of solitary confinement and set about having conditions changed.

72. Martha Vicinus gives a verse and part of the patter in *The Industrial Muse*, p. 244.

73. For some account of McGonagall's experiences, especially his first performance as Macbeth, see *Poetic Gems, Selected from the Works of William McGonagall, Poet and Tragedian*, first published in two parts in 1890 and many times reprinted. Reference is here made to the fourteenth impression (two parts in one, Dundee, 1966). McGonagall explains how he came to play Macbeth in Giles's theatre in Dundee. He cannot give the exact date but it was 'a very long time ago' (p. 5). It was, in fact, about 1847. Giles required £1 as a fee to allow him to go on the stage and McGonagall's fellow handloom weavers in the jute mill where he worked contributed this. Though McGonagall tells of the great success he achieved — 'the applause was deafening, and was continued through the entire evening, especially so in the combat scene' (p. 6) — the audience could scarcely contain itself for laughter.

74. V. C. Clinton-Baddeley, 'Wopsle', *The Dickensian*, 57 (1961) 156. He quotes from Hazlitt's review of a Mr Edwards, an amateur who performed at Covent Garden: 'It was one of those painful failures, for which we are so often indebted to the managers.'

75. *The Wandering Patentee*, vol.ii,pp. 233–4. J. W. Robinson (ed.), *Theatrical Street Ballads*, gives another example and reproduces a good song on the subject of an amateur, a Mr Pritchard, who wished to be

an actor on the professional stage about 1844. Neither 'the supporting players nor the audiences would necessarily look kindly on the attempts' (p. 92). These are stanzas from the song:

I reach'd the house — began to dress, but the actors full of gambols,
Pour'd water in my boots, so I was forc'd to put on sandals;
I rush'd at once upon the stage, the audience did hiss hard,
'Cos I went on without my trunks when I came out in Richard.

I found they all determin'd were to have of fun their whack, sirs,
They slily came behind and pinn'd a paper on my back, sirs;
Twas set on fire, it caught my wig, now really I thought this hard —
It singed the hair all off my head when I came out in Richard.

The author's advice is much the same as Arthur Murphy's:

So all stage-struck young gentlemen, take this advice from me, sirs,
What'er in life your station is, contented with it be, sirs,
On the world's great stage play well your part — 'twere well for me
    if this had
My maxim been throughout my life, so don't come out in Richard.
                                                                    (p. 94)

76. Compare the danger of reading novels in George Colman's *Polly Honeycombe* (1760), reprinted in *Eighteenth-Century Drama: Afterpieces*, ed. Richard W. Bevis, with Mary's reading Ibsen in O'Casey's *Juno and the Paycock* (1924).
77. *The Modern British Drama* (1811) vol.v,p. 181.
78. Jackman's *All the World's a Stage* is printed in *The London Stage*, vol.i.
79. *The British Theatre*, ed. Mrs Inchbald (London, 1808) vol.xx, p.10. Willoughby was played by Macready. When Still played this part, he 'suddenly discovered in the combat scene that he had left his rapier behind the scenes but compensated for this absent-mindedness by improvising as follows when a large basket-handle sword was thrust to him from the wings: "Ah! lucky circumstance; someone has left a sword sticking in a tree"' (Quoted by Thornton S. Graves in 'Some Aspects of Extemporal Acting', *SP*, xix (1922) 429–56).
80. Compare Ellen Terry when describing Henry Irving's taking over the management of the Lyceum from Mrs Bateman in 1878: 'I dare say he found it difficult to separate from Mrs Bateman and from her daughter, who had for such a long time been his "leading lady". He

had to be a little cruel, not for the last time in a career devoted unremittingly and unrelentingly to his art and his ambition' (*Ellen Terry's Memoirs, with Preface, Notes and Additional Biographical Chapters*, by Edith Craig and Christopher St. John, p. 118).

81. 'Shakespearian Burlesques', *Shakespeare Quarterly*, 16 (1965) 60. Burlesques of Shakespeare do still occur. Thus, the anti-Vietnam play, *MacBird!* (1965–6) by Barbara Gerson, was based mainly on *Macbeth*, Macbeth and Lady Macbeth being President Johnson and Mrs Ladybird Johnson. Chief Justice Earl Warren was given Hamlet's line (as the Earl of Warren), 'O cursèd spite! / That ever I was born to set things right' (Harmondsworth, 1967), pp. 38–9.

82. The text of *Hamlet, with Alterations* is to be found in Jesse Foot's *The Life of Arthur Murphy Esq.*, with a preliminary account of how the parody came to be written (pp. 252–74). Foot says that the manuscript 'remained undisturbed in the portfolio of Mr Murphy, till it came into my possession at his death' (p. 252). Martin Lehnert includes the text in his 'Arthur Murphy's *Hamlet* Parodie (1772) and David Garrick', *Shakespeare Jahrbuch*, 102 (1966) 97–167.

83. Wells, 'Shakespearian Burlesques', p. 61, quoting V. C. Clinton-Baddeley, *The Burlesque Tradition in the English Theatre after 1660*, p. 109.

84. *The Burlesque Tradition in the English Theatre after 1660*, p. 90. Clinton-Baddeley gives an account of Thomas Dibdin's attempts and the failure of his *Bonifacio and Bridgetina* (1808).

85. *Early Victorian Drama*, p. 76.

86. *The Extravaganzas of J. R. Planché, Esq.*, ed. T. F. Dillon Croker and Stephen Tucker (London, 1879) 5 vols. The passages quoted come from vol.II. For a recent account of Planché's work, see M. R. Booth's introduction to *English Plays of the Nineteenth Century*, vol. V, pp. 10–18.

87. Reynolds, *Early Victorian Drama*, p. 60; he refers to D. Macmillan, 'Some Burlesques with a Purpose, 1830–70', *PQ* (July 1929). The dates of Robertson's plays should be borne in mind with respect to those of Ibsen's 'social' dramas, e.g. *The Pillars of Society* (1877), *A Doll's House* (1879) and *Ghosts* (1881). *Play*, incidentally, is not in the tradition of *The Muse's Looking-Glass*. The word is glossed as 'make-believe' (particularly, 'playful flirting') and also refers to a Salon de Jeu in III.ii, and to Amanda being a player — not at the tables, but on the stage. This inter-relationship of meanings is characteristic of Robertson.

88. In 1809 riots took place at Covent Garden for sixty-seven nights

following J. P. Kemble's raising of the prices for admission.

89. Allardyce Nicoll quotes a few lines of this scene in *A History of English Drama, 1660–1900*, vol.IV: *Early Nineteenth Century Drama, 1800–1850*, p. 150.

90. The reference is to 'A man who could make so vile a pun would not scruple to pick a pocket', John Dennis (1657–1734).

91. Planché, *Recollections and Reflections*, vol.II,p 73.

92. Ibid., vol.II,p. 69.

93. *The Merry Wives of Windsor*, I.i.115.

94. *When Crummles Played*, with an Introduction by F. J. Harvey Darnton.

95. *The Deep Blue Sea with Three Other Plays*, p. 122.

96. No better idea of Planché's seriousness of approach can be gained than by reading his account in *Recollections and Reflections* of the way a happy ending was given against his will to *The Red Mask* (1834), which was based on Fennimore Cooper's novel *The Bravo*. The press claimed that his original ending was too violent. He rejects strongly the idea that he would write a mere coup-de-théâtre or 'propose any exhibition tending to brutalise the people'. He believed his ending served moral ends, branding with infamy a fiendish government. The result of the softened ending meant that 'the political lesson [was] unread' (vol.I,pp. 218–22). Planché's attitude and analysis, the way action was imagined which never took place, and the actions of reporters (one inaptly named Francis Bacon) in putting pressure on the manager of Drury Lane to have the ending changed, make salutary reading. Even great creative writers can imagine they have seen things in the theatre that have never taken place. Jean-Paul Sartre saw *US* and, according to Peter Brook, 'thought he saw a red curtain fall and wrote about it' — *The Book of US* (London, 1968) p. 211.

97. James Branch Cabell once offered a provocative comment on the closing of the theatres in 1642 which indirectly highlights one quality of drama that does not hesitate to break the dramatic illusion, making the audience conscious it is watching a play: 'It should always be remembered in favor of the Puritans that when they closed the theatres "realism" was sprawling upon the stage'. Joe Lee Davis, who quotes this paggage in *The Sons of Ben* (p. 235, n.1), points out that 'This sentence does not appear in earlier editions of *Beyond Life*.' It was added in *The Works of James Branch Cabell* (New York, 1927–30) vol.I,p. 26.

98. An exception occurs in a burlesque already referred to: *Hamlet! The*

Ravin' Prince of Denmark!! (1866) (see pp. 67–8). When the stage is littered with the dead at the end of the burlesque, the Prompter enters and gives each actor a shake, but to no avail. Then he speaks to the audience:

> But as I see you in a state of fog,
> I'll 'speak a piece' by way of epilogue.
> [*Coming forward*] — And now kind friends, whatever can we say,
> For having murdered Shakespeare in this way?   (p. 138)

He begs the audience to applaud in order to bring the actors back to life — shades of Tinker bell! — and when the audience responds, and the 'dead' have come back to life, all join (including, of course, the ghost) in singing the finale.

99. One contemporary example of the intermean deserves a mention, if only in a footnote. I am reminded that no *Muppet Show* would be complete without the comments of the two old gentlemen in the theatre box.

Select Bibliography

This bibliography lists primary works, other than plays, and secondary works which have been referred to directly or indirectly. Texts of plays quoted are given in the notes and details are not repeated here unless reference has been made to their introductory matter. A separate list is provided of acts on record (see Appendix II). Most of the plays and acts discussed are not well known (hence the fairly full quotations) and as a supplement to the sources given in the notes, it was thought that a chronological list would be more useful to the reader than a separate bibliography. Quotations from Shakespeare, if not from early quartos or specified editions, are from W. J. Craig's Oxford one-volume edition. Jonson is quoted from C. H. Herford and P. and E. M. Simpson's edition (Oxford, 1925–52). Useful annotated bibliographies of eighteenth- and nineteenth-century plays are to be found in Frederick M. Link, *English Drama 1660-1800* (Detroit, 1976) pp. 13–16, and in L. W. Conolly and J. P. Wearing, *English Drama and Theatre, 1800-1900* (Detroit, 1978) pp. 357–84. Conolly and Wearing direct the attention of readers of these anthologies to R. Crompton Rhodes, 'The Early Nineteenth-Century Drama', *The Library*, IV,no.16 (1936) 91–112 and 210–31. I have made much use of texts in anthologies in my possession: *A Selection of the Most Esteemed Farces and Entertainments* (Edinburgh, 1784) 4 vols; *The British Theatre* (selected by Mrs Inchbald, 1808) 25 vols; *The Modern British Drama* (London, 1811) 5 vols; *The London Stage* (London, *c.* 1824) 4 vols; and *The British Drama* (London, 1828) 2 vols. No attempt is made to represent here the wealth of scholarly work on all the drama discussed in this study. That would imply a degree of detail which the broad lines of my argument forbid.

Amory, Hugh (ed.), *Sale Catalogues of Libraries of Eminent Persons*, vol.7: *Poets and Men of Letters* (London, 1973).

Armin, Robert, *Collected Works,* ed. J. P. Feather (New York and London, 1972) 2 vols.

Armstrong, W. A. (ed.), *Elizabethan History Plays* (London, 1965).

Avery, Emmett L., 'Fielding's Last Season with the Haymarket Theatre', *MP*, 36 (1939) 283–92.

Avery, Emmett L. and Scouten, Arthur, *The London Stage 1660-1700* (Carbondale, 1968).

Axton, Richard, 'Popular Modes in the Earliest Plays', *Medieval Drama*, Stratford-upon-Avon Studies, no.16 (London, 1973) pp. 13-39.

Bancrofts, The, *Mr and Mrs Bancroft On and Off the Stage* (London, 1891).

Baum, Paull B., 'Chaucer's Puns', *PMLA*, 71 (1956) and 73 (1958).

Bede, Venerable, *Historical Works*, Loeb Classical Library, trans. by J. E. King (London and Cambridge, Mass., 1930).

Belden, M. M., *The Dramatic Works of Samuel Foote* (New Haven, 1929).

Bentley, Gerald E., 'Randolph's *Praeludium* and the Salisbury Court Theatre', *Joseph Quincy Adams Memorial Studies*, ed. J. G. McManaway, G. E. Dawson and E. E. Willoughby (Washington, 1948) pp. 775-83.

_____, *The Jacobean and Caroline Stage* (Oxford, 1941-68) 7 vols.

Berry, Francis, *The Shakespeare Inset: Word and Picture* (London, 1965).

Bethell, S. L., *Shakespeare and the Popular Dramatic Tradition* (London, 1944).

Bevington, David, *The Macro Plays* (New York and Washington, 1972).

_____, 'Popular and Courtly Traditions on the Early Tudor Stage', *Medieval Drama*, Stratford-upon-Avon Studies, no.16 (London, 1973) pp. 91-107.

Bevis, Richard W., *Eighteenth-Century Drama: Afterpieces* (Oxford, 1970).

Boas, F. S. and Reed, A. W. (eds), *Fulgens and Lucres* (Oxford, 1926).

Booth, Michael R., Introduction, *English Plays of the Nineteenth Century*, vol.v: *Pantomimes, Extravaganzas, and Burlesques* (Oxford, 1976).

Boswell, Eleanore, *The Restoration Court Stage, 1660-1702* (London, 1932; rev. edn 1966).

Boswell, James, *The Life of Samuel Johnson* (London, 1898).

Brand, John, *Observations on Popular Antiquities*, with additions by Sir Henry Ellis (London, 1913).

Brecht, Bertolt, 'Alienation Effects in Chinese Acting', in *Brecht on Theatre*, trans. by John Willett (London, 1964).

Brooke, C. F. Tucker, *The Shakespeare Apocrypha* (Oxford, 1908).

Brooks, W. S., 'The Théâtre du Marais, Quinault's *Comédie sans comédie* and Thomas Corneille's Illustres enemis', *French Studies*, xxvii (1973) 271-7.

Brown, Arthur, 'The Play within a Play: an Elizabethan Dramatic Device', *Essays and Studies*, n.s.13 (1906) 36-48.

Brown, James, 'Eight Types of Puns', *PMLA*, 71 (1956) 14-26.

Burke, Peter, *Popular Culture in Early Modern Europe* (London, 1978).

Busby, Olive Mary, *Studies in the Development of the Fool in the Elizabethan Drama* (Oxford, 1923).

Caputi, Anthony, *Buffo: the Genius of Vulgar Comedy* (Detroit, 1978).

Chambers, E. K., *The Elizabethan Stage* (Oxford, 1923) 4 vols.

Charney, Maurice, *Comedy High and Low* (New York, 1978).

Clarence, Reginald, *'The Stage' Cyclopaedia: a Bibliography of Plays* (London, 1909).

Clinton-Baddeley, V. C., *The Burlesque Tradition in the English Theatre after 1660* (London, 1952).

_____, 'Wopsle', *The Dickensian*, 57 (1961) 150–9.

Collins, Howard S., *The Comedy of Sir William Davenant* (The Hague, 1967).

Colman, Adrian, *The Dramatic Use of Bawdy in Shakespeare* (London, 1974).

Comte, Edward Le, *A Dictionary of Puns in Milton's English Poetry* (London, 1981).

Craig, Edith and St John, Christopher, *Ellen Terry's Memoirs, with Preface, Notes and Additional Biographical Chapters* (London, 1933).

Craik, T. W., 'The Tudor Interlude and Later Elizabethan Drama', *Elizabethan Theatre*, Stratford-upon-Avon Studies, no.9 (London, 1966) pp. 37–57.

_____, *The Tudor Interlude: Stage, Costume, and Acting* (Leicester, 1967).

Creeth, Edmund (ed.), *Tudor Plays: an Anthology of Tudor Drama* (New York, 1966).

Davies, Norman, *Non-Cycle Plays and Fragments* (London, 1970).

Davis, Joe Lee, *The Sons of Ben: Jonsonian Comedy in Caroline England* (Detroit, 1967).

Davison, P. H., 'The Theme and Structure of *The Roman Actor*', *Aumla*, 19 (1962) 39–56.

_____, '*Volpone* and the Old Comedy', *MLQ*, 24 (1963) 151–7.

_____, 'The Serious Concerns of *Philaster*', *ELH*, 30 (1963) 1–15.

_____, 'Contemporary Drama and Popular Dramatic Forms', Kathleen Robinson Lecture, University of Sydney, 1963; printed in *Aspects of Drama and the Theatre*, Richard N. Coe *et al.* (Sydney, 1965).

_____, 'La Dramaturgie en Angleterre à la veille de la Guerre Civile: John Ford et la comédie', *Dramaturgie et Société*, ed. J. Jacquot (Paris, 1968) vol.II,pp. 805–14.

_____, *Songs of the British Music Hall: a Critical History of the Songs and their Times* (New York, 1971).

_____, 'Popular Literature', *Encyclopaedia Britannica*, 15th edn, vo.xx (Chicago, 1974) pp. 804–7.

_____, 'Henry V in the Context of the Popular Dramatic Tradition', *Contexts and Connexions* (Winchester, 1981).

_____, *Contemporary Drama and the Popular Dramatic Tradition in England* (London, 1982).

Dean, Leonard, 'Richard II: the State and the Image of the Theater', *PMLA*, 67 (1952) 211–18.

Donaldson, Ian, *The World Turned Upside Down* (Oxford, 1970).

Downes, John, *Roscius Anglicanus* (1708), ed. Montague Summers (London, 1929; facsimile, New York, 1968).

Dumont, Frank, *The Witmark Amateur Minstrel Guide* (Chicago, New York and London, 1899).

Ellis-Fermor, Una, *The Jacobean Drama* (London, 1958).

Eliot, T. S., *The Complete Poems and Plays, 1909-1950* (New York, 1952).

Evans, H. A., *English Masques* (London, 1906).

Fenton, Doris, *The Extra-Dramatic Moment in Elizabethan Plays before 1616* (Philadelphia, 1930).

Fielding, Henry, *The Works of Henry Fielding Esq.*, ed. Leslie Stephen (London, 1882) 10 vols.

Foot, Jesse, *The Life of Arthur Murphy Esq.* (London, 1811).

Franklin, Benjamin, *Autobiography* (New York, 1965).

Graves, Thornton S., 'Some Aspects of Extemporal Acting', *SP*, XIX (1922) 429–56.

Greenfield, Thelma N., *The Induction in Elizabethan Drama* (Eugene, 1970).

Greg, Sir Walter, *Marlowe's 'Doctor Faustus': 1604-1616* (Oxford, 1950).

Godwin, Thomas, *Romanae Historiae Anthologiae* (Oxford, 1614).

Happé, Peter, *English Mystery Plays* (Harmondsworth, 1975).

Harbage, Alfred, *Annals of the English Drama, 975-1700*, revised by S. Schoenbaum (London, 1964).

_____, *Shakespeare and the Rival Traditions* (London, 1952).

Harington, Sir John, *A Supplie or Addicion to the Catalogue of Bishops to the Yeare 1608*, ed. R. H. Miller (Potomac, 1979).

Hopgood, E. R., *An Actor's Handbook* (New York, 1963).

Hoy, Cyrus, 'The Shares of Fletcher and his Collaborators in the Beaumont and Fletcher Canon, iv', *SB*, 12 (1959) 91–116.

Hughes, Leo, *A Century of English Farce* (Princeton, 1956).

Hunter, G. K., *John Lyly: the Humanist as Courtier* (London, 1962).

Jeffrey, David L., 'English Saints' Plays', *Medieval Drama*, Stratford-upon-Avon Studies, no.16 (London, 1973) pp. 69–89.

Jenkins, Harold, 'Playhouse Interpolations: the Folio Text of *Hamlet*', *SB*, 13 (1966) 31–47.

Johnson on Shakespeare, vol.VII of *Yale Edition of the Works of Samuel Johnson*, ed. Arthur Sherbo (New Haven, 1969).

Jones, Gwennan, *A Study of Three Welsh Religious Plays* (Minneapolis, 1918).

Jonson: The Complete Poems, ed. Ian Donaldson (Oxford, 1975).

Kern, Jean B., *Dramatic Satire in the Age of Walpole, 1720-1750* (Ames, 1976).

Kirschbaum, Leo, 'The Good and Bad Quartos of *Doctor Faustus*', *The Library*, IV, 26 (1946) 272-94.

Klein, David, *The Elizabethan Dramatists as Critics* (New York, 1963).

Kornfeld, Paul, 'Epilogue to the Actor', *An Anthology of German Expressionist Drama*, ed. Walter H. Sokel (New York, 1963) pp. 6-8.

Lamb, Charles, 'Popular Fallacies, ix: that the Worst Puns are the Best', *The Works of Charles and Mary Lamb*, ed. E. V. Lucas, vol.II. (London, 1903).

Lawrence, William J., *Pre-Restoration Stage Studies* (Cambridge, Mass., 1927).

Lea, K. M., *Italian Popular Comedy* (Oxford, 1934) 2 vols.

Leech, Clifford and Craik, T. W. (eds), *Revels History of Drama in English*, vol.VI: *1750-1880* (London, 1975).

Lippincott, H. F., *A Shakespeare Jestbook: Robert Armin's 'Foole upon Foole' (1600)* (Salzburg, 1973).

McDowell, J. M., 'Tudor Court Staging: a Study in Perspective', *JEGP*, 44 (1945) 194-207.

McGonagall, William, *Poetic Gems, Selected from the Works of William McGonagall, Poet and Tragedian*, two parts in one (Dundee, 1890; quoted from 1966 impression).

Maidment, James and Logan, W. H. (eds), *The Dramatic Works of Shackerley Marmion* (London, 1875).

Manly, J. M., *Specimens of the Pre-Shakespearean Drama* (New York, 1897).

Morgann, Maurice, *Shakespearian Criticism*, ed. D. A. Fineman (Oxford, 1972).

Nelson, Robert J., *Play within Play: the Dramatist's Conception of his Art: Shakespeare to Anouilh* (New Haven, 1958).

Nethercot, Arthur H., *Sir William D'Avenant, Poet Laureate and Playwright-Manager* (Chicago, 1938).

Nicoll, Allardyce, *A History of Eighteenth Century Drama, 1700-1750* (Cambridge, 1929).

———, *A History of English Drama, 1660-1900*, vol.IV: *Early Nineteenth Century Drama, 1800-1850* (Cambridge, 1955).

Noyes, Robert Gale, *Ben Jonson on the English Stage, 1660-1776* (Cambridge, Mass., 1935).

Orgel, Stephen, *The Jonsonian Masque* (Cambridge, Mass., 1967).

_____, *The Complete Masques of Ben Jonson* (New Haven, 1969).

_____, *Selected Masques of Ben Jonson* (New Haven, 1970).

_____, and Strong, Roy, *Inigo Jones: the Theatre of the Stuart Court* (London, Berkeley and Los Angeles, 1973).

Partridge, Edward B., 'Ben Jonson: the Makings of the Dramatist (1596–1602)', *Elizabethan Theatre*, Stratford-upon-Avon Studies, no.9 (London, 1966) pp. 221–44.

Paulson, Ronald and Lockwood, Thomas (eds), *Henry Fielding: the Critical Heritage* (London and New York, 1969).

Planché, J. R., *Recollections and Reflections* (London, 1872) 2 vols.

Puyvelde, Leo van, *Flemish Painting from the Van Eycks to Metsys* (London, 1970).

Rattigan, Terence, *The Deep Blue Sea with Three Other Plays* (London, 1955).

Redfield, Robert, *Peasant Society and Culture* (Chicago, 1956).

Redwine, James D. Jr, 'Beyond Psychology: the Moral Basis of Jonson's Theory of Humor Characterization', *ELH*, 28 (1961) 316–34.

Reiss, T. J., *Toward Dramatic Illusion* (New Haven, 1971).

Reynolds, Ernest, *Early Victorian Drama* (London, 1936).

Righter, Anne, *Shakespeare and the Idea and the Play* (London, 1962).

Roberts, Arthur with Morton, Richard (eds), *The Adventures of Arthur Roberts by Rail, Road and River* (Bristol, 1895).

Robinson, J. W. (ed.), *Theatrical Street Ballads*, the Society of Theatre Research (London, 1971).

Sanders, Norman, 'The Comedy of Greene and Shakespeare', *Early Shakespeare*, Stratford-upon-Avon Studies, no.3 (London, 1961) pp. 35–53.

Sarris, Andrew, *Interviews with Film Directors* (New York, 1969).

Saunders, J. W., 'Staging at the Globe, 1599–1613', *Shakespeare Quarterly*, 11 (1960) 401–25.

Schelling, Felix E., *Elizabethan Drama, 1558-1642* (London, Boston and New York, 1908) 2 vols.

Scott, Virginia P., 'The Infancy of English Pantomime, 1716–1723', *Educational Theatre Journal*, 34 (1970) 125–34.

Somerset, J. A. B., 'The Comic Turn in English Drama to 1616', unpublished Ph. D. thesis, University of Birmingham (1966).

_____, '"Fair is foul and foul is fair": Vice-Comedy's Development and Theatrical Effects', *The Elizabethan Theatre*, vol.v, ed. G. Hibbard (Waterloo, 1975) pp. 54–75.

Sorelius, Gunnar, '*The Giant Race before the Flood*': *Pre-Restoration Drama on the Stage and in the Criticism of the Restoration* (Uppsala, 1966).

Spencer, T. J. B. (ed.), *A Book of Masques* (Cambridge, 1967).

Sprague, Arthur Colby, *Beaumont and Fletcher on the Restoration Stage* (Harvard, 1926).

Stanford, W. B., *Ambiguity in Greek Literature* (Oxford, 1939).

Stoker, Bram, *Personal Reminiscences of Henry Irving* (London, 1907).

Summers, Montague (ed.), *Shakespeare Adaptations* (London, 1922; facsimile, New York, 1966).

Swift, Jonathan, 'A Proposal for Correcting the English Tongue', *Polite Conversation, Etc.*, ed. Herbert Davis with Louis Landa (Oxford, 1964).

Tarlton's Jests, ed. J. P. Feather (New York and London, 1972).

Thomas, Keith, 'The Place of Laughter in Tudor and Stuart England', *TLS* (21 January 1977) 77–81.

Thompson, Elbert N. S., 'The English Moral Plays', *Transactions of the Connecticut Academy of Arts and Sciences*, 14 (March 1910).

Towsen, John H., *Clowns* (New York, 1976).

Trussler, Simon, *Burlesque Plays of the Eighteenth Century* (Oxford, 1969).

Vicinus, Martha, *The Industrial Muse* (London, 1974).

Weimann, Robert, *Shakespeare and the Popular Tradition in the Theatre*, ed. Robert Schwartz (Baltimore and London, 1978; German version, Berlin, 1967).

Wells, Stanley, 'Shakespearian Burlesques', *Shakespeare Quarterly*, 16 (1965) 49–61.

_____, *Literature and Drama with Special Reference to Shakespeare and his Contemporaries* (London, 1970).

_____, with Kimberley, M. E., *Nineteenth-Century Shakespearean Burlesques* (London, 1977–8) 5 vols.

Welsford, Enid, *The Fool* (New York, 1961).

Wickham, Glynne, *Early English Stages 1300–1660* (London, 1959–).

_____, *English Moral Interludes* (London, 1976).

Wilkinson, Tate, *The Wandering Patentee* (1795; facsimile, Menstone, 1973; with index prepared by C. Beecher Hogan, London, 1973).

Williams, Ioan, *The Criticism of Henry Fielding* (London, 1970).

Wilson, F. P., 'The Diction of Common Life', *Shakespeare Criticism, 1935–1960*, ed. Anne Ridler (Oxford, 1963) pp. 90–116.

Wood, Harvey H., *The Plays of John Marston* (Edinburgh, 1934–9) 3 vols.

Young, Steven C., *The Frame Structure in Tudor and Stuart Drama* (Salzburg, 1974).

Index

Plays are indexed under their own titles and not under names of their authors. Alternative titles of plays are not usually indexed. Characters in plays are only exceptionally indexed (e.g. Falstaff). Strictly bibliographical references in the notes are not indexed. The Select Bibliography is not indexed. Relevant topic headings will be continued in the index to *Comtemporary Drama and the Popular Dramatic Tradition in England.*